Angels in the
Wilderness

YOUNG AND BLACK IN NEW ORLEANS AND BEYOND

D1508896

Angels in the
Wilderness

YOUNG AND BLACK IN NEW ORLEANS AND BEYOND

WILLIAM BARNWELL

IMAGES BY CHERYL GERBER
FOREWORD BY LAWRENCE N. POWELL

2017
University of Louisiana at Lafayette Press

Images © Cheryl Gerber

Front cover: Troy Simon
Back cover: Robert Burnside

http://ulpress.org
University of Louisiana at Lafayette Press
P.O. Box 43558
Lafayette, LA 70504-3558

Printed on acid-free paper

Library of Congress Cataloging-in-Publication Data

Names: Barnwell, William Hazzard, 1938- author.
Title: Angels in the wilderness : young and black in New Orleans and beyond /
  by William Barnwell.
Description: Lafayette, LA : University of Louisiana at Lafayette Press, [2017]
Identifiers: LCCN 2017005939 | ISBN 9781946160034 (alk. paper)
Subjects: LCSH: Church work with African American youth--Louisiana--New
  Orleans. | African American youth--Louisiana--New Orleans. | Youth in
  church work--Louisiana--New Orleans. | Young volunteers in community
  development--Louisiana--New Orleans. | Toleration--Religious
  aspects--Christianity. | Racism--United States. | United States--Race
  relations.
Classification: LCC BV4468.2.A34 B37 2017 | DDC 362.7083/0976335--dc23
LC record available at https://lccn.loc.gov/2017005939

"The Spirit immediately drove Jesus out into the wilderness. And he was in the wilderness forty days, tempted by Satan; and he was with the wild beasts; and the angels ministered to him."

(Mark 1:12-13, *Revised Standard Version*).

Praise for William Barnwell's
Angels in the Wilderness

"As I read this wonderful book, I cried. I cried because someone loves the people of New Orleans enough to seek out the stories that are the lives of a few mirroring the lives of many. My friend, William Barnwell has brought the skill of listening to a new level. One definition of the word listen is 'paying attention to.' By re-counting the experiences of youth and young adult African American New Orleanians, William pays attention to the current motivating and challenging influences of the city.

"For people of faith, we are reminded that the concept of church really does embrace Christians being and living Christ's love alongside the culture, gifts and challenges of communities. Thank you, William for courageously sharing examples of the Church at work for justice and righteousness in the face of tough realities. The book does such a great job emphasizing the intersections of faith, family, culture and community relationships across all levels.

"As you read the book, allow yourself to feel the rhythm of life, love and promise of your own city!"

–Linetta J. Gilbert

"There are two types of people who come from Louisiana, preachers and storytellers. Although he's an Episcopal clergyman, William Barnwell falls in the storyteller category.

"Just as the Bible conveys its messages through tales and parables, Barnwell helps us feel and celebrate the situation of our less-privileged brethren through their stories. He is not only a master storyteller, he is able to help others become storytellers. By knowing how to listen and by venturing out into the neighborhoods of New Orleans, he is able to encourage, with his genial and loving manner, other people to relate their own experiences.

"Alex Haley once said that the most powerful phrase in the English language was, 'let me tell you a story.' Barnwell empowers others and deepens our sense of love and justice by letting those whose voices that are sometimes not heard tell us their stories. We should read this book daily and be inspired by it."

–Walter Isaacson

Table of Contents

Acknowledgments

First, I thank the inspiring angels, young and older, who made this book possible and who are now showing the way. Here they are in order of appearance in the book: Ms. Briana Brown, Mr. Ed Buckner, Big Chief Tugga Cloud, Gang Flag Eric Smith, Ms. Shedren Burnside, Mr. Robert Burnside, Ms. Tia Cage, Mr. Malik Brooks, Ms. Tayler Payton, Ms. Kaila Holloway, Mr. Alonzo Booth III, Ms. Candace Gautreaux, Mr. Troy Simon, Sgt. John Johnson, Mr. Derrick Strong, Mr. Yahmel Bey, Mr. Jonathan Lewis, Mr. Pat Bryant, Ms. Kristen Rome, Mr. Steven Kennedy, Ms. Nakita Shavers, Mr. Derek Rankins, Ms. Lindsey Ardrey, Mr. Mark Walters, Mr. William Gillispie, Mr. Trevor Bryan, Ms. April Williams Bryan, Ms. Nancy Hampton, The Rev. Dr. Dwight Webster, Mr. Jarvis DeBerry, Ms. Kelly Harris DeBerry, Ms. Ashleigh Gardere, and Mr. Orlando Smiley.

Second, I thank my wonderful editors and consultants: Ms. Shannon Ravenel, founder of Algonquin Press and my longtime editor; Ms. Corinne Barnwell, my wife; Mr. Jed Horne, author of *Breach of Faith* and *Desire Street*; Mr. James Wilson, associate director of the UL Lafayette Press; and Ms. Mary Karnath Duhé, production manager at the UL Lafayette Press.

And third, I am privileged to have worked with the following, all who contributed to the front and back covers of this book: Ms. Cheryl Gerber, the photographer; Prof. Walter Isaacson, author of *Steve Jobs*, *The Innovators*, and others; Dr. Lawrence Powell, author of *The Accidental City*; Ms. Linetta Gilbert, beloved member of Christian Unity Baptist Church and citywide leader; and Mr. Troy Simon and Mr. Robert Burnside, angels.

Foreword

People who know Charleston-born William Barnwell might be astonished to learn he isn't the first Barnwell of South Carolina legend to have landed in New Orleans on a racial mission. Preceding him to these parts more than a century earlier was a collateral ancestor by the name of Robert Barnwell Rhett. Historians of secession—the sectional crisis that disrupted the Union, drenched the South in blood, and led to the freeing of four million slaves—rank Rhett among the most radical fire-eating secessionists in American history. He was still blazing with white nationalist fury when he relocated to New Orleans during Reconstruction, hell-bent on rolling back equal citizenship rights for African-Americans. Whatever tree William's apple may have fallen from, it was country miles from Barnwell Rhett's orchard.

This marvelous book isn't about William Barnwell, however, even though he was the major force behind pulling it together, never mind the central interlocutor in the stories that follow. Rather it's a book about life-changing stories, mostly by young black people who have seldom gotten a fair shake in life, let alone much of a second chance. They are poignant tales, often gripping. Some will amaze you, others grab you by the gut and refuse to let go. Most of the stories are about coming of age in New Orleans, a city that has learned to live with tragedy. Katrina—or the federal flood of 2005, as locals often refer to it—is one of the great caesuras in the city's history. There's *before Katrina*, and there's *after Katrina*. New Orleans has been cast in several different lights over the years—as painted lady or sportsman's paradox; as the murder-rate capital of these United States, or the central conveyor belt for Louisiana's overstuffed jails and prisons. But one characteristic is easily overlooked: its irrepressibility. Resilience is practically tattooed on New Orleans's soul. That stiff upper lip comes across in the stories Will Barnwell persuaded his book's interviewees to share with its readers.

There are rules about spoiler-alerts, but I can't resist mentioning a few of his book's stories—for instance, Big Chief Tugga Cloud of the city's youngest Mardi Gras Indian tribe, the Red Flame Hunters. One day his mentor is teaching him how to fish for eels, the next day the instruction involves the patient art of sewing Indian costumes. "The Indians used to be fighting back in the day," seventeen-year-old Big Tugga says. "But now it's about the needlework. The needle and the threads." Then there are the College Track success stories like Tia Cage, whose near-death experience with bone cancer left her disabled but unbowed; or Robert Burnside, who nearly died at the hands of overzealous police who mistook him for an alleged gun-toting criminal who happened to be sporting a red hoodie similar to his own. The legendary and seasoned organizer Pat Bryant turns up. So do several veterans of the Undoing Racism collective, the Peoples Institute. Then there is the born-again rap artist and Icon for Peace, Derrick Strong, who has risen, rather miraculously, from the mean streets of pre- and post-Katrina, and with gunshot wounds to prove it—yet without the coruscating anger that most mortals would have had difficulty quelling.

And that is what's so remarkable about this anthology: the willful banishment of anger. Rejection of revenge goes against the grain. The urge to strike back against violence, whether witnessed or experienced, can be all consuming. But these are remarkable people—mostly young, but some old; generally black, but a few white. And all of them have elected to bend their energies toward mitigating violence rather than fanning its flames.

For all of the tragedy that has befallen New Orleans over the years (and since Katrina there has been a gracious plenty), *Angels in the Wilderness* is an indispensable reminder that light can still pierce the darkness. It's a book worth reading then contemplating.

–Lawrence N. Powell,
Professor Emeritus of History at Tulane University;
author of *The Accidental City: Improvising New Orleans*
(Harvard University Press, 2012)

Introduction

So, why am I, this older white guy, writing about young African Americans from my longtime home, New Orleans? There is an expression in the black community here regarding supposed white liberals like me: "He's going to tell us all about colored people and what colored people should do, imagine that!" I hope I don't fall into that category. My purpose here is simply to pass on the stories of young people, stories that need to be told to inform and inspire us all—black and white—in New Orleans and beyond. In my work in South Carolina, Boston, Washington, D.C., and, for many years here, I have been amazed at how little my white sisters and brothers know about most of the black leaders and potential leaders, both young and old. These stories come from young people and their mentors, coaches, and faith leaders in organizations such as:

- The Red Flame Hunters Mardi Gras Indian tribe—the only all-youth tribe
- College Track, the afterschool program supported in part by the Aspen Institute
- The Icons for Peace—young people who have been or could have been incarcerated
- Justice and Beyond—a coalition of African American justice seekers in the city
- Four Styles of Working for Racial Change: 1) The People's Institute for Survival and Beyond; 2) The Louisiana Episcopal Diocesan Commission for Racial Reconciliation; 3) Micah, a grassroots reform coalition that is part of the national PICO; and 4) a young historian
- St. Luke's, an historically black and historic Episcopal church
- Christian Unity Baptist Church, a place centered on both faith and justice-seeking action

Most of the young people don't know others outside of their particular group: don't know the other stories, the other missions—another reason to take on this project. All the storytellers, both the young people and their advisors, I claim as friends—some new, some longtime. My challenge has been to choose only twenty-eight stories from the many I have read and heard.

I hope these stories add to the powerful stories already out there by black writers in New Orleans, including the recent memoir by former first lady of New Orleans, Sybil Morial (*Witness to Change: From Jim Crow to Political Empowerment*) and a narrative of Hurricane Katrina by actor Wendell Pierce (*The Wind in the Reeds: A Storm, a Play and the City that Would not be Broken*).

I hope also to encourage readers in other cities to get to know the young and older African American leaders and emerging leaders in their own communities.

In my work as an Episcopal clergyman, I have been leading storytelling groups in white churches, black churches, secular reform organizations, and prisons—most particularly the Louisiana State Penitentiary at Angola. My custom is to read short passages from my favorite gospel, St. Mark, and ask those gathered, "How does your story connect with the story Mark tells? You know," I say, "our personal story is the most important thing about any one of us. And Mark gives us a focused way to tell some of that story." Jesus heals a man paralyzed with guilt by forgiving his sins (Mark 2:1-9). "Can you talk about a time," I ask, "when guilt left you 'paralyzed' so to speak and/or a time when guilt—'gadfly guilt' I call it—nudged you into right action?" On a mountain top, Jesus is "transfigured" (9:2-8). So I ask, "Can you talk about a mountaintop experience when you, like the disciples, had eyes to see and ears to hear?" Secular participants respond as well as people of faith.

I often start with Mark's Prologue: Jesus is in the terribly harsh wilderness for forty days. Satan and wild beasts are after him, and then, we are quietly told, "the angels ministered to him" (1:12-13, *Revised Standard Version*). "Can you talk about a wilderness experience, a harsh time in your life when the angels—people—ministered to you, helped you out?" I ask. I love the answers to the Mark-inspired questions, especially this one about the angels. But I don't stop there. I ask the storytellers to keep going, to write down something of their stories; or to let me turn on my tape recorder as I listen to them. William Gillispie, himself young and African American, has transcribed many of the stories for me and tells some of his own story in chapter 5. The storytellers talk about *their* angels in the wilderness, but I have come to realize that all of them are, for New Orleans and beyond, *our* angels. As I keep saying, you do not need to be perfect to be an angel to others.

That this book's theme should be about angels and the wilderness came to me when I was leading a small group as part of an Episcopal program at a women's prison—Lowell Correctional Institution, near Ocala, Florida. This was in May of 2015. I was asking the nine or ten ladies (as they like to be called) in the group about their wilderness experiences and who were those angels for them. As usual, I was blown away by the responses, but one I will always remember. Holly had hardly said anything in the first two days of the in-prison retreat, but when it came her turn to speak about the angels, she said this:

> When I came to this prison thirteen years ago, I was pregnant and just nineteen. I didn't know who the father was and my own family had long ago abandoned me. When the child, a girl, was born, they took my baby from me. You can imagine that wilderness experience, sentenced to prison for many years and losing my only child. But then, a family from a Christian foster care organization agreed to take my little girl into their family. And then an amazing thing happened. They started visiting me in Lowell Prison regularly, making me part of their family. And when my child, Alice, was old enough they started bringing her to see me most every month. Alice is now thirteen . . . and she calls me Mom. I am her mother.

And then Holly, who will be in prison many more years, burst into tears—as we all did—as she tried to say the words about her "angels in the wilderness."

Gloria Steinem and I have our differences in regard to faith, marriage, and what she, at eighty-one, calls "wonderful sex," but I love the way she describes a turning point in her life. She calls that experience "Ask the Turtle"—the "mantra" she lives by. When she was a first-year student at Smith, one day on a field trip, she found a large mud turtle on a riverbank. Thinking she was saving the turtle's life, she picked it up and carefully lugged it down to the river and slipped it in. A professor saw her just as the turtle disappeared in the water and explained that she had done the exactly wrong thing. "The turtle had been making its way to dry land for a reason," he said, "in order to lay its eggs—and now it is going to take the turtle months to lay them."

"It was a lesson I learned to apply to people a few years later, in India," Steinem went on, "though I didn't realize it then. I was going from village to village with Gandhian women-organizers, listening to them [say to the village women], 'Tell us your stories. You've lived them, *you're the experts.*'" It has taken me more years than it took Steinem to learn the lesson of the turtle, but at least now I know who the experts are on African American life in our cities.

As I listen to the wonderful stories of the young and black in New Orleans and their advisors, I try not to interrupt or change the conversation. But after the stories are transcribed, I do respond as to how they touch my life either directly or indirectly. (I make the same kind of response when the stories come to me in written form.) I hope you, the reader, will consider and respond to the stories in the same way: how they touch your life, how they connect or do not connect with your views and experience. Your responses and reactions to the stories will likely be quite different from mine, but will contribute to your reflections on your own story, angels and all.

Though I try not to brag, I am right proud of my moving from early beginnings in white segregated Charleston, South Carolina, in the forties, fifties, and early sixties, to my appreciation of just how much black lives do matter and how much our nation needs those black lives to move forward. It has been a special grace that I can still love those from Old Charleston who were my close friends and family in my growing-up years—some of my angels, imperfect for sure.

In these last two years, I have been trying to get the attention of important publications, like the New Orleans *Times-Picayune*, the *Washington Post*, and the *New York Times,* by writing op-eds in response to today's black movements from the point of view of a white liberal, yes a do-good white liberal. Here is one of my op-eds that was rejected by all three newspapers as well as several others. I wrote it after the Charleston massacre/tragedy, in which nine African Americans were murdered in the Emanuel African Methodist Episcopal Church (Mother Emanuel), June 17, 2015. It was also a time when the nation began to pay attention to the rising anger over police brutality.

A White Liberal Responds to Black Lives Matter

Of course all lives matter, but like many fellow whites I am taking seriously and appreciatively the Black Lives Matter movement. So how should we liberal whites respond to what is rapidly becoming a new movement? For the last fifty years I have been working across race lines, preaching both justice and empowering love, stumbling along, but so far, not quitting. Here are some of the questions I am asking myself these days and others from the white community.

First, why are we white liberals always seeking to recruit black folk to be part of *our* programs but seldom think of joining effective black advocacy groups? I have found this true in all of my work places as an Episcopal clergyman. One of the most dynamic African American advocacy groups that I have encountered anywhere is right here in New Orleans—Justice and Beyond. Most Mondays, I am privileged to meet with black leaders from across the city. Preachers, union and neighborhood leaders, and various justice advocates attend and bring their issues for discussion and action.

Of the hundred or more people who gather each Monday evening at Christian Unity Baptist Church, only a handful are white, even though everyone is invited. It does not seem to occur to my fellow white Episcopalians and most liberal whites for that matter that they could learn a lot by being part of Justice and Beyond and, when they agree, joining in *their* efforts.

Second—and I'm talking about myself as well as fellow white liberals— why haven't we made a clear distinction between overcoming personal racism (bigotry) and overcoming institutional, structural, and cultural racism? When I ask white friends about why there is still so much racism, they often say things like this: "What do you mean racism? I have a first cousin who married a fine black lady, and she's part of the family." Or, "We have a wonderful black family in our congregation and everyone loves them." Or, "Some of my colleagues at work are black. In fact one of my supervisors is African American." When I visit the public charter school my kindergarten grandson attends, I see a class half white, half black carrying on beautifully. If the children notice color, I don't see it.

That's all great, but overcoming personal racism is a lot different from working steadily for city-wide and country-wide racial justice. Some of the best souls I know give only fleeting attention to sad, *un-American* facts! Like the number of African Americans who fill our prisons (in Louisiana the number of incarcerated African Americans is close to 80 percent in a state with 32 percent black citizens). Like the number of black children who grow up in poverty and attend under-performing schools. Like the percentage of unemployed black males. Overcoming personal racism, of course, helps, but it is not the full answer. And sometimes, I think it blinds us to the *underlying* racism in our society.

Third, why do we white liberals—again I include myself—often write off political conservatives even though *they* may be showing the way toward personal racial reconciliation, if not overcoming cultural and institutional racism? I spend much of my so-called retired years in prison ministry, especially at the Louisiana State Penitentiary (Angola), north of Baton Rouge. I never see anything close to racism among the many white and black volunteers in the Kairos Prison Ministry International I work with as they relate to one another and to the inmates we serve. Some volunteers call themselves "flaming conservatives" to counter my "flaming liberalism." But it is those same conservatives who, along with the moderates and the liberals, spend three twelve-hour-day weekends with mostly black inmates, as everyone tries to carry out the Kairos slogan: "listen, listen love, love." And they—we—succeed, at Angola and at over four hundred prisons.

If we white and black liberals are going to strive for racial justice, I believe it imperative that we seek allies across political, religious, and cultural lines. In these times of crisis after the Charleston murders at Mother Emanuel Church in 2015, then in Dallas, Chicago, Baltimore, Baton Rouge, and Queens, in 2016, we have no time for self-righteousness, refusing to partner with those we differ with politically—they may have a great deal to teach us.

So fellow liberals, let's join with all who seek racial justice and love, as we move toward that Promised Land that Dr. Martin Luther King Jr. talked about the evening before he was assassinated, that place where, as the prophet Micah taught us, we "do justice, love kindness, and walk humbly with our God" (6:8). We may not get there in our generation, but, like Dr. King and Moses before him, we will know what the Promised Land looks like and we will know which way to walk.

Having talked, preached, and written about racial justice for years, I am the first to admit to my mistakes. Recently, at a planning meeting for Justice and Beyond—the strong African American advocacy group that I am part of—I spoke of "those people" who had been released from prison and their need for our support. The young man sitting across from me, whom I had seen before but did not know, said, "What do you mean Rev. Barnwell by *those people?* I am one of them and we do not accept being called *those people.*" I apologized and learned a new phrase: "Formerly incarcerated persons,"—FIPs, right along with VIPs. We moved on, and I was not thrown out of the meeting or further criticized. New Orleans, by and large, is a forgiving place when you make mistakes like this.

Besides that forgiveness, our city—with all of its problems—is full of jolly interactions between whites and blacks. When I buy a loaf of bread, an African American saleslady will say, "Thank you Sweetie." "My pleasure," I'll say, "and thank you Honey Pie." One reason for this forgiveness and jolliness is that we in the Big Easy have so much in common: the unsurpassed food, jazz, of course the Saints—win or lose—Mardi Gras, and informal second-line parades that arise for any occasion. And everyone knows someone's cousin.

But I have not experienced that forgiveness and jolliness in other places, at least in regard to race matters. Recently, I was giving a book reading and signing at a Manhattan mid-city Unitarian church for my book, *Lead Me On, Let Me Stand: A Clergyman's Story in White and Black.* I found no forgiveness from some of the people attending when I made a mistake. Maybe it *was* because of subconscious, long indwelling racism. I was going around the room of twenty-five or so, asking both white and black participants to introduce themselves with two or three sentences. I managed to skip over a black lady, not asking her to introduce herself. When I finished going around, she told everyone that by my skipping her, I was showing the real problem that we white people have: "You don't even see us! We are invisible to you. I don't care what book you wrote about race. You are just like all those other so-called liberal whites." Several participants nodded in agreement.

I, of course, apologized. "Yes, that's what you white people do," she responded, "apologize, but it doesn't do any good. You keep from seeing who we are!" I wanted to say in a squeaky, guilty voice that could have come from one of my grandchildren, "But, but I have worked hard at this for many years. I do see you and all people."

As you can imagine, it was pretty hard going forth with the book-reading and leading the discussion after that. At the end, I thought the encounter was over, but the last words just before we adjourned came from the same lady saying the same thing. Again several people nodded. Again I apologized. Again, she refused to accept my apology. And then I thanked everybody for coming and, with my head hanging low, went back to the place we were staying and was comforted by family members, angels for sure.

Now, that's my introduction to me, angels, and the Big Easy. Here is how Briana Brown, a twelfth-grade student, introduces our city in a book of student writing published in 2012 by College Track, the highly esteemed afterschool program. Briana says she is passionate about writing "both to inspire and entertain." She writes, she says, "for her own personal release and self-examination." In this essay, she gives a pretty typical picture of how young African Americans view New Orleans. She says she loves our city, but she also says, "People often see only the good in New Orleans in books, but not necessarily the whole truth of it."

> If you want to write about New Orleans, be sure to include all the of the flavorful food and festivals and, of course, Mardi Gras. The Krewes of Endymion, Bacchus, Rex, and Zulu are great parades to enjoy at carnival time. But does your reader really want to know their history? Do they care to know that the Krewe of Rex parade was originally segregated and meant for socially elite whites only? Do they really care to know that this segregation was why the all-black Krewe of Zulu was created?

> You may not want to inform your reader that equalizing racial pay is still a work in progress, even now. When talking about the carnival attire, it's all right to talk about the Indian headdresses and feathered boas, but don't go into too much detail for your reader. Refrain from focusing on the attire the rich white male krewe captains wear as they trot along on their horse and toss out doubloons to the screaming crowds. The white silk blouses and white masks may remind some readers of a very different group's clothing. Instead write about parties and our famous Southern hospitality, safe topics for any season.

> It's a must that you incorporate jazz as it is one of the most important aspects of New Orleans. After all, jazz began right here in New Orleans' own Congo Square. Don't leave out Voodoo either because your reader will want to know all the juicy details on that as well. You can write about the beautifully crafted buildings in the French Quarter, but by all means do not focus on the black man's hands who built them. Also avoid the crime that goes on in the city and the statistics of how many people are shot dead every year, as such facts may unnecessarily disturb the reader. And don't focus on the fact that there is more space here holding prisoners in jail than space holding students in college. The hands that once crafted the bars on balconies now grip the steel bars of a prison cell. Such facts will only discourage visitors.

> However, feel free to inform your reader about the importance of the Mercedes Superdome that draws tourists from miles around to enjoy concerts and Saints football games! *Who dat!*[1]

> But pay no mind to the sign within the shadow of the Superdome that reads "Future Site of the New Orleans Police Dept. Forensics Lab," for it is not a part of the revitalization of the city, and this sign is nearly completely

---

1. "Who dat say dey goin' to beat dem Saints" is the longtime favorite cheer for the New Orleans Saints football team.

covered in weeds as it has sat in an empty lot for five years. Please don't reveal to your reader that the city doesn't even have the means to perform fingerprinting analysis for the people they do throw into jails. Instead, maybe focus on the charming folk art and the museums, as these are located in safe neighborhoods and will help you get to your fairy tale ending. . . .

The streets in the Quarters are filled with beautiful buildings and the fresh scent of beignets and chicory coffee. The people are friendly. The gumbo is great. The music is jazzy. The parades are wildly fun and the football games are exciting. *Laissez les bon temps rouler!*[2]

If you want to write about New Orleans, this is all your reader needs to know.

Other College Track students tell some of their stories in chapter 2. Now that I am focusing on Briana, I have to include one of her poems in the same College Track book. It is entitled "Letter to My Child."

> Dear Elliot, Benjamin, Sabastian, Ryan, *or* Bella,
> Before I could hold you
> Before I could comfort you when you cried,
> Before I could hear you speak your first words . . .
> Before you could crawl
> Before you could walk
> Your knees, feet, and legs were taken from you.
>
> Before I could see you off on your first day of school
> Before I could sit down and help you with your homework
> Before I could applaud and watch you
> Perform in the school play . . .
> You were gone.
>
> Before you could fall in love for the first time
> And cry after the break up
> Before I could wipe your tears and tell you everything would be ok
> Before I could hear you speak of your hopes and dreams
> Before I could marvel at any awards you may have received
> Or see you walk across the stage and smile with your college degree
> You were gone before you were here.
>
> I wish I could have tucked you in at night
> And I wish that in the morning for breakfast I could have given you the
> World on a silver platter
> But I couldn't feed you because
> I didn't have the money

2. *Laissez les bon temps rouler!*, meaning "Let the good times roll," is a common New Orleans mantra.

And I couldn't tuck you in because
I was asleep myself
And I couldn't wipe your tears because
I was too busy crying
And I couldn't help you with your homework because
I had some of my own.

I wish I could have given you the best
Life possible. But I couldn't. . .
I wish I would have met you, but not
At age 16.

In early December 2015, I began to realize that the angel conversations were leading me to many other experiences in black and white New Orleans that I needed to write down—if not for others, at least for myself. I have been diagnosed with what I call "old-age anxiety." It's a good thing when the anxiety drives me forward releasing a lot of energy, not so good when I find myself either not challenged or bored. My moving around in black-led groups gives me an opportunity to cross not only race but also religious, class, political, and generational barrier lines as well. I hope I can bring some healing as I mostly listen to all kinds of voices.

**Note: Many of the younger and older storytellers in this book speak of how they were displaced after Hurricane Katrina struck in late August 2005. Over 1,800 of our people died as the waters covered our city, in some places over twenty feet deep. The estimates vary, but most agree that at least 125,000 residents were never able to return after they had fled the "Storm," as people here call it. Of the 125,000 displaced residents, between 75,000 and 80,000 were African Americans; some say even more than that. (Three weeks before Katrina, Corinne and I had left for Washington, D.C., where I worked at the National Cathedral as the "canon missioner"—Episcopalese for community minister. Our home flooded, but we were able to fix it up before we returned to New Orleans in late 2008.)

I use formal titles, like Dr., Pastor, or Ms. when the storytellers prefer those titles. For everyone else, I use first names. While some insist on calling me Father Barnwell or Reverend Barnwell, I actually prefer William or Will, or, my favorite, Brother Billy.

Many of the storytellers refer to various places in the city. I try to identify those places as best I can.

Finally, I avoid capitalizing "black" as I would then have to capitalize "white" all the way through. I do make exceptions when the storytellers want the capitalization.

Chapter One

The Red Flame Hunters

Long ago, American Indians rescued many runaway slaves in the forests outside of New Orleans. Eventually, Indians and former slaves had children together, introducing yet another mixed race in Louisiana to add to the already colorful mix of Creoles, Cajuns, whites, blacks, and free men and women of color. As a way of honoring the Indians, black leaders in New Orleans organized the Mardi Gras Indians in 1885. They would have their own "tribal marches"—*their* celebrations—to support their heritage, as opposed to the largely white and nationally popular Mardi Gras elite with their balls and parades. The Indians would march, walk, and dance with drums pounding wherever they chose in New Orleans, not bothered very much by law enforcement.

Today, as then, the Mardi Gras Indians spend many months sewing their brightly colored "Indian" suits. (Some say this is racist because the flamboyant suits are exaggerations of what Native Americans actually wore.) In earlier days, when a Mardi Gras Indian tribe would meet a rival Indian tribe on the streets on Fat Tuesday, they would often end up in fights, some lethal. Today's forty or so Mardi Gras Indian tribes are made up of from six to forty members each. Their "suits" get more elaborate—prettier—each year, and for the last hundred years, the highest compliment an Indian could receive would be that his suit was the "prettiest." Indians today, macho adults and young alike, vie for the title of the prettiest suit.

Mr. Edward Buckner is the founder and coach of the only Mardi Gras Indian tribe that is solely composed of teenagers and younger children. The young people in "his" tribe call themselves the Red Flame Hunters. Their Indian suits, which they wear for only one year, are as lavish and as pretty as any in the city. The Hunters meet in Mr. Ed's home five afternoons a week, sewing their suits, talking and listening to Mr. Ed tell his stories, often to the great glee of the Indians. Sewing the elaborate suits requires quite a lot of discipline that the young people take with them in other areas of their life—so important in low-income New Orleans, where gangs roam freely.

I first met Mr. Ed at a conference called by Mayor Mitch Landrieu in December of 2014. The mayor is trying to bring together various groups to support each other as they/we work more successfully to relieve poverty and combat racism in the city. I was representing the Episcopal Diocese of Louisiana and found myself in a breakout group with Mr. Ed, who was complaining that city and foundation money was not going to help the young people most

1

in need in the Seventh Ward, his part of the city. He talked briefly about the Red Flame Hunters and said there should be more money available to help his Indians write their stories for a book that should be published. After the workshop, I cornered Mr. Ed and told him about my background teaching writing at the University of New Orleans—long ago—and offered to help.

He accepted my offer and invited me to come any weekday late afternoon when the Hunters would be sewing their suits. I could get them to start their writing then. I began meeting with the determined young people at Mr. Ed's home, listening to their stories and encouraging them to write and write some more. Some of the Indians wrote a little, most wouldn't write at all. Nevertheless, we became friends and they invited me to walk—and dance—with them on Mardi Gras Day, February 17, 2015. I didn't do much dancing.

I asked Mr. Ed to tell some of his story as I recorded it and then asked seventeen-year-old Big Chief Tugga Cloud and Gang Flag Leader Eric Smith to tell theirs. The positions in Mardi Gras Indian Tribes almost always include Big Chief, Assistant Big Chief, Wild Man, Spy Boy, Gang Flag, Flag Boy, and the Queen—all of whom you will come to know as Tugga tells his stories.

Mr. Ed Buckner: From Homelessness to Angel in the New Orleans Wilderness

On November 24, 2015, I first met with Mr. Ed in his home in the largely black Seventh Ward. He is a longtime community activist, volunteer football coach, and coach/mentor of the Red Flame Hunters, consisting of a dozen or so teens. Mr. Ed is one of the jolliest persons I have ever known. About fifty-five, he lost the fingers on one hand in a work accident over fifteen years ago. He makes his living baking and selling pies, especially delicious pecan and sweet potato pies. I think he must have eaten a lot of them over the years, but weight does not matter at all to his family and friends, certainly not to the Red Flame Hunters, who adore him like a father.

We met in his kitchen, where on the weekends various family members, young and older neighbors, and the Red Flame Hunters walk in and out all the time. Mr. Ed was preparing his pies and putting them in the ovens as we talked. Every now and then I had to turn off the recorder as someone was calling to order a pie for Thanksgiving. Mr. Ed and I have gotten to know each other pretty well over the last year, especially when I marched but did not dance with the Red Flame Hunters last Mardi Gras. In this transcript I did not try to "correct" what I used to call "community English" when I taught mostly black students at the University of New Orleans, back in the eighties. I asked Mr. Ed to begin by saying what he wants people to know about him.

"Mr. Ed" Buckner, founder and coach of the Red Flame Hunters

Mr. Ed: Well, the main thing I want people to know is that I'm a good person, and I'm a concerned person about everyone and everybody. Don't matter if it's your family, next-door neighbor, or person passing on the street. I've been to the lowest points that a person can ever be in their life by becoming homeless. So I welcome everybody, no matter who that person may be. I don't have picks over people. I just love all the people. That's what I want people to remember me—in my end, when people think about me. I want them to know I am a civil servant, I am there really working for them.

Where did you get that from? Not everybody has the kind of drive that you have.

My family. I had great men in my family. My uncle Jo-jo Williams. My uncle Johnie Johnie Williams. My uncle Lofton Johnson, who is my mama's brother, and my uncle Smokey Johnson, whose name is George Johnson, and we used to call him, "Uncle Little Joe." Those were the men who were instrumental and with my father, Mr. Johnson, they were very instrumental, strong, positive people.

My father was so kind that he would go outside every day and give all the kids in the project courtyard a quarter. Just 'cause he knew they didn't have a quarter. Somebody may not have a quarter to get a little frozen cup. You know what they called back in the day Hucklebucks.[1] So they would get those frozen cups, and you know, kids were wanting for it because it was hot outside. And my dad was the kind of guy that, when he came outside, the kids knew one thing. Mr. Bully got a quarter. In our house we called him Bully. Some of his friends called him by other names, like Mike. You know, so he had all those names that his friends in the Tremé section of town called him.[2]

My mother was a very polite woman, worked twenty-seven years for the New Orleans School Board. She was a baker, twenty-seven years baking in that kitchen. She was really good—back in the day, when I was a really little boy, my mom used to walk through the Seventh Ward projects, to John F. Kennedy High School, over two miles each way. There was no bus at that time. And she'd go cook in the morning time (six in the morning) to make sure kids got breakfast in the morning. Otherwise, they would miss breakfast. And so those are the kinds of inspirations who inspired me to be who I am, because I had these kinds of people in my life.

My mother was the only girl, and she was a motherless child. She didn't have no mother; her mother left her at an early age. And after her mother left town and moved to San Francisco, my mother lived with her grandmother from about eight or nine years old. All of her life her grandmother took care of her. And the most incredible thing was for her to be able to raise us in a loving way and to be so caring and while she worried about things all the time. You know it took a certain kind of grandmother to bring that on. Because I wouldn't have been that caring man, I wouldn't have been saved, Mr. Barnwell!

Another thing I want people to know, that if I'm supposed to do something for you or do something with you, I'm going to definitely do it. I coached football for the New Orleans recreation department. I've been coaching for the past thirty years as a volunteer. So I've always tried to show the kids and all the young people that I touch in their lives, that I will be dedicated to them, and I will have no end in my dedication. Not only to the people, but I'm dedicated to the programs I have served.

When I was a kid, eight years old, I was out running on the field at playgrounds and everything, getting ready to play football. So I know what it meant to have them older guys to be my mentors and come out and work with me on basic and fundamental stuff and teaching me how to organize things with other children and other people. So it was so very important, and Mr. Leroy Thomas, one of the men at the playground, Coach Labeau, [Josh Labeau] who we used to call Coach Shafie or Brother Shafie. They really worked us and trained us and ran us. We never had an organized team in our community. And we wanted to play ball. And they decided that we would have a ball team at the playground.

Then I met Endesha Juakali, who was the person who taught me how to

1. "Hucklebucks" are a Louisiana treat consisting of frozen Kool-Aid served in a Dixie cup.

2. Tremé is now widely known from the outstanding television series by that name.

read and write though not a school teacher, because that guy, he was more about you learning how to read books and write and stuff like that. He just was this guy that was trying to put and build an educational piece in young men's mind. He had a group of us. We were called "Together Brothers Youth Organization." We dealt with political issues and all kinds of things. We were part of the "Take Over City Hall," when the guys took over the control of the mayor's office in City Hall.[3]

I had a strong community. In the Seventh Ward housing projects, where I grew up at, 'cause it wasn't just men that were great mentors to you, but women also, like my mother. Besides working for the School Board, she was also the pool manager in the summertime for the kids who went to swim in the public pool. So in the summertime, she would deal with all the kids I knew and all the kids that was older than me and younger, and manage them when they'd come to the pool. She'd make sure they had their bathing suits and showered and all this stuff. So that was a great piece for me because I got to know everybody. Yeah, I got to know everybody.

When I got out of high school and graduated. I just sat around not doing nothing. And just not doing nothing, but then I started working at Reliable Janitorial. I was just a young kid, nineteen or so, but was going to work every day, doing what I needed to do, stuff like that there. Then it came to that point where I started hustling but still working, like eight years on the job. They used to do high-rise janitorial cleaning on Charity Hospital, Charity School of Nursing, City Hall; all those places they did the work.

Then I decided to just quit everything and stop working, and I'm going to sell drugs all the time. Actually, indulging in and getting more involved in drugs got me to start *using* the drugs. So I started using cocaine. And at that time, there was a big movement toward cocaine. It was prevalent in all the nightclubs, and I was with that whole scene of going out, partying, smoking, snorting cocaine, and stuff like that. But when I realized about five or ten years down the line that I had done wasted that much time on an addiction—and it wasn't so much that coke was an addiction but just a recreational substance. It was just so readily available that I just loved to do that drug at the time.

I stopped one day and realized I had wasted so much time, and I wanted to get clean. I couldn't think of anything else. I didn't want to go to no family members' houses because I was using drugs. They invited me to come to their houses. I didn't go. Instead I went on the street. I won't forget that first night, homeless and hungry for home . . . hungry, hungry. Still didn't get nothing to eat. Second day, hungry as hell. And I'm up around the Canal Street area. And I'm saying to myself, "What if the drugs have done messed me up?" They just

3. My wife, Corinne, was working at City Hall during the demonstration, on the staff of Dutch Morial, the first black mayor of New Orleans, 1978-1986. The demonstration was a general complaint against racism; "black lives matter," we would say today.

had done took a toll on my life.

So I decided that I wasn't going to use no drugs. So I went on the street. And I was toughing it out on the street. And I was looking for work and I got some work. At this time, I had done lost my fingers on the job at a bag manufacturer. I was still using drugs. Stuff like that. My head had gone in space. Then I lost my best friends. I lost my friend Crago and his little brother Bam. They was murdered on the street. And I lost my friend J.C. He went to jail.

I had two good friends murdered, and another that went to jail, got sick in jail and died. That was my friend Jerome, J.C. That was my guy. Him and I, we would be in a house in the project and when our moms wasn't at home we'd be cooking all kinds of stuff. We tried to cook and everything. This was my guy. But, those guys had done died off. And it was just like . . . I was still trying to coach football; still working with the kids at the time.

I had to go to football practice, every day. And the kids didn't know I was getting loaded because I'd walk to football practice, a couple of miles from the Riverfront Moonwalk where I was sleeping under some shelter. The field was next to Philip Junior High School, right there at that time. And I would get to the field there right before school let out, and I would see all the kids coming out and sit on the bleachers. And when I'd see the school totally clear, I would walk that field—that big old field—and pray. Every day. I'd pray to God that I wanted a house. I wanted to get my house to help my own children. I had two boys and a girl at that time. I needed a house 'cause I wanted to be off drugs and I wanted a place to stay, so I didn't have to sleep on the street anymore and see the trash that I was seeing happen on the street.

So when the football season came to the end that year, I decided "Okay, since I'm homeless, I'm going to go find whatever work I can and I'm going to work all of the summertime. I'm going to work my butt off. I'm going to get myself a house by winter. So I went to Morgan City,[4] where I was told they had work. So when I got to Morgan City, a guy gave me a ride and brought me to a house. And in the house they had about thirty men living in what was a three-bedroom home.

But I got there and the first week I worked for forty hours to get paid on a Friday and then realized that nobody was going to get me any pay. My whole pay—my whole forty hours—went to room and board. I had never read the rules or never knew anything. After I have my forty hours in and they took my money, I knew I needed to make at least eighty hours. So the following week, that next week's pay, I had only had forty hours, but the third week, I had actually done hustled up seventy-five hours, so I had some money in my pocket.

We were a temporary work service run by white guys, who were in cahoots with the white police, and we couldn't leave the house, or at two in the morning, they would put us way out on the road where you had to walk back

4. Morgan City is located in south central Louisiana, roughly eighty-five miles west of New Orleans.

two or three miles back to town if the alligators and snakes didn't get you.

So from being homeless, I hadn't had no good shoes. I only had one pair of old work shoes. And I was stinking in those work shoes. But the people in Morgan City were so hard, they wouldn't give you an opportunity to go nowhere, because they were afraid you were going to run, and not be there to do work. And also not be able to pay your room and board to them. So I went to work for that whole month. And I felt that I had actually put myself in slavery. All the guys around me smoking crack. Getting loaded and everything.

"Man, I don't want no more crack," I said to myself. "I don't want no more Jack Daniels. I don't want nothing that has to do nothing for us." No. I was out here in Morgan City, being homeless. I was totally set up. I felt like drugs again had me in another episode of a bad piece of life. But now I'm in slavery and I walked myself into slavery. Let me ask you. Do you think it's right, you have to work eighty hours and only end up with forty of the eighty hours of pay? And I'm getting (eating) actually a sandwich and some Kool-Aid in the evening when I do get dinner. 'Cause I'm so tired after working sixteen or twenty hours a day, I end up falling asleep 'cause I'm too tired to eat. And finally one time I got paid on Friday about a month after I started working eighty hours. And I asked them, could they give me a ride to pick me up a pair of shoes. So they gave me a ride to get me a pair of new shoes.

Let me back up a second, when they would bring us to the work site, I would always see the bus station. I knew the bus station was behind the tennis shoe store. So every day they brought me to work I would look at that bus station. And I was going to run. Believe me Reverend Barnwell, I was going to run. I felt like I had done put myself in slavery and I ain't no damn slave! And I never would have been a good slave back in that day. I would have cut off my feet or somethin'. So I knew that this wasn't going to happen long. I got that money, and I got that check cashed, and I asked them, could they take me and let me go buy some shoes. By this time I had made about a thousand dollars, saved up in my pocket for working so hard. So I got to the store to get the shoes, and they say they gonna pick me up.

I'm not going to tell you a word of lie. I ran around the back and bought me a bus ticket. And ran out and hide behind some cars. I sat there after I got the bus ticket and waited there all day until seven that evening. And that bus pull up. And I ran and jumped on that bus. And I have not even drove nowhere near Morgan City since. I don't even drive down that way. That's like the wrong turn and shit like that. You know, it was totally bad. I was mad at myself because the people at Morgan City done put me through that. I was on drugs, hard-headed, and not doing what I needed to do. I was still indigent. I knew what I needed to do. I'd gotten homeless. I thought about all them steps I needed to have to go through to get back up.

And I felt like God was chastising me for being disobedient like I had been being. And I knew God was doing this. And I didn't get mad with God 'cause God didn't give me none of the dope. God didn't give me none of the things I was doing wrong. God didn't do it to me. I had done did it to myself.

So when you came back from Morgan City, was that when you began to get your life back together?

I went to my oldest brother's house, Leonard Johnson. And I talked to Big Toy we called him. I named my son after him. I went to Big Toy's house. I had called him and told him to be looking for me soon 'cause I was coming back to the city. His thing was, I want you to stay over by me. My thing was, I still felt like I was still on drugs, and I didn't need to be at no one's house 'cause I was afraid I might steal somethin' for drugs. I don't want anything to come up missing and I'd be blamed for it.

When he asked you to come to his house, did you go eventually?

I went! I went. But I couldn't stay long. 'Cause see, let me tell you something about being homeless. Going on and living in someone's house and getting comfortable and things may not work out will put you back homeless. At that time I wasn't ready to trust nothing other than where I was going and I was finally getting my sobriety. So I wasn't ready to be really trusting. Being that it was my brother, who I love dearly, I had done trusted him all my life, I gave him the opportunity to help me because if anybody in the world that was going be there to hold and help me it was going to be him. And I gave him that opportunity. And my brother truly, truly helped me. But I kept going back to the street. I wouldn't stay there. If you talk to him, he'll tell you. I kept coming back to the street because I would tell him, I can't get comfortable. I was still homeless in my mind!

Finally, I get work and still practicing with the kids. And I had a little change. Coach Flea, which is Pastor Lionel Roberts, he knew I wanted a home, and he takes me over to the house that he had. Now granted the house didn't have no front door. The house didn't have no back door. Almost all of the windows was out in the house. But when I looked in the house, I had seen glory. I had seen glory. The house was in such bad condition that he didn't charge me no rent. Told me to get the house together. So I worked on that house for about four months. And all of a sudden, I went to smoking crack again. I went to smoking crack again! Reverend Barnwell...

I'm listening!

I went to smoking crack again! Now I'm smoking more than I ever smoked. I got a house so now I can invite other crackheads to smoke at my house. So we smoking and having a party. Ba-bam! One evening, my disability kicked in for my loss of fingers. Got my disability money. I was still working and stuff. Got some disability cash. I had done saved up $10,000. And I planned to smoke it all up.

Then something hit me when I got down to about $8,000. I keep going to my neighbor who was holding all my money for me. I went to my neighbor and asked her not to give me another dollar. 'Cause I was going to get my shit together. Those were my exact words. I don't mind you recording that or that being recorded. I was going to get my shit together. I walked around the corner, which is on Elysian Field Ave. I got down on my knees and begged God to forgive me in tears, crying, sobbing all over everywhere. Went from there around the corner, walked from there to the Moonwalk steps,[5] where I had been sleeping for almost a year and a half. I went and let myself see those steps and asked myself, "Do I want to go back to these steps again? Do I really want to be on those Moonwalk steps again? Do I really want to come up here at night and count the ships that pass in the night?"

Reverend Barnwell, I'm gonna tell you something. It took a mighty God. I went home. I don't tell many people this. And you'll forgive me. I don't tell many people about this because this stays between me and the Lord. I went home and I prayed some more at home. I prayed to God. I went to bed that night. And I woke up the next morning. Didn't answer the door for nobody.

Went to bed the next night, woke up the next morning didn't answer the door again for nobody. When I answered my door again, I knew one thing. I was not inviting that devil, Satan, across the steps again. He was not coming across my door-seal to my house. He was not entering. So I decided at that time, Reverend Barnwell, that I wasn't smoking no more. And I meant that. The last dollars I had, I was going to do something good for myself and my house and everything. I was going to have something.

I went across the street to Mrs. Glory Biggas. God bless that day. Mrs. Glo told me, "Son, glad you're feeling better. You're going to make it." And she kept saying—she was a Catholic—"The Lord is going to be with you." And I worked on it and worked on it and prayed. So I stopped smoking. I didn't go to rehab, I felt like God granted me a miracle in the night I prayed. I didn't have the urge again. I didn't want to. I didn't go back to smoking crack no more. That was it.

It sounds like Mrs. Glo came along just at the right time, when you were ready to hear someone who really cared about you, the perfect angel.

Well, yeah, she was around the right time. But, Coach Fat was around the right time. Pastor Roberts was around the right time. You know, my brother Toy, Big Toy was around at the right time. They were supporting me in the right way. They weren't giving me money. They weren't making me cut out nothing or fussing at me or telling me I'm a fool for all that I had done. They weren't doing that. They helped me manage my finances. They helped me start getting myself on track by keeping better company with them instead of the crowd I had been keeping company with. So once I started getting my things together, I was able to receive help in a greater way. And them guys, God bless them, were there first. And I received the help I needed. Reverend Barnwell.

---

5. The Moonwalk steps are located on the Mississippi side of the French Quarter.

I'm listening!

I will tell you this. And I'm not trying to bring nobody closer to God. And I'm not trying to tell people to be about God 'cause I'm not an evangelist. My life still ain't a hundred percent right. I don't smoke crack no more, but I won't say I'm not full of myself sometimes. I try not to judge the other man. But I tell everybody, if you run into a crisis, if you need help, you need to get on your knees and get true. Because remember how I told you about this, about how I walked on that field at Philip Junior High and prayed to God. [A pause to check on pies.]

When I got myself right and I got my life right, God brought me this house, here at 1823 Elysian Fields. So I have a dedication. I owe the Red Flame Hunters. I owe the kids at Willy Hall playground, where I coached all those years. Because God has a special thing for me to do. He could have taken everything away from me, but he stayed with me, through all the hell. Through all the waves and bad water I was swimming in and drowning in and when I needed help.

He kept me for a reason. That's why you see the Red Flame Hunters sewing their suits most every day of the year. And that's why you see my dedication to law and order with them. Because I know where I come from that they could go there. And I know God say help the next brother. Reach out. Don't forget what those brothers done for you a long time ago. You might have went astray but the foundation that your mother and your father and your uncles and all those have built for you was the basis that helped me come back. I only want to help them build a good foundation.

I don't know where the Red Flame Hunters gonna go or where it will lead them. But hopefully that's the foundation and the education that I'm helping these young men get. I'm hoping that it will carry them better through their life than I did for myself. And I hope that through my mishaps that I tell them about all the time, that they don't go through it. Because see, it's a hard thing to tell somebody you got a miracle if you went back to doing what you were doing before. I can tell you this here, I don't know if anybody else in the world got a miracle before but I know that when I woke up the next day that long-ago time, I never smoked crack again. And I'm talking about this about a long time since that time.

Let me ask you another question. How much does racism play into your story? If we hadn't had so much racism in New Orleans, would you have had those same problems?

Well, racism didn't cause my problem. I do recognize there is a lot of racism. I could have been a part of the negativity of what black men felt about the white race because of the things that had happened. And I was brought up around some militant brothers that made you know how they felt about what had happened to our black people, and the oppression that had went on in that time. They would go to war over that.

The thing is, I can't wage the war that I wasn't there to fight and battle at that time. I can't wage that war. I can only wage the new war. What I can do is help keep our young brothers in a safe place and do what basically older brothers done for me. Because of the war that they fought. I believe we have made great progress as a country, don't get me wrong. But then we do things that go backways as a country a lot of times.

I was mentioning this to another man, and we was talking about guns. We were talking about the accessibility to guns and how easy it is to buy guns. Well, my black guys don't get to buy the guns from the gun store, where the white guy buys guns from. My black guys have to buy guns off the street. When the white guys run out of the crack money, then they sell us these big old forty caliber guns that black kids can't get in the store. That's how guns get into the community. When we were coming up, we all got charges for trespassing and everything else by the time we get to eighteen. We'd get the trespassing charge because the cops, at some point, would just stop and arrest us because we were black. That was racism.

What I am doing is that I want the young men that I am working with to understand people for people. I'm not trying to give them the street talk that I had when I was younger. I think that would make them more prejudice against a lot of things. I want to give them a book that Endesha Juakali gave me, like *Malcolm Speaks* and *Jim Crow Diary,* and let them be able to read and decide things for themselves. I want to give them the type of books and writing and education to be able to make choices.

You see, so many times, these kids are not able to make a choice. And the thing is, to take and give them a chance to make them choices—see, the Mardi Gras Indians is a good thing. When you talk to these young men in here when you visit, these guys are on the principal's honor roll and doing great things in school, and because the Indian thing is that I ask a lot of them. I ask "Don't come around me being no dumb Indian. We need to do the things we need to do to be good people and Indians but do it the right way." [Another pause to check on the pies.] But I teach them to be good Indians and good people. And see, the thing is, the Indian is an avenue to discipline that I can use that will help them in life.

As a person, to spend your first two or three weeks homeless on the streets when you are at your weakest point and you just can't seem to get anything right, there is no love, nowhere, that seems to flow your way. I wanna make sure that what I have in me, that the Lord gave me, the strength that I have, I have to pay back in full. I don't believe what he did, in saving me, through all the dope, trials, fighting, shooting, and people taking people's dope and all of the carnage that happened, I don't think he saved me to be here doing nothing. To be wandering and not doing

When I go to sleep at night, I don't have a doubt no more. The drugs don't haunt me to smoke the crack. What haunts me is to do better every day to help the young people every day. That's the things that haunt me now. I got a better spirit that gets on me now, better than to have that one that got on me and took me through all the carnage that I went through all the years. Without the help of all those people and the help of God, I wouldn't have been that caring man I am today, I wouldn't have been saved, Mr. Barnwell

I sure like the way you talk about "being saved." It's not something you just do with your head. It's how you, Mr. Ed, live. That'll preach!

Reaction:

In my responses to the various stories in this book, I say what I might have said in the conversations but usually didn't. The stories are not about me, but they often connect with my life in some way as I hope they will with anyone who reads this book. So here is my reaction to Mr. Ed's story:

When I was growing up, my mother drilled in me the optimism I live by. "William, always look for the good in other people. And William, remember, it is never too late to do the right thing." Over the years, people like Mr. Ed have made me know that she was right. He was homeless and addicted in his mind even when he was no longer homeless or addicted. And yet he was able to receive what he calls "God's glory," especially when he was given that broken-down house with no front door, no back door. Eventually, he was able to rebuild those doors, keep Satan outside, and find his way to coach the Red Flame Hunters—to give back what he had been so generously given in his growing-up years.

I appreciate the way he talks about being saved, something he does with his redeemed life, not just claiming a new belief. Too often, we in the church think of belief as something we do only with our heads, our minds. Lately, I have very much appreciated the way Sister Helen Prejean, of *Dead Man Walking* fame and a friend, speaks of belief. The interviewer on the program, *I Believe*, asked her how she knows what she believes. She answered something like this: "I think back on what I have done and not done over the last few days, weeks, and months, that is what I believe." She and Mr. Ed have a lot to teach me, all of us.

I also appreciate Mr. Ed's determination that each of his young Indians have options in life. They are not stuck in poverty and injustice. Throughout this book, storytellers emphasize the importance of their friends and family members having options, and of how they will live their lives.

And the pies were great. I bought several for Thanksgiving Day friends.

Big Chief Tugga Cloud:
Prettiest Indian in All Downtown

Tugga, now seventeen years old, has been the Big Chief of the Red Flame Hunter Tribe for seven years. Slightly built, he may not look like a Big Chief, but he surely has the pride and respect of one. As I walked with the tribe last Mardi Gras, I was careful to stay well out of the way; the young Indians want and deserve all the respect they can get and don't need fascinated people like me talking to them, getting in the way. Tugga, like the other Indians, had worked on his suit for the eleven months before Mardi Gras Day. With the crown and all the carefully sown beads and sequins strung together on dental floss, the beautiful green, feathery suit weighs an amazing ninety pounds and spreads out three-feet wide. During much of the parade, Big Chief's Gang Flag, Eric Smith, had to carry the heaviest headpiece ever worn since they adorned King Arthur's knights. The lettuce-green suit still hangs in Mr. Ed's living room along with six other suits from past Mardi Gras.

Tugga began our conversation this way: "How ya'll doing out there? I'm the Big Chief of the Red Flame Hunters Youth Mardi Gras Indian Tribe." We'd been talking about his one-and-only fishing trip that Mr. Ed had taken him on. That was what he wanted to talk about when I asked him to tell me about himself. I didn't "pretty up" his language, just as I didn't put Mr. Ed's in so-called standard English. This is Tugga's story, and I want to pass it on the way he told it to me.

"Big Chief" Tugga Cloud, longtime leader of the Red Flame Hunters

Tugga: Well, me and Mr. Ed went fishing, and first we had to climb down this hole under the Danziger Bridge.[6] It was like a small hole on the creek side, opening in the woods, and they got a lot of trees down there. And there is a little small space where you got to throw your cast out, you got to just toss it out. You can't really lunge it out, you got to just toss it out there. And we catching fish out there. We put our bait, shrimp, on the hook.

And Mr. Ed taught me how to put the shrimp on the hook and tie the knot and all that. So, as I'm putting my shrimp on the hook, I throw my rod out there. So my pole is sitting in the water. Then Mr. Ed put his shrimp on his hook, then he threw his out there. And about one second later, he got something biting on his before they biting on mine.

Then about two seconds later, his phone start ringing. And he said he had to take it, so he said "Tugga! Grab my pole for me! Grab my pole, Tugga! Reel it in, I got something big!" I'm thinking he playing at first, so I grab his pole and he on the phone—that was his wife calling—he on the phone with his wife. And I'm reeling the pole in and I'm reeling, and I keep on reeling, and it's getting stronger and stronger. Then I see something coming up to the shore . . . and it's a great big old eel!

I said, "Mr. Ed! We don't want that! Put that back in the water!" I thought it was a big old snake at first. A big old eel. Then he like "Get that off my line, boy!" And I'm like, "We don't need that!" and he's like, "It's got a lot of meat on it!" Like we in survival mode, like we trying to survive or something. I was scared. I thought it was a big old snake.

Tugga, tell me more about yourself, where you are in school and all.

Alright, I go to McDonough 35. And I'm about to be out. Me and most of the tribe. We got a lot of us graduating this year. And we need to graduate. It's a must. It's our last year, we been going all this long, and we got to do it. I'm doing good at McDonough 35. My grade point average is a 3.1. So I'm doing very good.

If I get this book published and it spreads around, people will ask, "Who is this guy, Tugga?" So who are you, and what do you want people to know about you?

I just want people to know that I come from the Seventh Ward in New Orleans, and it's a real tough neighborhood and it's a real tough area. And I just want people to know that I'm the Big Chief of the Red Flame Hunters, the only all-youth tribe where we try to help the youth in our community. There's a

---

6. The Danziger Bridge is just outside of New Orleans where the infamous police shooting of several fleeing African Americans took place during Katrina; one man was killed.

lot of gun violence and robberies and a lot of criminal activity going on in our neighborhood. I haven't had problems with criminal activity, but my family members have. They've been a part of gun violence…

Tugga didn't want to go into any details about that violence though his neighborhood is one of the most violent in the nation. So I asked him how he found the Red Flame Hunters?

Well, I had some old friends and we used to be riding some bikes around, catching the chickens and roosters and hens and all that. Yeah, we used to be crawlin' under people's house or under people's fences, grabbing them all out the air, and grabbing them roosters and hens. And they had a community center called the Porch. And that was where them chickens used to sleep at. They used to sleep in a big old tree up back by the Porch. And the Porch was where Mr. Ed was the director of the community center. So we used to be all in the Porch backyard, catching all them little chickens and all that and Mr. Ed caught us in the backyard catching the chickens.

Instead of fussing at us very much, he asks us if we want to be Indians. And I said "Yeah!" I used to be scared of the Mardi Gras Indians. But I said yeah, and all my other friends said yeah. And that's how we became Indians. Then we started going back to the Porch, the community center. Then meeting at Mr. Ed's. Sewing our Indian suits, learning step by step. Being an Indian made a real difference because I got a lot of younger kids that look up to me, and I can't do nothing bad because that's setting a bad example for the younger kids that are looking up to me as the Big Chief. This year we have a total of seventeen Indians so far. And it's probably going to get bigger as the year goes on.

To somebody not from New Orleans, how do you explain what the Indians are?

The Mardi Gras Indians of New Orleans are black Indians and we are paying homage to the Indians that helped the slaves through the tunnels and through the underground caves and they hid the slaves when they were going toward freedom. And the Indians helped them. I started the Red Flame Hunters, and I came up with the name Red Flame Hunters. It was about the first thing that came to my imagination.

We spend most all year sewing our suits because we want our suits to be pretty. And I want to be the prettiest thing walking out the door on Mardi Gras Day. And on Mardi Gras, we sew so people can *see* because a lot of the kids don't sew. And we are the only kids' tribe that really sew. After I learned to sew, the game was over. Sewing is now easy after sticking my finger so many times.

We want people to see that not just the grownups but also the kids tribes can sew too. The Uptown Indians do flatwork, which is beaded flat work with sequins. The Downtown Mardi Gras Indians do three dimension suits. That's the artwork that pop out at you. Now the Red Flame Hunters, we are Downtown but we do both. We do a mixture of Uptown showing the pretty beads and pictures and like Downtown Indians that do the three-dimension suits.

The Red Flame Hunters brings me and the other friends together in so many ways because I'm meeting new friends 'cause I get a lot of my Indians from school and I tell a lot of kids at McDonogh 35 school that I have an Indian tribe. And every year we get new members, young people, to come and make new suits and come up with their own artistic design. And another thing is that a lot of family members get involved too. Yeah I have a cousin and my cousin, he was talking about bringing some more friends.

You said earlier that some of the young people you know get in bad trouble. What's going on?

Well, sometimes, it is that they don't have nothin' to do. When I come home from school, I go to Mr. Ed's and sew my Indian suit. Maybe if they had something to do, maybe they wouldn't be into the gangs like that. As long as I got the needle and thread, I'm out of trouble. As long as I got that needle and thread.

And what are some other ways that young people do some constructive things if they are not in a Mardi Gras Indian tribe?

Well, a lot of people, a lot of kids, they are either in a band at their schools or on the basketball team or football team. My friend Eric, the Gang Chief in the tribe, is on the football team. And they played Easton, Warren Easton. And they going to be playing them for the second time and Warren Easton won the first game and hopefully McDonough 35 can win this time.

Now I was with you last year, during Mardi Gras. I wasn't there the whole day, but I know you are very serious about this and I was following along—this old white guy following along—but if you are telling somebody what happened Mardi Gras day what would you say?

Mardi Gras Day last year was awesome. My suit was elaborate. It was big and green, taller than me. The suit had rhinestones all over. Being the Big Chief of the tribe, Red Flame Hunters, takes a lot of leadership and calls for respect. Even though you are wearing the prettiest suit, you have to have a big brain. Mardi Gras morning, when the Hunters proceeded out of the door, we had drums banging, tambourines ringing, and the Big Chief singing.

Wildman, whose job it is to protect the Chief, was acting wild in his orange Indian suit. He was not letting anyone get to me. He was really doing his job. The Spy Boy's job is to spy for other tribes. The Spy Boy walks down the street by himself looking for other tribes. The Gang Flag is closest to the Big Chief. That's Eric Smith. They had a lot of people out there waiting for us, and we were walking down the street banging drums and chanting, singing our songs. It was freezing cold, but we were still out singing and chanting like it was regular temperature, like it was hot out there. We had our feathers on walking up and down the street, dancing.

Then my Flag Boy, he saying that he's "the prettiest Flag Boy from way Downtown: Prettiest Flag Boy won't back down—be he black or be he brown." He's saying he the Flag boy, he gonna put a hole in the ground for the flag. Then I got Spy Boy telling me the Wild Man coming from another tribe, but we got our Wild Man, and we ain't got no reason to fear. We didn't have a Queen this year, but the Queen's job is simply to look pretty. Can't forget about Mr. Ed. He's not an Indian, but he's like the Red Fame mentor. He keeps us on the right track.

Finally, you have the Big Chief and I'm looking pretty, rearing back singing, throwing signals to my Spy Boy. I came out the door screaming. I'm a real Big Chief, 'cause I suit up every year. And everybody just singing and chanting and hollering with the tambourines ringing. And you got the drums banging and you got the cowbells. And everybody just singing and whooping.

So last Mardi Gras, I saw you all walking and singing and saw what happens when you meet the Big Chief from another tribe. All the other chiefs are grownups, right?

Right. Most of them are grownups. So when I meet another Chief, I just looking at his suit and trying to see whose is prettier. I know I'm prettier than him though. So I'm looking at his suit, seeing how his bead work is and how his three dimensional work is—does it pop out at you? We dance around hollering, like we angry with each other, but at the end of the day, we gonna shake hands and back off 'cause it's all about the bead work, and it's not about the violence. Back in the day, the Indians used to be shooting and fighting and grabbing each other up. And shooting each other in the head with a shotgun.[7]

And they used to have their shotguns wrapped around with feathers. And you would think it was a fake gun. But the whole while it was a real gun. And they would go off and shoot a shot in the air, and Indians used to be fighting back in the day. But now it's about the needlework. The needle and the threads. So when I meet another Big Chief, I'm trying to see who has the best bead works.

So, what else do you want people to know about the Red Flame Hunters?

---

7. The violence Tugga talks about was real, but now it's an all-for-fun war dance—for fun, but very serious.

Well, especially from last Mardi Gras, I remember that big old heavy crown that I had on. That's the thing I remember, 'cause I went home and my neck was hurting. I want people to know that we sew our own suits. And we have children in the Hunters that are six years old, seven years old, some of them five years old. We had a four-year-old before, and he just trying to pick up a needle and thread, trying to start sewing his own suit. Unlike all the other children that are in the tribes out there, they don't sew their suits out there. We of the Red Flame Hunters sew our own suits.

We're the best tribe out there. And we're the prettiest tribe out there, coming every year. I think for the rest of my life I'm going to be masking as an Indian. So every year I'm coming out the door. It's already been seven years so far, and we got a lot of years to go.

Let me ask you another kind of question: How do you see race relations in New Orleans now? I know the Mardi Gras Indians help people come together, but what about the big picture? Do you run into much racism still in New Orleans?

Naw, the only racism I see is the penitentiary. That's the only slave type thing I see. You got to suffer your consequences, but I think that's the only racism thing I see going on. Like, if you do something, like if you kill somebody, you got to suffer your consequences, you got to go to jail. But jail is like slavery. And racism is all through that part of things, in jails. I just mean like the racism has a part to do with the jail system because it's not run by black people. It's run by white people.

I think that is a big part of the problem, most things being run by white people. So have you run into racism or prejudice in your own life or with the Mardi Gras Indians?

No, I think we all bleed the same blood color. We all the same.

So, what else do we need to talk about? Tell me about your family, Tugga.

Oh, uh, my family doing good. My momma sews our under-suits that we put under our Indian suits. She sews that for the whole tribe every year. And my sister, I'm trying to get my little sister to be an Indian. She is about three years. Yep, I brought her a little bitty tambourine. She walking around the house talking about sharing her food with momma and Big Chief Tugga. So I think in the next year or two, I'll let her be an Indian. I have two nephews, they want to be Indians. They running around the house talking about Wild Man and Flag Boy and Big Chief. Little bitty nephews, four and five years old.

We sing all the time on Mardi Gras, and I make things up as we go along, like this:

Big Chief Tugga, early in the morning,
Big Chief Tugga, what they talking 'bout,
Big Chief Tugga all on fire,
Big Chief Red Flame Hunters,
Big Chief prettiest Indian in all Downtown

After Mardi Gras we had dressed up and performed at the Jazz Fest[8] and in the summer flew up to Boston to dance and sing. They'd never seen anything like that. So we told them all about the Indians. They didn't have a clue at all. Usually they invite the Brass Band[9], but last summer they invited us. This Mardi Gras, we getting bigger and better every year. On Mardi Gras morning, we need to start early so we don't get back so late at night.

How would you describe Mr. Ed? He wouldn't mind me asking.

Mr. Ed, he's like a father and friend. He's a real cool guy. He's always there when I need him. Like if I need some pearls or beads or dental floss, he's going out and get them. Sometimes when I'm down or somethin', say I'm aggravated with my momma or somethin', I go see Mr. Ed and he gets me laughin' and I forget all about it.

Mr. Ed was helped out by a lot of father figures when he was young, and now he wants to pass that on to you and the Indians and you will pass it on to others. Not that this is important to me, but I am curious: Are you part of any church community?

No, I'm not but the Red Flame Hunters are my church, and Mr. Ed's home is my church building.

Reaction:
It's pretty clear who Big Chief Tugga's special angel is, and how he, Tugga, is now passing on his prettiest self to others.
Since we lived in serious-minded, often humorless Boston for six years, I can imagine just how amazed and delighted the people there were when they saw the Red Flame Hunters in full regalia singing and dancing and hollering out their Indian calls, suited in their prettiest best. Tugga didn't remember

8. The very popular Jazz and Heritage Festival is held in late spring each year in New Orleans.

9. The legendary New Orleans Preservation Hall Jazz Band

the name of the group that flew them to Boston, but "they were very nice."

When Tugga began our conversation talking extensively about his fishing trip with Mr. Ed, I was getting a little bored, wanting to move on. But then I realized how important such a trip was for a teenager who had seldom left his neighborhood. Being at that fishing spot where "they got a lot of trees," tossing out the line, and the eel that looked like a snake—those things were as important as anything.

Besides, when I was Tugga's age, I probably would have talked about my summer fishing near Fort Sumter in Charleston Harbor with Pappoo, my grandfather, and how he called me Shipshape since I made such a mess of things in the boat, and how once we put a string of fish over the side to keep them alive and a how a great big old shark I could have touched almost got them and my fingers as I pulled in those fish. I still dream about that shark.

Finally, I do appreciate Tugga's determination not to be a bad example for young kids in his "tough" neighborhood. I wish we in churches could reach those young kids like the Red Flame Hunters do.

Gang Flag Eric Smith and How God Spoke to Him

Until last fall Eric was a regular participant in the sewing afternoons at Mr. Ed's. He is an outstanding football player—outside linebacker on his high school team—so he wasn't able to come to many sewing sessions while football practice was going on. When I met with him after Christmas, he didn't want to talk or write very much about the Red Flame Hunters, but he did want to write about one of the most important experiences in his young life. Here is what he said about himself and the Hunters, followed by what he wrote about his friend Bouncer, who died tragically.

> **Eric:** What I want people to know about me is that I am an all-around person, that I am active and I want to do things. Like someday I wanna go skydiving. I also like sewing my suit. My football experience has been great. A lot of college coaches have been coming to see me all month to see if I will play with them. I hope to go to Nicholls here in Louisiana.
>
> I found the Red Flame Hunters through some friends and have been active in it about five years. I am the Gang Flag. I give orders to everyone from the Chief and try to keep everyone straight when we meet another tribe or when we're just singing and dancing along the street. I am the Big Chief's right hand man. I like sewing and getting ready for Mardi Gras because it keeps me focused and calm, stuff like that. Being an Indian also helps me have patience. And in school, I really did need to learn a lot about patience. I learn patience by sitting here sewing one set of beads at a time. You can't hurry that up. My mom and papa are the most important people to me, and they like me being an Indian.

Here is what Eric wrote about his friend Bouncer. (When Eric writes about "second-lining" in New Orleans, he is telling of another long tradition in the black community—the times when young and old alike follow brass bands and members of clubs—the first lines— through the streets, singing and dancing, playing instruments, and twirling parasols).

Growing up in New Orleans, teens died by the week. My family and I grew up in church. The church I go to is called House of Healing. I have been a junior usher there for three years as time passes by. For a while I stopped going to my church and started attending second lines every Sunday. One day I got sad news saying my friend Bouncer was gunned down in a crossfire at the Chocolate Bar on Broad Street. He was only nineteen. Bouncer and I went to the same church and took part in second lines and always talked about sports and other things that made our friendship stronger.

Some days after his death, I would go outside and think of the good memories we had. His death was like losing one of my sisters. We joked all the time. My mom pulled me to the side when Bouncer died and said, "Son, I can talk to you about Christ, but you have to start coming back to church on your own." As I think about memories of me and Bouncer, I realize life is short so I pray every morning thanking God for me living each and every day.

The Wednesday after Bouncer died, my mom told me to go to Bible study because my pastor could talk to me. Pastor George Green sat down with me and we started talking. And he said, "Eric, why would you stop coming to a place where blessings and prayers come from?" And I said, "Pastor George, I really don't know." I learned that everyone has got to die some day, so why should I jeopardize my life from a second line? Before pastor and I stopped talking, he said, "You can go to second lines, but just put God first." And after our talk that was how I started doing things.

It seems a long time since Bouncer passed. I still have my moments when I am talking to him, his spirit. Until this day, I still don't know why he died at an early age. Everyone always tells me to stay in church and your blessing will come. I know that that could be a good start for me. Some days I'm thinking about all the bad things that could have happened to me, but I know that God has my back. If I didn't learn anything else from God, I learned to keep my head up and keep moving. And I am glad I am here with Mr. Ed and my friends.

Reaction:

Even though I tried to get Eric to talk more about his Indian experience, I had to respect what he wanted to talk and write about. He didn't call either Pastor Green or Mr. Ed his angels, but it was pretty clear that they were.

Chapter Two

The College Track
Afterschool Program

In the spring of 2015, Jed Horne, who wrote perhaps the best book on Hurricane Katrina (*Breach of Faith*), put New Orleans native Walter Isaacson in touch with me to see if I might help students in an afterschool program write their personal essays for college admission. As I had taught English to so-called remedial freshman students at the University of New Orleans for many years, I readily agreed to assist in the program and am still working with the students one evening each week. With a lot of support from Isaacson, College Track, New Orleans, got underway in 2008. The program introduces itself this way:

> College Track is a national college completion non-profit that empowers students from underserved communities to graduate from college. From the summer before ninth grade through college graduation, our ten-year program removes the barriers that prevent students from earning their college degree by providing them with comprehensive academic support, leadership training, financial and college advising, and scholarships. Our students learn the skills necessary to succeed in college and beyond.

> Over the past seventeen years, national College Track has demonstrated a record of success. Over 90 percent of our students are admitted to four-year colleges and our students graduate from college at 2.5 times the national average of their lower income peers (defined as PELL grant eligible). In the 2014 to 2015 academic year, we served over 2,000 students across seven sites in California, Colorado, and New Orleans.

> We know a college education has the power to create a completely different life path for our students far beyond earning a degree. College Track alumni leave their campuses, not just as graduates but as the new standard for their friends, families, and neighborhoods. In making college a reality for one, we make it an expectation for all.

Sherdren Burnside, the director of College Track from 2008 to May of 2015 and a former English teacher herself, gives her introduction to the College Track this way: "I've witnessed the shock and frustration of college freshmen who, after receiving top marks in local high schools, entered first-year essay classes without skills to keep up. So far behind, many of these students withdrew. College was simply too late and too demanding for catching up on basic skills. We often hear the catchphrase 'writing as process'; however, I'm not convinced that we regularly model our own advice. *Our* students write not because they have to, but because they want to, and because we are offering them an audience for their ideas. They have evidenced discipline and patience. I am hard-pressed to think of any quality more important in a writer. I am very proud of them."

In this chapter, eight College Track students share their writing. Unlike most of the stories in this book, these eight stories came to me as essays, most of which I helped guide. I am including these from two sources. The first six stories come from the 2014 and 2015 graduation booklets (nicely produced with seven stories from the students and their pictures); the last two stories , much longer, come from a book that College Track published in 2012: *Young in America: New Orleans*. (I include Briana Brown's essay and poem from *Young in America* in the Introduction.) I introduce each story briefly and at the end of each story, I describe how these stories touched my life and, I hope, will touch the reader's life. While most of the students don't use the word *angels*, it is usually clear who their angels are, and I believe they—the young people—will be angels for the next generation.

- -

Robert Burnside:
Breaking Chains and Moving Forward

Sherdren's son wrote this piece for the 2015 College Track graduation booklet. I had the privilege of working with him on his story, doing my best not to get in the way. Robert focuses on the greatest problem in New Orleans, our murder rate, often the highest of any city in the nation. Robert graduated from International High School in May of 2015 and now attends Southern University and A&M College in Baton Rouge. "Breaking Chains" is his title.

Surrounded by red, white, blue flashing lights I froze at the approaching white officer's command. In that moment, time stood still. The sound of police sirens grew louder and louder as two more police cars pulled up to the curb and officers jumped out of their vehicles. Every single police officer looked the same: white pale skin, light blue shirt, with hands on their firearm. Though frozen I could still hear my friend Alonzo trying to explain to the cops as they swiftly surrounded me about how we were just students. Alonzo and I were on a corner waiting to catch the bus to College Track.[1]

My heart began to race as I wondered about my fate. Prior to this day I had never been stopped by a cop. As an officer frisked me for weapons or drugs, I thought to myself why am I being treated as if I were a criminal? I don't know

---

1. Alonzo tells his story later in this chapter.

Robert Burnside, proud member of College Track

where it came from, but I mustered the courage to ask the officer, "Why am I being stopped? Did I do something wrong?" Yes, I had worn a red hoodie over my school uniform on my way from school to College Track.

In those moments I experienced the effects of a society mired in discrimination. I became aware of the discrimination all around me that I previously did not notice. I became aware of the perception that others held of me. I resolved not to become bitter, but to become better. The officers, six of them in three cars, were responding to a call reporting that there was a man with a gun wearing a red hoodie in the area.

I am an International Baccalaureate student at the International High School of New Orleans. I like to play basketball. I volunteer at my church and in my community. I will attend a four-year university, excel, and graduate. I have aspirations of becoming an engineer. To the responding officers, I was a suspect. To them I was an African American male, wearing a red hoodie, armed and dangerous. Having found no drugs or weapons on me and being satisfied with my story that I was traveling from school to an afterschool program, I was released. One of the officers apologized, his initially hostile tone now calmed.

Day after day I hear reports of black males being arrested, shot and/or killed. In 2013 there were over two hundred murders in New Orleans. Ninety percent of the victims were African American and 86 percent of the suspects were African American. There are fourteen thousand youths between sixteen and twenty-four years old in New Orleans who are not in school and are not working. My peers, young men who look just like me, are overrepresented among the city's criminals and victims of crime. I now realized I am a member of an endangered species. In those few frozen moments, I made a decision to be not what society portrays me to be. Being criminalized by the police liberated me. It fueled my passion to break the cycle of discrimination and violence that exists in my community.

Today, I am working with my church to help eliminate youth violence in my community through a violence awareness campaign called Stop Killing People (SKP). My goal is to ultimately eradicate racial discrimination and youth violence in my community. This will take what College Track calls "GRIT": Guts, Resilience, Integrity, and Tenacity." I got GRIT!

Reaction:

When Robert talks about the unfair—and probably racist—"stop and search" and how it changed his whole attitude toward life for the better, I couldn't help but think of the Joseph story in Genesis. His brothers had sold him into slavery when he was young. They did not know that over the years Joseph rose from the chains of slavery to become the equivalent of Egypt's prime minister. When there was famine in the land of Israel and his brothers came to Egypt seeking food, they met with Joseph, whom they did not recognize. When Joseph finally revealed who he was, he said to the brothers: "What you meant for evil, God used for Good" (Genesis 50:20). You enslaved me, he was saying, but I became the very person to save you and our families from starvation.

If only all of us could discover the "good" in the most frightening experiences! We could learn from both Joseph *and* Robert, who strives to become "not bitter but to become better." If only.

--- --- --- --- --- --- --- --- --- --- --- --- --- --- --- ---

Tia Cage: Differently Abled

Tia Cage graduated from Lake Area High School in 2015 and is now attending Xavier University of New Orleans, Louisiana. I got to know her at College Track and urged her to tell some of her story for the 2015 College Track graduation booklet.

The summer of my sophomore year, I was nominated by my geometry teacher for the National Youth Leadership Forum on Medicine. I was accepted and stayed on the UCLA's campus for a week and a half, where I had the privilege to speak with doctors in different fields. There was a pediatrician who stood out to me, but I wanted to become a nurse because they're a little more involved with the patient than a doctor. It was then I did some research and realized what I aspired to be: a pediatric nurse practitioner.

Tia Cage, College Track member, now "differently abled"

It wasn't long after that trip that I was diagnosed with metastatic osteosarcoma, a form of bone cancer. At first, my doctor recommended amputating my leg because the cancer was located in a very difficult area on my pelvis. I told the doctor not to go through with the amputation. I didn't know it then, but my life was drastically changed. The only time I had spent at the hospital before was for volunteer work. I had spent over sixty hours as a volunteer worker that summer alone. Soon, Children's Hospital became my home away from home.

The first few months of my treatment were exhausting. Having to be in the hospital for days then leave to be sick at home only to be right back in the hospital was not how I imagined my junior year of high school, but I didn't want that to stop me. In the beginning, I met with tutors as much as I could, as I wasn't allowed to attend school because of how the chemotherapy affected my immune system. After my surgery, though, it was somewhat more difficult to keep up with my lessons. Because of where the tumor was located, the four lower vertebrae of my spine were fused together, the right side of my pelvis was removed, and a few nerves were cut leaving me unable to move or feel my right leg. In June of 2014, I completed my chemotherapy treatments. Today, I am cancer-free.

Getting back on track with school my senior year was harder than I had hoped. I am mostly wheelchair bound, and although my right leg isn't functional, I am learning to walk with assistance (with a brace, walker, and crutches) in physical therapy. My heart was set on nursing, but I've questioned whether I would ever be able to do something that rigorous. I think about how my life would be different if I weren't diagnosed with cancer. I would be working with JUMA [a special program for teens] at the Superdome, where I would get to see my favorite football team, the Saints, while saving money for college. I would be helping my family in any way I could. I would be a member of the varsity volleyball team at Lake Area High School, a loyal volunteer worker at many different places, a better friend, daughter, sister, and aunt.

I wouldn't change a thing, though. I surprise myself with the goals I accomplish every day. I have also found the career I would be more than happy doing for the rest of my life, which is social services. One day, I will start my own non-profit organization helping those I've learned to call "differently abled teens," like me. I am still striving to have some normalcy in my life. It's just the beginning though. I know that I have so much more to look forward to, and whenever I get discouraged, I have to think about the fact that everything I have gone through has made me stronger. My trials and tribulations have only increased my faith.

Reaction:

For me, the most moving passage here comes when Tia imagines how life would be different if she were not stricken by cancer. She would be working at the Superdome, saving money for college, playing on the varsity volleyball team; she would be a loyal volunteer and a better friend, daughter, sister, and aunt. Of course, we, her readers, suspect she has been a wonderful friend and family member and will succeed in her chosen profession.

Tia introduced me to the term "differently abled." I love that and wish it for all young and older people who are "disabled" in any way. Tia's story made me think of Carlos, a differently abled wheelchair user I taught years ago in a remedial English class at the University of New Orleans. I used his essay as an example of strong "argument" writing in my 1983 textbook, *Writing for a Reason*. He was making the point that wheelchair users must band together to seek their Constitutional rights. Carlos ended his essay this way: "Divided we stall, united we roll." Patrick Henry could not have said it better.

Malik Brooks: A Healing Gift

Malik wrote this personal story for the 2014 College Track graduation booklet. He is now a student at Louisiana's historically black Grambling State University. As Malik tells his story of how he was able to offer a kind of healing to a devastated mother who had lost her child, he does not emphasize the gift he made but rather the gift that was given to him as he brought the mother and son together in a wonderful re-made photograph.

Sweat rolled off my face while pushing the level down on the heat press. The shop could get pretty hot between stacking shirts, printing banners, pressing images, and taking orders. I had been working at Exclusive Tees in downtown New Orleans for about two weeks during the summer of my sophomore year. I had experience in graphic design, but I'd never physically made a product. I also had to get used to hearing customer requests such as these:

"I need a shirt for my daughters' Strawberry Shortcake party."
"My church is having a fundraiser on Sunday. We need a banner."
"We're having a family reunion and need two hundred shirts."

These were some of the orders I took, but many were far more emotional:

"My father passed away."
"Last week my boyfriend was killed in a car accident."
"My brother got shot."

I'd heard that last line a lot. In New Orleans it's a tradition to get a shirt made in memory of a loved one. New Orleans has a bad history of crime, and at one point it was the murder capital of the United States. When I was eleven, I witnessed my first shooting from my front porch. When I was fourteen, my little cousin was shot. When I was fifteen, another student pulled a gun on me; he didn't like the way I looked at him. At sixteen, I had grown numb to violence. I was a kid with the mentality of a hardened soldier. This culture of violence had taught my generation not to care unless we were directly affected and even then to quickly move on.

So when a lady walked in and asked me to make a shirt for her son who'd passed, her request didn't strike me as anything unusual. I handed her a sheet to fill out.

Date of Birth:
Date of Death:
Pictures to be used:

She handed me the form back. His name was Shone. He was sixteen like me. Then she handed me two pictures. The first was a picture of Shone standing in the street alone. Tall. Light-skinned. Red gym shorts. He smirked at the camera. The second image was of Shone and his sister hugging each other.

"This is a beautiful picture." I told her. Shone's mother explained that she had moved to California when he was small; she didn't have many photos taken with him. "I just wish I had more happy moments with my son." Her head dropped as if speaking about it exhausted her. I noticed how much her son looked like her. Same skin color. Same cheekbones. She gave me her email, and I told her I'd be in contact.

Her anguish lingered with me. I understood the void that she felt, that longing for more time with her son. She didn't even have a picture with him to reminisce upon. I could have just done the job with what was provided, but I felt compelled to make her something special. Logging onto Facebook, I directly went to search her email. I found a picture of her sitting at a table with her arm stretched out. The background was easy to create, but the challenge was piecing Shone into the picture. I moved the cursor back and forth, from his arm to her shoulder, while adjusting the contrast until I couldn't tell they weren't originally one image. I searched for flaws, but all I could see were the two smiling faces of a mother and her son holding one another.

When Shone's mother walked back in the shop and unwrapped the shirt with the picture of her and her son, tears clouded her eyes. I had thought maybe it was a bad idea to make the picture. A tear landed in a crease in her cheek. But she was smiling. She hugged me, and I held her for a long time. Her pain was real, and I felt as if Shone was my own brother.

Reaction:

As a student of the Bible, I am struck by the creative way in which Malik offered his healing, using his skills and compassion for sure, but also thinking something up that was outside-the-box creative. All through the Bible, God surprises everyone over and over again, stimulating our imagination and hope.

Who would have thought that a small group of slaves could successfully escape from Egypt? Or that, as they approached the Red Sea about to be destroyed, they would find that a strong east wind had blown the waters back, allowing them to escape, or that the water would return just in time to stop the pursuing Egyptians? Who would have thought that Jesus, whether someone's savior or not, would move from carpenter's son in a minor Roman province to becoming the most famous person who has ever lived? Who'd have thought that Jesus, through a favorite parable, would counsel leaving ninety-nine sheep to possible—probable?—danger to seek out the one who was lost? I marvel at these surprises and also the ones I come to know up close, like Malik's finding just the right way to offer healing to a weeping mother he didn't even know. No question as to who her angel was.

Now some sad news. Just before this book was submitted for publication, Malik was shot and seriously wounded in a drive-by shooting. He is now recovering.

Tayler Payton: An Attitude of a Warrior

I worked with Tayler when she wrote this for the 2015 College Track booklet, but I didn't need to offer her much help. Tayler graduated from one of the premier public high schools in New Orleans, maybe anywhere, Ben Franklin. She is now attending Tulane University.

As I progressed through my academic career, I faced obstacles I had to figure out on my own. Certain situations were easier than others, but they all required a certain character I gained through exposure to these obstacles. During middle school, my grandmother was diagnosed with lung cancer. She had been battling with a habit of smoking cigarettes for the majority of her life.

Three months after she had stopped smoking, she started experiencing an intense cough, and we had to take her to the hospital. The doctors discovered that she had stage-four lung cancer and would only survive for a couple of months. And so as time progressed, she got in worse shape and began to deteriorate and fade away.

During this time I was able to help her and make things easier for her. As I fixed her food, I can remember thoughts flooding through me. "I hope she has a good day today and eats something." After I set my grandmother up with food, I would ask her if she wanted to take her morphine. I always knew when she was in the most pain because those were the only times she wanted that dreadful medicine.

My grandmother passed right around the time I had to take the Louisiana Educational Assessment Program (LEAP) test in the eighth grade and was going through my application process for acceptance into Benjamin Franklin High School. My grandmother's illness had a tremendous toll on me and began to interfere with my academic performance. The day of my grandmother's funeral was BFHS's registration day and was mandatory for incoming students. Due to my state of mind and the grief I was experiencing, I didn't want to attend registration and began to forget how vital this opportunity was.

This situation left me with a decision to either give up and lose sight of my goals or push through the pain. Thankfully, with motivation and a lot of determination, I did exceptionally well on the LEAP test and achieved the necessary requirements to get into Benjamin Franklin High School. I gathered the willpower and strength to go to the registration directly after the funeral with my head held high and an attitude of a warrior.

Dealing with my grandmother's illness and death bettered me as a person and helped develop my character. As a result of my experience, I have gained tenacity and ambition. My grandmother was very vital to me and gave me knowledge, wisdom, and love that I will carry with me the rest of my life. She always expected the very best from me because she had no doubt in her mind that I could accomplish many things.

Every time that I feel discouraged or inadequate, I revisit some of the heartening words she would say, and it gives me comfort and strength to persist. She would often say, "Tayler, God would never bring you this far to leave you." After losing one of my biggest supporters at the worst possible time in my life, I then realized that with dedication, resilience, and ambition, I could overcome anything.

Reaction:

In recalling her grandmother's belief in her and expectation for her, Tayler is able to call on what I have come to call a Kingdom of God treasure. When I hold forth on the subject in churches and prisons, I talk about Jesus's parable of the buried treasure (Matthew 13: 44-46). A farmer is digging in a field and by chance finds a treasure, one that makes him know he has found the Kingdom of God. He sells all he owns to buy the field so he will have the treasure forever. And then, he buries the treasure again. The people in the town see no difference in the man, except that now he is poor. But he knows that treasure is always there to be rediscovered, dug up. No one can take that Kingdom of God treasure away. Among her other treasures, Tayler always has her grandmother's love, talent, and hope to reclaim, dig up. Her angel lives on.

Though never coming close to criminal activity, Tayler reminds me of many of the inmates I get to know at the Louisiana State Prison at Angola. Through the international Kairos Prison Ministry, I see inmates uncovering long-lost memories of transforming love from many years earlier in their lives. The long Kairos weekends, full of love themselves, give inmates a different kind of treasure as they move back on Mondays to dehumanizing prison life. The love experienced through Kairos is always there to be rediscovered, dug up, once again inspiring and giving hope.

Kaila Holloway: How My Grandmother's Cooking Helped Me Survive Hurricane Katrina

I often say that in spite of all the underlying racism in New Orleans people get along, day by day, year by year because of our common culture. Everyone loves jazz, the city's parks, Mardi Gras and second lining, the Saints—win or lose—and the great food. This essay is about how our food redeems! Kaila wrote it for the 2014 graduation leaflet. I never got a chance to meet her, though I feel I know her. Kaila is now a student at Howard University.

"MeMe what are you cooking?" I ask my grandmother. The thick aroma of the Cajun "trinity" (onion, celery, and bell pepper) cooking in the frying pan fills the air. In another pan, her sweet barbecue sauce softly pops.

"Jambalaya and barbecue ribs," she smiles; she knows jambalaya is my favorite food. Her knife clacks against the cutting board as she slices links of Andouille sausage.

My love for cooking began with my grandmother. While other children looked forward to Friday and Saturday, my favorite day of the week was Sunday, the day MeMe and I cooked. Starting at the tender age of five, I spent every weekend at MeMe's house assisting in the kitchen. I often chose the most complex dishes that I could think of, like omelets or French toast. Once I finished in the kitchen, I would prepare my makeshift restaurant. I handcrafted menus, set the table, and acted as the waitress for the day. My most pleasant childhood memories started in MeMe's kitchen: the scent of her spice cabinet, taste of her crawfish étouffée, and the thin smile across her face.

Our Sunday tradition came to an end on August 29, 2005. Hurricane Katrina stole the only life and community I had ever known. It would be a month until I saw MeMe again, but I refused to let our ritual die. In my temporary home in New Roads, Louisiana, I put my skills to the test. This was the first time I cooked spaghetti and meatballs without MeMe's help. I seasoned the ground meat with a combination of salt, pepper, Tony Chachere's, garlic, and onion powder, then proceeded to roll it out into perfect spheres like she taught me. While baking the meatballs, I recreated her homemade tomato sauce, making sure to add her secret ingredient, a pinch of sugar. I made a mental list of everything that I needed to make dinner perfect: set the table, make menus, and plate the food. The smells brought me back to my Sundays in MeMe's kitchen.

Returning to New Orleans, I found my home destroyed, my school closed, and my friends scattered throughout the country. Yet MeMe's recipes prevailed. The only part of my old life that remained was my culture, in particular, food. Because MeMe relocated to Baton Rouge after Hurricane Katrina, I rarely saw her anymore, but I refused to let our distance stop me from cooking. The kitchen has become my safe haven, the one place where I am perfectly content.

When I am cooking, my confidence is at its zenith. I love the feeling of satiating someone's taste buds with the food that I create. Regardless of location or circumstance, the kitchen will always remind me of my childhood spent within the white walls of MeMe's domain.

The kitchen's significance lies in what it does for people. My entire family convenes during the holidays at the dinner table. We all sit as one to reconnect and reminisce over delectable cuisine. Food not only has the power to unite families around the dinner table, but to bridge cultures around the world. Often, our first experience of another culture is a taste of it—mole sauce, curry, lemongrass—enabling us to connect with other cultures through the senses.

On a much more personal level, MeMe's influence persists today. I now aspire to own my own restaurant, a place where families can come together over a nice meal. As an early start on this dream, I began a baking business, Kaila's Creations, using recipes for Italian Cream Cake and mini pecan pies learned during my many weekends at MeMe's house.

"Kalia, what's on the menu?" I imagine MeMe asking as she walks through the doors of my new restaurant. A wide smile flashes across my face. "Everything you taught me."

Reaction:

Kalia helped me know just how important it is to recall long-ago stories from family members who raised us. For her it was the confidence and perseverance that her grandmother instilled in her as they cooked wonderful New Orleans food together. For me, as I think back, it was my grandfather, Pappoo, who took me fishing most summer days in Charleston harbor with my older cousin, Neddie. Pappoo would tell us stories and quote sayings from the past. Like the old man who could not stand moving to Upcountry, South Carolina: "There ain't no mullet in the creek, no marsh on the bank, and it's always ebb tide." Neddie would cringe with embarrassment when Pappoo would interact with other fishermen when we were out close to Fort Sumter. "How many fish you caught, Ned?" an old friend would ask. "Well, I'll tell you Galliard, when I catch this one that's about to bite and another one, we'll have two." I could go on and on about Pappoo and will in my journal—the good and the not-so-good.

— —

Alonzo Booth III: Why I Write

Alonzo graduated from high school and College Track in May of 2015 and now attends Franklin and Marshall College in Lancaster, Pennsylvania. He has been one of the most promising College Track writers and, with Walter Isaacson's help, was able to attend the Aspen Institute Summer Words Conference in both 2012 and 2013. He wrote "Why I Write" for the 2015 College Track graduation booklet. I helped him with it, but he didn't need much. Here is an excerpt from the essay and two of his poems: "First World vs. Third World" and "New Year's Eve in New Orleans." With all of the beads, the flashing, the costumes, the jazz, "New Year's Eve" could describe multi-cultural Mardi Gras Day in "the city that care forgot," the Big Easy.

Besides the natural beauty, Aspen is one of the first places I ever wrote poetry. I discovered my ability to channel emotions through words and to affect audiences with the power of my language. I write anything that comes to mind whether it is a poem or a profound idea that captivates my imagination, a skill that was not a part of my academic upbringing.

Growing up, the New Orleans school system did not encourage me to write. I was rarely challenged by the overly-simplistic assignments given to me by the English teachers. Even the teachers committed to instilling a love of reading and writing always seemed too stressed or overworked to pay much attention to me or my writing. This environment, while not ideal, forced me to grow as a writer. With that lack of structure I developed my own individual sense of how to write. This had pros and cons, because while I developed a way of writing that was entirely my own, I lacked the critical feedback that comes from being part of the rigorous academic setting that I craved.

In eighth grade, I did encounter a teacher who profoundly shaped my academic career. My English teacher was a hard grader who asked us to write, write, and then write some more. I was surprised by how much I loved this challenge. If you had told me at age ten that I would grow up to love writing poetry, I would have laughed hysterically.

For most of my childhood I immersed myself in the virtual reality of video games because the clear rules of each game and deviation from my everyday life felt empowering. It was only through the process of trying to write poetry myself that I began to see that the incomprehensible feat was not frightening, but exhilarating. I wanted to escape the life into which I had been born. Poetry gave me a means of escape from circumstances that confined me, but unlike video games, which are passive, poetry is active. Instead of diving into a world created for me, I want to shape worlds that leave my readers in suspense of what will happen next.

Reaction:

Of course the first angel in this story is the eighth grade English teacher who forced Alonzo to "write, write, and then write some more." In my conversation with Alonzo, I heard about other angels, especially those who staff College Track.

Alonzo finds his freedom in writing poetry; I find mine in listening to stories from all kinds of people and then writing them down. But we seek the same kind of freedom in our everyday lives, freedom "from circumstances which confine." As a young man, he fears that confinement; for me the older I get (now seventy-seven) the more I realize that if I let it, the world will close in on me. This project of listening to the "angels," supporting them when I can, and writing about them is keeping me from giving in to what I call that old-age anxiety. The inner voice is saying, "Barnwell, write, write, and then write some more." Here are two of his poems:

First World vs. Third World

So listen closely as the things I'm going to tell you I want you to take personally
Us humans live in a world where everyone takes the little things for granted
But what if you were the young boy or girl in poverty
Wondering when the next meal was coming

Knowing that they have a disease that can be cured but don't have the money for the antidote
Or the Indian woman who sells her whole head of hair just to keep her family fed
While you use that hair to grab a dude's attention who doesn't give a damn about you most of the time
Little children stealing from tourists because they want that apple on the stand
In tattered clothes the most worn out shirt would be a gift to them

But you really have the audacity to complain about not having hot water
They cannot get CLEAN WATER!
You complain because you can't get the next pair of Jordans that just came out
But they just want a pair of shoes
You complain that you don't have a ride anywhere
But they walk almost everywhere they need to go and are at longer distances than what you drive

You complain that you wanted steak instead of chicken
But honestly these children would take bread by itself and think it's a five star meal
You complain that there isn't Wi-Fi in the area
But they wish just to see basic cable
While you buy the next new gadget that everyone wants
They get the next best thing to keep them from getting sick or even worse

Before you want to complain about the little things you don't have
Just know that there is someone somewhere worse off than you.

New Year's Eve in New Orleans

10 minutes left
Thousands of people crowding the neon lit streets
The different alcoholic beverages all over the paved streets
From beer to the famous New Orleans Grenade[2]
A man with a bunch of colorful beads sings "O Happy Day"

2. A popular New Orleans drink made with gin, green alcohol, melon liqueur, rum, and vodka.

Down the next block, a group plays on their drums and guitars
Women in their early 20s flash a crew for some beads
They must have been tourists

Another man passes you but you take a second glance
He wears a neon green wig, a green tutu, eyeliner, carrying a wand, and has
pink wings on his back

But the only indicator that allows you to assume it was a man is the full grown
beard on his face
Bars filled with intoxicated youth in their early 20s
The overwhelming stench of alcohol and pee fill your lungs like a rushing wind

5 minutes left
Jazz music fills the French Quarter with the urge to get everyone tuned up
Everyone has their last drink of this year
Time to get my last plate of beignets before the new year
The warm, flaky beignets with the sweet white powder fills my mouth with
such intense flavors
That may lead to a severe sugar coma
Trying not to exhale while eating the beignets so the sugar doesn't get all over
my blue polo shirt

1 minute left
The final countdown is coming
Everyone finds the person they want to kiss, same or different gender
There was this hazel-brown-eyed young lady with luscious brown curly hair
that had the skin complexion of caramel
Her lips covered in red lipstick screaming, "Come kiss me!"

Final 10 seconds
We were all ready to bring in the new year
Her voice was as sweet as an angel playing a golden harp
10, 9
We looked deep into each other's eyes not breaking eye contact
8,7,6
Slowly moving, the world starts to slow down as if we were the only ones on
Earth
5,4,3
Centimeters away the warmth from her lips brushes the nerves on mine
I wrap my arms around her

Happy New Year!

Candace Gautreaux:
From Mentee to Mentor, Candace's Miracle

Candace wrote this essay for the 2012 College Track publication *Young in America: New Orleans*. She graduated from McDonogh 35 and attends Delgado Community College in New Orleans with plans to transfer to Dillard University. She wants to pass on what a teacher gave her as she reaches out to others. Candace also writes about a grant she received for her writing and how she has used it to start a mentoring program aimed at lowering high school dropout rates.

"Here is a boy with five small barley loaves and two small fish, but how far will they go among so many?" proclaimed Andrew, Jesus's disciple (John 6:9). Andrew thought that five loaves and two fish would not be enough to feed the thousands of hungry people who followed Jesus. Hearing that his sacrificial offering was not enough must have made this young boy feel the way I felt many times in elementary and middle school.

In school, I was alienated and ostracized by my peers. I had been retained twice, once in second grade due to major surgery to correct a limb length shortage. Although my absences were excused, my mother felt I had missed too many days and needed to be retained. In fourth grade I did not pass my Louisiana Educational Assessment Program (LEAP) test. I felt like I was the dumb, sickly child in my family. Students, including my younger siblings, would tease me and tell me I would never make it out of high school. I hated school. I had let my little sister catch up to me. We even shared some of the same classes. Still I was averaging D's. I needed help from my sister, but was too ashamed to ask. I thought to myself, I'm the big sister. She should be coming to me for help. Slowly, I was giving up on myself.

Sitting in my eighth-grade math class in New Orleans, I felt like I had been dropped in the middle of Tokyo. My teacher was speaking, but his words sounded like a foreign language I didn't comprehend. "Does anyone have any questions?" he asked.

I had a million questions racing in my head, yet not the courage to ask a single one. I would just sit and look around, believing that I was the only one who didn't understand. I was caught between frustration and shame. Raising my hand would mean letting others know how little I understood. Instead of choosing to do something, I opted for the easy way out. I concluded school just wasn't for me. I was done. As soon as I could, I would drop out.

Many students encouraged me to get a General Education Development (GED) credential rather than try to persevere. People would say things like: "If I were in your shoes, I'd drop out" and "You must be the dumb one in the family to let your little sister catch up with you." I wasn't catching on in school. I had insecurities about it, and their comments put the icing on the cake. However, when Mr. Fruga, my eighth-grade teacher, heard that I wanted to leave school, he pulled me aside. He had been like a father to me—giving me attention, warning me about boys, and motivating me.

Mr. Fruga looked at me with his brown eyes. He ran his hand along his trimmed beard. "I know school seems hard, but you can make it. I believe in you." Mr. Fruga made me promise to do some research on high school dropouts and their chances of success. Little has changed for this group since 2008. In Louisiana, 53 percent of students who enter ninth grade will leave high school without a diploma. Annually, their earning potential will be less than $20,000 in an already depressed economy. Having someone to believe in me when I didn't believe in myself saved me from becoming a part of this statistic.

The disciple Andrew was right! Five loaves and two fish were not enough to feed the multitude. Feeding the five thousand required a miracle, and that's exactly what Jesus did for the multitude and for me. My academic skills and willingness to succeed weren't enough to keep me from giving up on school. Having a caring adult who believed in me made all the difference—that was my miracle. I got the courage and strength to believe in myself when I blocked all of the negative comments out and started focusing on my education and myself. Once I did that, I started seeing good results in my academics.

When my principal, Mrs. Mitchell, and Mr. Fruga saw that I was improving, they encouraged me to apply to College Track, an after-school program for college-bound high school students. For the past four years, I have attended after-school tutoring sessions Monday through Friday even though the program requires only three days per week. The extra help I got at College Track has indeed kept me on track.

While participating in the program, I also seized other opportunities to better my writing skills. I wrote a proposal and received the "My Idea Grant" from America's Promise Alliance to start my mentoring program called "Mini Butterflies." I started this program for ten- to thirteen-year-old girls to help lower the high school dropout rates. I know that it was important to reach out to younger girls because eighth grade was a hard time for me. It was when I first began to think of dropping out of school. My academic abilities seemed inadequate because I learned differently and at a different pace. The challenges and setbacks I experienced in school discouraged me.

I didn't believe I was smart enough to go to college. However, at College Track I found staff like Ms. Sherdren Burnside and Dr. Hamilton, who also believed in me and continued to push me to reach my goal of going to college, just like Mrs. Mitchell and Mr. Fruga did in middle school. My mentors inspired me to pass my miracle forward to my Mini Butterflies.

When they had all had enough to eat, Jesus said to his disciples, "Gather the pieces that are left over. Let nothing be wasted." So they gathered them and filled twelve baskets with the pieces of the five barley loaves left over by those who had eaten. After the people saw the sign Jesus performed, they began to say, "Surely this is the Prophet who is to come into the world" (John 6:12-14).

Jesus fed the multitude and still had enough left over to fill twelve baskets. My miracle could have stopped just with me getting the encouragement
I needed to stay in school. But it will not! I'll continue to tell others my story and
let them know that they too can make it.

Reaction:
After receiving just the right kind of support, Candace will multiply the
loaves as she helps others know they too can make it. She reminds me of
how a single teacher can make all the difference in one's life. I'm thinking of
Alexander Mays, who taught me English at Christ School, my prep school
near Asheville, North Carolina. We would have long arguments on integration. This was in the 1950s. As a loyal white Charlestonian, I would think of
every argument imaginable to disagree with his "liberal"—some said "Com-
munist"—positions. Then I would take his arguments home to argue with
family and friends on the same issue. It wasn't until I was at an Episcopal
seminary in the 1960s, however, that I began acting on what "AMaze" (as we
called him) had taught me. I never got to tell him how much difference he
had made in my life, confronting but also caring. I hope Candace has told
Mr. Fruga just how he changed her life—from mentee to mentor, her miracle.

Troy Simon: Snatch and Run

Troy, one of the best young writers I have known, wrote this story, based
on true events, for *Young in America: New Orleans*. He has changed names
and a couple of the situations to protect others. Troy was unable to read until
he was fourteen, but then College Track discovered him. In just four years,
he was writing well enough to win a full scholarship to Bard College in New
York. In June of 2016, he graduated and is on his way to Yale Divinity School.
He and I are working diligently on what will be his stunning memoir.

I'm glaring out of the window during math class, thinking about the last
eight days of my life. I'd spent them in prison. It was a place I'd been before, but
only for tapping[3] in the French Quarter, never for theft. I knew the consequences
for stealing, but I chose to ignore them. I should have never jacked that woman's
purse. I should have just walked off. How foolish I was, thinking that I could make
a quick getaway through the crowds on Bourbon Street. But hindsight is perfect.

And now I'm stuck in seventh grade with this box-like computer around
my right ankle. The police are able to track my every move.

My friends think the bracelet is silly. They crack jokes about how I took a

---

3. Illegally tap dancing on the street for handouts

bath with it on. How I sleep with it charging around my ankle, how I tuck and hide it with my school pants. They rib me to cheer me up. However, everywhere I go, I'm embarrassed. Out on the streets I see how people watch me. They look at my face, but then their eyes drop down to check out my ankle.

The other students ask me questions, disturbing the class: How did the cops arrest you? Did they slam you on the ground while you were handcuffed? Did they beat you? How did your friends get away? Did you snitch on them? How much money was in the purse? Did she know you were going to steal it?

Suddenly, our math teacher, Ms. Diane, yells across the room, "Leave that damn boy alone! Nosy children. Can't you see he's trying to talk?" She glares at the students. Ms. Diane's voice chases them back to their seats. She keeps her students in line. If anyone talks out of place, she points out the repercussions to them. No questions asked.

Ms. Diane sits back in her swivel chair and knits her eyebrows together. She crosses her legs under her beige skirt and slips her fingers through her long black hair. One of her toes points from under her desk. Even though she wears blazers and skirts, she has told us who she is. Don't get it twisted. I'm from the Seventh Ward. "Go Troy!" she says, pointing a red nail at me. "Tell your story to yourself and then write it for us."

"Okay." I close my eyes and bring myself back to that sound of Lionel's voice. And I begin to tell my story. It goes like this:

*****

My cousin Darnell blew smoke from his weed cigarillo at my face. "We need money, son." Thin, white trails flowered from his nose and mouth.

I stood with my right leg against Darnell's porch, thinking about how to come up with money to pay Ruben. Ruben was seventeen, five years older than me, six years older than Darnell. We owed Ruben for taking the charge and lying to the cops and saying he'd stolen some hats from the Walgreens when it was us. The cops confiscated his taps and fifty dollars from his pockets and drove him to the juvie. Ruben called us before he got out and said he wanted triple for taking the charge. So now we had until sundown to come up with $150. Ruben was serious about getting his money. We had seen what happened to those who didn't pay up. Visible scars. Black eyes. Broken noses.

"Puff! Puff! Give!" James yelled and leaned in. He snatched the cigarillo out of Darnell's hand.

"Y'all want to go tapping?" Darnell danced with his bare feet on the concrete porch.

"Yeah, son!" I said. I thought we could go down to the French Quarter and dance for money. We'd done it plenty of times before. Maybe this was our chance to pay Ruben back.

We left Darnell's house in the Bywater and went downtown to the Florida projects. We needed some nails to attach the taps to the bottom of our shoes. I heard that my girlfriend Niece was looking for me around the corner. I immediately decided to take a swing over there. I'd told Darnell and James I was coming back.

Troy Simon, from tapping in the
French Quarter to winning a scholarship at Yale Divinity School

"There's my girl," I said to myself as I walked inside the black gates and saw Niece sitting on the concrete steps of her aunt's porch. She was red-skinned, short.

"Wuzzam!" I laughed.

Niece rolled her light brown eyes. "What! So that's how you talk to me now? Like I'm a stranger?"

We kissed and hugged. I ran down with her what I was about to do.

"Why Troy?" she demanded. She reminded me that I could get picked up by the cops. It had happened before.

"But I need the money," I explained. Over her shoulder, a dozen screaming kids ran after the ice cream truck.

"What about me?" she asked. "I need you." She leaned in closer to my side and softly rubbed her nose across my shoulder.

"I know."

The tension flooded out of me. Niece was my heart. She always kept me out of trouble when I couldn't think for myself. We hugged for a long time and kissed. But she held her ground. If I went along with my friends, she didn't want to be bothered with me anymore. She was tired of me listening to my friends and not her. She worried that something would happen to me; she had night-mares about me going to jail or getting jumped.

"We'll hang out next time," I told her. I could hear her breathing as I edged closer, tracing her nose with my lips. "I promise."

She pressed her head against my chest, then pushed herself off and moved down the porch. "See Troy, that's what I'm talking about! You always getting yourself into something that you don't have no business doing."

She was right. I needed to slow down, but there was no backing out of the situation with Ruben. Not this time. Darnell and James were depending on me, and it was getting late. "I'm sorry," I told her. "This is my last time."

It was a lie. I knew tonight was just the beginning of how my life would end up. I was failing my classes. School wasn't the answer. I figured hustling the streets was the only future I had.

I met Darnell and James at the bus stop. James told me he'd borrowed some tap nails from Lionel, who would meet us in the Quarter. At that moment, I knew there was going to be trouble. Lionel was seventeen and known for jacking tourists out of their wallets. He would say, "They drunk anyway. What they don't know won't hurt them." But fighting the tourists when they were drunk wasn't cool, especially elderly men. One time we were tap dancing together, the flow of money wasn't coming fast enough, so he called it quits, snuck in the Hilton Hotel to steal Game Boys. In ten minutes he'd stolen $270 worth of stuff.

We'd hopped on the bus and saw the last person we wanted to see. Ruben sitting in the back. He pointed at the row in front of him, cocking his finger. Like obedient dogs, we all sat down.

"You got my money?" Ruben demanded, his jaw tightening into a hard edge. The light filtered through the window and lit his eyes. Acne scarred his forehead. Beneath his dry lips, a chain of pus-covered bumps erupted across his chin.

"No, not yet." I said. A chill slithered down my back.

"If you don't have my money by tonight, my boys and I will beat James, Darnell, and you to death." He leaned in. "And that's a promise."

I kept silent. James and Darnell bit their tongues.

"I'll be on Bourbon watching y'all." Ruben said, pushing his index finger in my face.

In my head I saw the bloody face of a guy who was late paying Ruben for weed. Ruben had the guy beat half to death, left him with a broken nose, a busted lip, and a swollen jaw. We had to pay on time or turn out like the other guy. None of us said anything, but we were afraid. I knew we wouldn't make $150 by just dancing. That was wishful thinking. So I thought about Lionel's way, about snatching a purse. It was worth a try. Even if I was caught, jail would keep me safe from Ruben's fists.

In the Quarter, we saw Lionel was already dancing. He wore a white shirt, black jeans, and yellow Adidas that showed off his footwork.

"What took you so long?" Lionel asked.

"The bus!" Darnell replied.

Lionel paused and caught his breath. Sweat covered his face and soaked his shirt. His arms bulged from weightlifting. Across his neck was a tattoo that read "Money Over Everything." His jeans sagged from the weight of the change in his pocket.

Lionel and I tap danced together while James and Darnel tapped alone. But no matter how hard we tried, the money wasn't flowing fast enough. After two hours, we had only fifty dollars and change.

Darnell threw his money box on the ground. "This ain't working. We got to fight Ruben."

"Yeah man. Ruben got me bent," James added, pointing a finger in my direction.

I sat on the curb and stared across the street at the trash blowing along the sidewalk. I knew we could fight Ruben together, but I also knew he wouldn't be scared off. He would just wait until we were alone and then come back twice as hard. He'd probably knock my teeth out and fracture my nose. Maybe he would break my jaw and crack open my chin. Maybe he'd just kill me. I refused to take that chance. Pressing my fingers against my temple, I knew we were out of options. We had to steal.

"I got a plan," I said.

I told Lionel about Ruben's threat. He agreed stealing was our only chance now. In truth, he seemed as if he was looking forward to teaching me.

"You ready to learn something?" Lionel asked, his eyes blazing with excitement. His cheekbones tightened with the force of his smile.

I glanced nervously. "Yeah, I'm ready."

We walked Bourbon Street looking for a corner bar, a place with two exits, so I wouldn't have to stop and double back. I told them I would steal the purse. I believed it was my fault that we couldn't pay Ruben on time. Either I'd steal a purse and we could pay Ruben, or I'd get caught and go to jail. Either way, I'd earn respect and save myself from being Ruben's punching bag. I knew it was a mistake to volunteer. I'd never snatched a purse before. Who knew what tourists might have hidden under their clothes? A can of pepper spray. A knife. A gun.

"All you got to do is snatch and run," Lionel told me. "Whatever you do, don't look back. It slows you down."

He gave me some tips. Keep my momentum. Grab the purse with one hand, pull it hard, then tuck it beneath my arms. Keep my face pointed forward so she wouldn't get a good look. I was to wait for his signal, three waves over his ear, then move. We had already picked our purse.

Snatch and run. Snatch and run. Then the adrenaline took over and pumped through my veins. I could hear my pulse beating in my ears, drowning out the sounds of Lionel's voice. I was blocking everything else out, focusing in on the task.

Suddenly, I ran without Lionel's signal. I grabbed and yanked the woman's purse from the bar counter. Someone pulled at my shirt. I felt the hem rip. Glass shattered on the floor. The woman fell off her stool. But I kept running. Behind me, I heard her scream. A man yelled, "Stop him!" As I jumped into the crowd on Bourbon Street, I ran full speed and never looked back.

When I reached the edge of the Quarter, I let myself pause to catch my breath. I looked at the black bag in my right hand, just to make sure it was still there. James, Darnell, and Lionel saw me run and found me.

"How much?" James asked, pointing at the back.

"Open it man!" Darnell said.

"Y'all better split fast!" Lionel told us. I should have listened to Lionel. Instead we stood where we were. There was a long pause as I opened the purse. I fished around the bag and came up with a credit card and a license. An identification card. There was no cash.

Darnel punched a set of wooden doors. "Man!"

Lionel laughed while James and I sat in disbelief.

"Now what?" James asked.

Snatching the purse was our last chance to pay Ruben. We were in serious trouble. Niece was right. I needed to slow down and think out my options. Now it was too late. We couldn't stick around the Quarter. Our only hope was gone.

We all went home in silence. I was angry that we let ourselves get bullied by Ruben. I was even angrier that I'd let my fear convince me to steal. It was time to stand up for ourselves. We couldn't spend our lives wrestling against fate. Even if we chose to run from our problems or ignore them, they'd only build and destroy us. I realized that all I'd ever done was run. I was so afraid of getting hurt by someone else that I ended up hurting myself. Now it was my time to fight.

When we made it to the projects, Lionel went home. The beef with Ruben wasn't his. I told Darnell and James I wasn't hiding anymore. They agreed to sit on Ruben's porch and wait with me. Beside the house, the garbage can had been overturned and wrappers blew across the side street. We sat watching, but Ruben never showed up. The sky had grown black; it was time to go home. We stood up from the porch, feeling as though we had escaped. Suddenly he turned the corner.

Ruben cracked his neck and pointed his finger like always. "Where's my money, son?"

I looked down. "We don't have it."

All the tough talk about standing up evaporated. Before Ruben could speak again, we did what we always did. Ran.

"Come here!" Ruben yelled behind us.

We split. James ran in an abandoned building, Darnell to his house. When I looked back, I could see Ruben gaining on me. My baggy jeans fell from my waist and my large shirt covered my elbows. My street gear was slowing me down. My heart burned. Suddenly, I tripped and stumbled into a fence.

Ruben grabbed me by my shirt. "Get up!"

My courage was gone. "Please don't hurt me," I begged, stumbling over my words.

His fingers snapped at my collar, ripping it off its seam. His breath smelled like an ashtray. "Shut up. You take me for a joke?"

I shook my head. Ruben dug through my pockets, looking for change. He slipped my crumbled cigarillo into his pocket. He held up my tap nails then threw them in the grass.

"Where's the money?" he demanded.

"I don't have it." I kept my head down. I was too afraid to even look at him.

The police car pulled up so quietly that even Ruben didn't see it until it was close. Ruben released his fingers from my shirt. He cracked his neck and whispered, "Pretend we're brothers."

Two cops stepped out of the vehicle. "Get on the ground!"

I didn't say anything, turning to Ruben for a sign. Sweat trailed down his neck. A smile pulled his skin, revealing his broken teeth. I stared at him, hoping to get his attention. He held his hands up as if the cops' words confused him, but kept a straight face. One of the cops pulled out his black stick from his belt. The other cop's hand hovered over the gun at his waist. These were no fat, donut-eating cops. They looked like bodybuilders. These cops were cut taller than Ruben.

"He's just my li'l brother," Ruben told them, "We were just playing. That's all." Ruben smiled and put his arm over my shoulder. I pretended to follow along, leaning into him. All of a sudden one of the cops rushed us. He grabbed Ruben and pushed his arms behind his back.

"That's my brother man!" Ruben wrestled.

"You're wanted for arrest!" The cop said.

The other officer dragged me by my pocket, murmuring beneath his breath. He twisted my arm and threw me in the back seat. My head slammed against the window. The cop shut the door. I saw them talking through the glass. The cop who shoved Ruben was holding him down on the hood of the car. The other yelled in his face. A crowd watched on the corner, others from their porches. When I sat up, I looked at my shirt. The fabric was torn in several places.

Suddenly, a cop opened the door. "Sit back," he told me. "We're going to the station."

The cell was freezing. The iron bunk covered most of the space in the room. The toilet was covered in urine, its inside clotted with feces. Gang signs scarred the walls. Some read "Blood Game," "Young Mafia," and "Uptown." I drew my fingers along the walls, trailing the dents. Then I sat on a small wooden bench. The ceiling was dotted with wads of tissue paper. I couldn't sleep. I was put on trial for two days before the jury convicted me. The judge sentenced me to three months for purse snatching. He told me I would have to serve my community by cleaning the streets. While on probation, I'd have to wear an ankle bracelet.

*****

When I finish the story, my friend Terrance sits back in his chair. "Man, I am just happy you didn't get hurt."

"I know, right?" I say.

"You could have been hurt bad," another student says.

Suddenly, Ms. Diane starts to teach the class. She reads from a paper in her hand and presses the dry erase marker against the white board.

"All right class, turn to page 162 in your math books," she says. "We're solving exponents."

I lean back, twist my dreads, and cross my leg. I feel the weight of the ankle bracelet. I stare out of the window as my teacher's voice fades. I hear Lionel again, his words echoing across my conscience. *Snatch and Run. Snatch and Run.* I knew if I continued to steal, I would end up in jail. I knew if I continued to be influenced by my friends, I'd end up in worse situations. The only choice was to make a new decision, my own decision, one that wasn't about either stealing or running. That life leads to drugs or jail or the cemetery. I thought about the road I was taking. I knew I had to find a different path, perhaps even forge my own way.

Six years have passed since I was arrested and decided I had to make a change. Not everyone came to the same realization as I did. The young men I knew have become sad and familiar statistics. Darnell and James have dropped out of high school. Lionel was gunned down while mugging someone in the Ninth Ward. Ruben became a thief and an addict and recently was shot to death by a drug gang.

As for me, I am changed, have let myself be changed, by education. I have put in the long hours required to begin to make up for all the years that I couldn't read or write, all the years I believed I couldn't learn.

I have attended afterschool and weekend programs for college-bound youth and surrounded myself with mentors. I have also turned to writing as a way of understanding my troubled past. Last December [2012], I was awarded a four-year scholarship to Bard College through the Posse Foundation. No more Snatch and Run. When I graduate, I plan to be an elementary teacher so that I can mentor and direct young people in the right direction.

Reaction:

In our long conversations as Troy writes his autobiography, he told me of the many things that have helped him make the change from criminal activity to serious student and writer, a young man who cares deeply for others. Besides being part of College Track, Troy was able to call on suppressed good things from his younger years. He converted to Christianity, after being counseled by a non-Christian fortune teller and one of his aunts, who told him that God had spoken to her and that God was going to fill him with knowledge and wisdom.

His story goes on and on and I look forward to many more hours of his sharing it with me. In all of his writing, including "Snatch and Run," he helps the reader—me—both see and hear what is going on, whether in the classroom, or in his tap dancing in the French Quarter, or his stealing the purse and, of course, his being caught. He is now writing about all those life-changing experiences, and I continue to be dazzled.

Here is a passage from his emerging memoir. He was seven at the time. His father was throwing his mother out of the house for the second time.

She had packed her clothes in a garbage bag and was trying to take Troy's little sister with her. His father is also named Troy, and Troy, the son, is nicknamed Moon.

"Troy," my mother said to my father, "you're listening to those people on the street about those men I'm supposed to be hanging out with." She began to cry harder. "They are all liars! It's all lies. Come on, Moon," she said to me. "Give me my baby."

My mother took my little sister, Naomi, by the hand, still holding her garbage bag full of clothes over her shoulder. I saw the hurt, the pain, the struggle. My father had put my mother out of the house before and told her to find another place.

I never understood it, but I knew that it had something to do with the man she was on the phone with earlier and another caller. I didn't bother to find out. We were kids. I knew that I would be beaten if I intervened. What my mother and father did was none of my business. I was just a kid and hardly knew what was going on. All I knew was that my mother and father were torn and broken. Their hearts were so far apart from one another that they couldn't see the hurt and pain that they were bringing upon their children. I cried, but not for my mom and my father. I cried for peace and an end to the madness and the pain I went through and was going through since the day I was born. I knew that, in some crazy way, they both loved each other and me!

An Update:
In May of 2017, Troy finished his first year at Yale Divinity School.

Chapter Three

The Icons for Peace

Formed in January of 2015, the Icons for Peace are, as they say, "Young leaders committed to PEACE through civic engagement and education." Most Icons are between seventeen and thirty-five. They meet twice a week at the popular multi-service Healing Center near the French Quarter in New Orleans, where they have been given ample space for their gatherings.

Here is how they describe themselves: "We are a Constitutional Citizen movement. We are students and professionals who are educated and trained to effect community change. We offer several organizing training initiatives such as: Organizational Leadership Training, How to Turn Research into Civic Action, Community Activism, Project Execution and Activism, and Neighborhood Project Planning. The Icons' primary goal is to build the capacity of local youth leaders to create a stronger civic engagement and advocacy infrastructure that give the youth of New Orleans power over issues facing their vulnerable communities. In the fight for equitable youth inclusiveness in policy decisions, we know firsthand that much work needs to be done at the grassroots as well as at the top level to achieve system change for the youth of the city, especially for young African Americans, the most vulnerable and marginalized population."

One of the groups I visit from time to time and support is the Isaiah Institute. It is built on the values and traditions of faith-based communities that take seriously the prophetic tradition in the Hebrew Scripture. The institute is named for Isaiah, who called on his people to "rebuild and restore the streets" (58:12). Like other organizations modeled on Saul Alinsky's Industrial Areas Foundation (IAF), Isaiah brings together those who have legitimate concerns over local and national polices and then helps the people organize to bring about the changes *they* think most significant. So it's not top-down, but bottom-up. The executive director of Isaiah and overall supervisor of the Icons is Joe Givens, a long-time friend.

Early last spring, I was visiting Isaiah during one of their organizing sessions, an evening when eight of the Icons told some of their story. Six young men and two young women, all African American, told how the Icons for Peace was helping them stay out of gangs, out of prison, off the street and how the program was giving them an opportunity to share their poetry, their visual art, and especially their music (such as their rapping) with other young people in New Orleans. The young Icons are able to reach many of their peers, including the so-called "street people," that even black churches can't reach. I love storytelling anyway and was inspired by the stories the Icons told that evening. So I set out to get to know the storytellers. Fortunately, I already knew their charismatic founder and coach, Sergeant John Johnson (Sarge) from my prison work—he works with formerly incarcerated persons as I do—so he made it easy for me to be accepted as part of their group. Me, this older white guy.

Here is some of Sarge's story and three stories from the Icons themselves—Derrick Strong, Yahmel Bey, and Jonathan Lewis. After they tell their stories, I make my response as though I were talking with them. I hope you, the reader, will consider your reaction as well, perhaps quite different from mine. This way we will keep the conversation moving.

Sarge John Johnson:
Advisor to Icons for Peace

Sarge returned to his home in New Orleans after serving thirty-six years in the Army. Besides his leadership in the community, he is one of the few African Americans active here in the Church of the Latter Day Saints. He seems completely comfortable with the term "angels in the wilderness" when speaking of the young Icons. We talked at his home, then ours, in early October 2015.

Sarge: I retired from the army Thursday, June the third, 2013, and came back to New Orleans, my home. I was in action here just after Hurricane Katrina and assigned to the 2nd Special Forces group. Our job was to secure major assets of the city. I was assigned to get Charity Hospital up and running, which we did—Charity was ready to be used by December 19, 2005. But, after all the work, the state chose not to use the facility. This made many low-income persons angry as they would lose excellent medical care. My next assignment was then to help rebuild Jackson Barracks, the National Guard Headquarters here in New Orleans. Because I was from here, it was convenient. My command central office allowed me to stay home as much as possible. But that soon came to an end. In 2007-2008 I was sent to Iraq. In 2009 I returned with my elbow injured from a combat mission.

The leader of my church, the Mormon Church—Church of Latter Day Saints—on St. Charles Avenue, asked us to expand our outreach work, so I started with the prison ministry in 2010 through an organization called Strength for Today. I got veterans involved, and we started going to the prisons. We went to Angola (the Louisiana State Penitentiary) and St. Gabriel's (the Louisiana Correctional Institute for Women). We also started going to Orleans Parish Prison and worked with chaplains. So I was connecting veterans and concerned citizens and church members going to the prisons. This was not the usual prison ministry, but what I call a "Constitutional Mentor Group."

The program I became part of, Strength for Today, teaches that individuals who live in the United States, or any country, have a responsibility to the constitution of their government and that inside most constitutions, especially the United States, the government can change based on the will of the people. We understand that, but most people don't even know what's in the Constitution.

So as mentors we show those in prison and others that through our own lives we can participate as citizens, as constitutional citizens, as the founding fathers did. We teach that in prison. We talk about the Thirteenth Amendment of the Constitution that says neither slavery nor involuntary servitude—except for punishment for a crime—shall exist in the United States and its jurisdictions. In other words, those in prisons are slaves! When I taught that to the men and women in prison, it was Niagara Falls. There were tears everywhere, there was whimpering and there was stony silence. For the first time, they saw themselves as slaves. Not de facto slaves, or kind-of slaves. They literally read what the document said and knew that they were slaves. Many have asked me why this is not on billboards all around the city.

And I just tell them, "You have to do that job." And they say, "How can we in prison get that done?" Well, part of the United States requires that those who register to vote have a vote. "I know you can't vote yourselves," I say. "But anybody can impact a vote. Be you a guy in jail, be you a guy down the street, be you a child who can't vote." So I teach these mostly black young men and women how to get their family members to engage in civic responsibility and civic action, get them to vote. So then they—the resident inmates—ask me, to take this to their kids. They say, "You sitting in here with us is great, but our kids need to hear it from you." So that's what I am doing.

Kids with parents in jail are seven times more likely to end up in jail themselves. Over half a million children have parents incarcerated in the United States. With the help of correctional officers, we came up with a plan. Now the mentors—the military guys, wounded warriors, and the church people—we are working with the inmates while in prisons *and* with their children. We do follow up ministry when the guys leave prison.

Meanwhile, as we were serving in this way, Joe Givens, head of the New Orleans Interfaith Peace Initiative and Isaiah, called for ministers and organizations to come together to find a way to bring real peace to New Orleans. I met many other members of Isaiah's Peace Initiative. They actually had me join their steering committee. And the committee gave a big push for a basketball league. They wanted young people, between the ages of eighteen and twenty-five, many of them in various kinds of trouble.

So we on the committee were all assigned our church areas to get youth. I ended up with sixty-nine youth from all over. I literally went to basketball courts, put on some spandex with my stomach out, some cool top tennis shoes, and a headband. I talked to the young people almost one-on-one. They were wondering what this old man was doing out here. I'm out shooting basketball, and I can't shoot and I got this bad elbow. I would go to a different area of the city for three days. And I did that for a full month. And then, working with my church, we ended up with maybe forty community kids and others who were like my church members. When we had the big basketball game that we had been planning, we were working with maybe ninety young people. So the game was held on July 3, 2014, and it was a beautiful event.

And those kids were excited! And the group we started with, they wanted to do more. The kids that played basketball began midnight basketball games, but they wanted to impact the whole community. So some of them started meeting at my house in August and September of 2014, coming to my house every week on Wednesdays. And I'd have dinner and stuff because that's another thing that we're big on in the Mormon Church, having people over to the house. Our church says if you are having people over to the house, you're going to show some love. Well, it grew from 10 to 15 to 40 or more kids, kids who got involved, in the fall of 2014.

And in January they came up with the name, Icons for Peace. All of the young people tried to come up with something that had "peace" in it, 'cause we talked about violence in the streets. They talked about how they could stop the violence because violence is what some people are into here. When we go about bringing about peace, then the violence will stop. And through that, and many conversations, we started going to Helen Cox High School and Park Community Center. And the Icons were talking to the younger kids. These older kids were talking to the younger kids.

So we identified seven leaders, and we set all seven leaders up in their own organizations, with their own point of view of how *they* wanted to achieve peace, *their* way, so we built on self-interest. So each one would go to a school at different times and talk to the civics class, or the art class, or the general assembly. And they would present their program and themselves as an Icon for Peace. So like, for example, Icons would go to a school and talk about how their dad is in jail and this and that and the other thing. And how they'd talked with other kids whose fathers were in jail. And how we have to band together, and we have to embrace love and we have to embrace our country so that we don't become slaves! Because the government has a mechanism in place for those who break the rules, they will become slaves. So those kinds of things.

To help the Icons—that wasn't their name yet—to be in touch with people, especially young people, we started doing giveaways. For Halloween we had a giveaway and gave away like $2,000 worth of stuff. We gave away candy that was donated from the New Orleans Baptist Theological Seminary. Yes, so the Icons went out, the young folks, everybody had all this candy, and we even got the Muslims to participate. The candy was like what some young people call "the glue of Jesus." It was kind of weird, but everybody participated. No one discriminated. It didn't stop. It was all about promoting peace, as long as it had Jesus's peace, or Jesus's love. We met other young people who became Icons, and giving out stuff gave our young people already Icons a way to serve others.

Then in November 2014, with the Orleans Parish Sheriff's Department, at the Convention Center, the Icons gave away over three thousand pieces of clothing that they had gotten from places like Men's Warehouse and other areas that donated. They gave all of these clothes away to the homeless.

Then in December 2014, at Hope Community Baptist Church on Elysian Fields, we gave away thousands of dollars worth of gifts to needy kids, including used Xboxes, Flat Screen TV's, and computers. We were hosted there by the fire chief, the chief of police, and the sheriff's office; they were the main speakers. And they were just telling the kids, hey look, we are not against you. They gave them applications for jobs; they told them that they banned the box, took away the box that asks if you are a felon when you apply for a job, for a lot of civil service jobs. So a lot of these hard thugs, a lot of these street kids, our guys, never knew that they could be helped. They never knew that these officers, these civil servants, police officers, the sheriff, sheriff deputies, firemen, that there was a place for them, the young people (the hard thugs and street kids). Many of these young people told their stories. So it was an instant connection.

That event galvanized our efforts. So then we became part of the Martin Luther King celebration. And we marched in the MLK parade. This was in January of 2015. We were at that big rally, we were all in the back and we were all dressed in blue or white or something. And so from that, we gave out "I Dig Empathy" cards. Joe Givens's organization, Isaiah, offered us a building for us to operate out of instead of meeting at my home. That was the Healing Center, on St. Claude. So we accepted that. That's the Icons for Peace. That's my backstory, that how Icons for Peace got to be what it is today.

When I came here after Katrina to help rebuild the city, I noticed that cooperation and collaboration was not going on. There was no coalition. There was no cohesiveness. With the exception of some small cell groups, it was almost like "every group for itself." In the immediate aftermath of the Storm, that was really obvious, because it was like abandoning the ship. As time passed, and people started coming back to New Orleans, they weren't trying to get together. There was this division. Why was Uptown, the mostly white part of New Orleans, this; and black people were not part of it? Without the basic communication being done. It was the black areas like the Ninth Ward that were being left out. It goes all the way back to redlining, where you can only buy land in a certain place and how much you can borrow. So my hope for New Orleans is to do the same thing as I did overseas, in my church and even with my own family. Get that communication going to bring about understanding. That's my hope for effective action and just change.

Icons for Peace has a contract, for all to agree to, and there are three parts to the contract: One, all Icons support every Icon's self-interest. That is how *they* want change to come—*their* interests are all included. Two, all Icons support the Icons for Peace *mutual* interest, which is peace, wealth equity, power, and knowledge. Third, every Icon has a nearby peer group that they're working with.

And when I say they need wealth, I don't want you to misunderstand, I'm not saying we're going to make you wealthy, but we do understand that you need to accrue some type of wealth in your life. We want poor people to be wealthy in this way, and we are pushing for that as well. We take on finding jobs, in construction projects, such as painting and building; we take on gardening and community development projects. We've worked with the Sutherland Plantation, jobs to clean the street from the interstate all the way to their business.

We actively engage in black rallies and have our own every ninety days. We have a peace breakfast once a month, where we bring in civic leaders and business leaders to showcase the new Icons. That's had a twofold effect: Number one, it lets the Icons know it's not just their advisors who care about what they're doing. Number two it shows the business community that the people who they are normally scared of—they call them the "Dreadheads" for their dreadlock hairstyle or "Deadheads"— these young people are actually conscious and self-aware individuals who have a future and they want their future to be bright.

Reaction:

I think it most important that Sarge arranges Icon events with sheriff deputies, police officers, and other officials. When I heard that the Icons told some of their stories with these officials, I realized that there was a new appreciation for the coming together of the law-enforcement people and the street people. That's what I keep saying all of us need to do: tell our stories and listen to those of others, especially the stories of those we see "on the other side." You can usually hear another's personal story without judgment. It's a way for us to find common ground in our deeply divided city, state, and nation. We need many more events like the ones Sarge has organized.

For the last fifty years, I have been quoting the educator, John Dewey, who said even longer ago than that: "People support what they help to create"—a platitude maybe but so important. It is fundamental to groups like Isaiah and the Icons. I have worked with such groups in South Carolina, Boston, Washington, D.C., and for a longtime in New Orleans. Sarge carefully makes sure all Icons know that they are a part of the "creation" process.

The more I move around the African American community in New Orleans, the more I hear very angry complaints, especially at the well-attended Monday night Justice and Beyond Coalition (the subject of chapter 4) that policy makers—whether in regard to charter schools or playgrounds or the police or incarceration—do not ask the people supposedly served to be part of the creation of the policies. Those most in need in our city are not appropriately included in the high-level discussions and decisions regarding the programs that are supposed to help them, their children, and their neighborhoods—or so the members of Justice and Beyond think. It is a big issue not only in New Orleans but around the country as I found out in the other states where I worked. In chapter 4, Kristen Rome describes in detail how the city's response to Hurricane Katrina was a disaster for many of the poor and black in New Orleans, as Sarge points out. "The people" did not help create the city's response to Katrina.

--- --- --- --- --- --- --- --- --- --- --- --- --- --- --- --- --- --- ---

Derrick Strong:
From Gang Leader to Icon for Peace

At twenty-six Derrick Strong has lived a lifetime of stories that should be told. He survived dangerous gang life as he grew up in New Orleans; then had turnaround experiences during and after Hurricane Katrina in 2005; then involvement in more crimes, which led to various prison sentences, eighteen months altogether. In prison, he came to be known as the Black Jesus. Now through his rap and poetry and visual art, he is reaching out to young people in the hope that they will hear and be transformed by his story of violence and redemption. Tattooed on his right arm is his mantra, in large script—the letters: GOREALLA, which I finally found out means "GO REAL LOUISIANA." He inked the tattoo himself. For some, his shoulder-length dreadlocks make him look dangerous. We talked on October 18, 2015, at our home. Besides his music offering, Derrick works where he can get part-time work. Recently, I put him in touch with a gardening service, where he is now working twenty hours a week.

Derrick: The thing about me is that I love people. To the point to where I put that as my priority for the greater good. I want to see other people smile. That's what makes me happy. Being in a role full of laughter and happy rather than a role full of misery and sorrows. So as I got older, I tried to push that be- cause, through lawful action, that's what brings good energy. I'm a real deep philosopher and thinker. I did a lot of things in the past that led to me being incarcerated for more than eighteen months. And during this time of incarcer- ation, I focused on advancing myself spiritually, mentally, and physically.

I did this specifically because my fifth-grade teacher had showed me mov- ies like *Roots,* like *Mississippi Burning,* and movies about Malcolm X and Martin Luther King. She told us about the Underground Railroad and what oppression actually meant. I came to realize that incarceration was slavery by a different name. Therefore, I tried to advance myself in those three aspects—mentally, spiritually, and physically—because I did not want the time to weigh me down. 'Cause that's what jail is, lost valuable time. Whenever you're taken out of so- ciety and put in bondage, it takes time out of your life, months, years, out of your life. That's something that can't be taken or given back. Time is that kind of concept.

Derrick Strong, from prison to serving as a leader in Icons for Peace

That's what I worked toward in jail, making my time count. I read every version of the Bible I could find in prison. That was the spiritual aspect. I read many different books, like the Koran. I also studied the thesaurus, the dictionary, and the encyclopedia. I was doing all this before I went to prison, but during my incarceration it increased because I was separate from society to the point to where all I had was this isolated time to think and read and reflect upon myself. I used this time to come up with a better plan and way of living and way of thinking of living.

I'm going to go back to the beginning, down in the nitty-gritty. When I was fifteen, right before Hurricane Katrina, I was a leader of a street gang. And we used to do a lot of mischievous things, like break into cars and steal bikes and stuff like that. And we used to get paid to fight, because we were boxers. And other drug-dealers would pay us to kick up their rivals. The city was a whole lot different back then.

Before Katrina it was a territorial type thing: Someone from the Eighth Ward couldn't go to the Third Ward and be there peacefully. The same thing if somebody was to go from the Third Ward down to the Eighth Ward. Any neighborhood. No matter where you were in the city, you faced opposition simply because you were from a different part of the city. That's how it was before the Storm. So you had to have a certain mentality in order to survive. You had to walk around with a chip on you shoulder, or be prepared to be attacked, randomly. I'd seen so many random beatings before the Storm that it seemed like a different world we were living in. So we became accustomed to that.

We all were boxing, and we used to make a game out of fighting people from other parts of the city sometimes with gloves, sometimes with bare knuckles. It was that physical altercation and combat that we'd seek. So when Katrina hit, I left town with that same mentality and my folks moved to Hebron, Mississippi.[1] My family there was more rooted in the Church than I was.

It was my last year in high school when Katrina hit. I was a senior going to John McDonogh. Earlier, at John McDonogh, in my ninth grade year (2003), a guy was killed at the gym. So my whole high school career at John McDonogh was more like a prison than an actual school. I had to take initiative to teach myself or to seek out teachers to teach me because teachers were at wits end, dealing with kids that didn't really want to be there, because of the way that kids were being treated or felt they were being treated. There were like armed guards at the front door of the school, police, pat downs, metal detectors, drug-sniffing dogs, and all sorts of stuff—all on a regular basis. There were big riots breaking out and crowds being maced and stuff like that. It was not a good learning environment 'cause there were so many distractions.

Not only that, but we still had to deal with the fact of territorial issues. There were many different wards and gangs and cliques at the school. Teachers were trying to find a way to teach us while the students were trying to find a way to be big and better and prove a point to each other. It was a big warzone at school. When Katrina hit, it was more like a blessing for some, and a curse for others. So it was a good and bad thing. In my aspect, I look at it like it was a good thing because if Katrina had never hit, I would have been stuck in the same life with that same gang mentality.

So when I went to Mississippi I reconnected to my folks out there. They were deeply rooted to the church to the point where they were deacons and ushers and, you know, stuff like that. The church was Old Palestine Baptist Church. I started to attend the church more, and it brought me closer to God, to the point where I started to seek out more wisdom and understanding for myself. But I later strayed away from Old Palestine just because I felt like I didn't want to confine myself to the beliefs of one particular congregation or one particular church. So I started to go to other churches to get a feel of what it truly is to be understood.

And this is still in Mississippi. But I was still stuck in a situation of not having nothing and could lose everything in one day. I was below the poverty line, you know, I was really living dirt poor so I had to get money any way I could. So here I am in Hebron, Mississippi, fending for my survival, and not only that, but I had to provide food for my mom and my sister 'cause my pops worked for the city, and he had to go back to New Orleans and get it up and running after the Storm.

1. Jefferson Davis County has a population now of less than five hundred.

Three years after Katrina, I stayed out there in Mississippi, taking care of my mom and my little sister. My pops was going back and forth from New Orleans and Mississippi. He would stay the week down in New Orleans, trying to get everything together, and then on the weekends, he would come to our house with food and some other stuff like that. And I was there throughout the week, keeping the grass cut, buying food, buying clothes, and other stuff, like working in a junkyard, but outside family members made me doubt my disposition on life.

They looked at me like, "Oh, he's going to fail at this, and this and that and the other," so I had to prove to them, not only to them but also to myself, that I can do it. So when I was going to school up there, I told myself I wasn't going to drop out, no matter what, and I graduated with art honors. I was gifted in art. I grew up with art since I was younger: I was a musical artist, martial artist, and visual artist. And I have worked in many different art exhibits, art projects, and stuff like that. I actually wrote my own book. It's called *Tales of Anarchy,* and it's a graphic novel. I'm actually going to publish it this year. My birthday is in December, so I'm going to publish it around my birthday. That way I can give it as a Christmas gift to some people. I don't actually have a publisher in mind.

I came back from Mississippi when I was nineteen. The churches in Mississippi eventually came to look at me as a "beacon of hope." But when I came back, I got back into the same arena I was in before I went to Mississippi. Therefore, with my new mentality I had to adapt to the environment I was in. I had a whole bunch of criminals in New Orleans, telling them about my progress and hope. Telling them about the things I learned in Mississippi. And they were telling me about all the things they did in Texas, because that's where many of them were after Katrina. There was a whole bunch of riots and fighting and stuff like that where they were. So our stories were different. We grew up together, these same guys that used to be boxing in the neighborhoods, beating up other people. So I was telling them that the way of Proverbs is to seek a higher knowledge. A Proverb says, "A fool rebukes knowledge. A wise man seeks understanding." (12:1)

So here you are, coming back, sounds like, as a different person, trying to help these young people you grew up with share in your experience in Mississippi.

Yeah, but not only that. I still had to deal with the rules of being a young black man in America. It was difficult because there were no resources. My home was still washed up because I lived in a Katrina flooded home. I had lived in the Eighth Ward. When Katrina hit, my house was thirteen feet underwater. So when I came back down to New Orleans, I had to live in a FEMA trailer until me and my pops literally rebuilt our house ourselves, me and my pops and my brother David [also a committed Icon]. The house we had been living in before Katrina, we had to go in there and gut it out. I put up the dry wall. My pops put in all of the wall studs. Then we added the texture, paint; we had to do everything ourselves, even get the water running. We hired a few carpenters, but the whole project was supervised by us. It was about a year and a half before we got it to the point where it was livable. It still wasn't complete. But once it was livable, we moved into it, and as we were working on it, we actually stayed there. This was me and my pops. My brother was in college at Southeastern Louisiana. My oldest sister was at LSU. My baby sister was in Mississippi with my mom. And then my pops was in New Orleans with me. So everybody was scattered.

Before that, I had moved into a FEMA trailer with a friend of mine. I was telling him about Proverbs, and he was telling me about all the gang stuff he had been doing in Texas. But I was still in the streets. I never did leave the streets. I just had a new sense of understanding. I still was part of a criminal element because of my situation. I didn't have any resources. I had skills, but there were no jobs developing for the skills that I had, especially for young black men. I would go to get a job, and they would find some reason to turn me around or some reason 'cause they don't want none of me. Whether it be my dreadlocks, certain credentials, a drug test, or this, that, and the other.

And I say that if you were to go to a similar situation, how would you deal with it? Some people go off and drink 'cause they can't stand it anymore. I like to roll up some marijuana and blow it all to the wind, leave it all to the air, and give it up to the Most High. That's what it is for me. It's not that it is an addiction or anything. It's more of a spiritual release, whenever I do smoke. When I came back down here, I finally got a job working at Louisiana Soup Kitchen. And I was the first one in my clique to do that. But I kind of fell back because my goals in mind were bigger than just working for just any job. I wanted more than just any career. There was something in my heart telling me that there was something greater in life for me. As I was going through the motions of life, I started selling drugs again and running with my gang.

So you had two forces pulling on you, one was the gang and getting in trouble with the law and the other was that part of you that you were beginning to discover.

Right, exactly. And this would have been about 2009 or 2010, like when the gang activity was real heavy, fighting in a lot in the neighborhoods. And you know, I was real, real good at fighting, one of the best in the neighborhood. I beat one particular guy up and he called Crime Stoppers on me. And he was supposedly a drug dealer himself, so by doing that, he broke the code of the street and ratted on me. I beat him up, and he ratted on me again for a charge that wasn't even related to me. But by him being so spiteful, he just was jealous, and dropped my name to Crime Stoppers. And the FBI labeled me a psychopath and all kinds of stuff like that. And after that I felt accosted by the authorities because I was labeled as such. Somebody lied on me. So I started going in and out of jail all the time because of drug possession or fighting or being a criminal suspect, all kinds of different reasons. And it seemed like no matter where I went in the city, I was targeted.

So it was a dramatic turn when a close friend of mine was killed, Earl, a guy I went to school with all the way through high school—he actually saved another friend's life at John McDonogh when there was a shooting there. After Katrina we came back and all got reconnected. I was living in that criminal element, but I had more of a sense of righteousness because of my Mississippi experience. I wanted to do better, but I couldn't seem to do better. I had to make do with what I could.

My friend Earl was killed just maliciously, because when he was getting off from work, a guy was beating on a car. When Earl protested, the criminal shot him. All my gang members took pride in being able to fight, and not resort to guns because we said that cowards hide behind guns. So when my friend was killed, it shook all us up because he wasn't like us. We were the violent ones, we were the ones getting paid to fight. He was the one telling us, "Chill out, chill out." And for him to get shot, in a situation such as this! So he was the one that was shot, and it threw us all for a loop. This was Earl, the friend, who saved another friend when we were at John McDonogh, ended up getting shot himself. It messed us all up.

We all had plans to run businesses together. And I was actually going to a school at the time for business management with a minor in music. When he got killed, I couldn't really focus on studies anymore. I was more focused on revenge than redemption and just trying to find acceptance in the fact that we can't bring him back, which was a hard thing for me to do because of all the things we planned on doing together. I was twenty-two, he was maybe twenty-three. We always celebrated our birthdays together because his birthday was in late December and mine was in early December so the whole month we'd be partying.

But when he got killed it took my mind off of studies and more on trying to find a way to get revenge. Once I found out the murderer went to jail, I purposely went to jail for a while so I could find Earl's murderer. I didn't know what I was going to do when I saw him, but I was just intent on seeing him and get revenge.

But the Most High actually showed me more about myself. So that's when I really started to seek divine intervention. It was real crazy. But in prison they take all your possessions, your cellphone, ID, everything. All you have is your booking papers. So when I went to jail, and I was rapping, there was a guy in there, who was like "Oh, you're like Black Jesus man." I was like "Don't do that man 'cause that's blasphemy, man." And he was like, "Nah, nah, man, you the Black Jesus." When they moved me to the "Tent," which was a huge tent that houses the overflow of inmates, I was staying with a different set of guys, not even connected to the other guys, not even knowing what they were talking about. And they said the exact same thing: "Hey, you're like Black Jesus" And I was like "Come on now!"

They said that because they could see the caring side of you?

Yeah, and not only that but they understood that I was seeking wisdom. I realized that every single day is a lesson to be learned. It's up to you to teach that lesson and tell others. So, when I was in jail, I tried to seek my friend's killer. I saw him once, but did nothing.

Another time I was incarcerated for arson and burglary of a church. I didn't intend for that to happen. But through my influence on other people that happened. In the midst of that act, I spoke to the Most High. And he showed me that I had two choices, I could continue to wreck my life or I could walk with him. I was learning something while I was committing that crime. See, before I was a gang leader, and I used to have teenagers doing criminal acts for me. I used to send them out. "Go do this, go do that," and they'd come back, and it was a loop. I'd send them with others. It got to the point where I was even out there doing some things. Me and my friends, we'd go out to the French Quarter and we'd be knocking tourists out. And this was something that we did because we felt deprived of our own resources in our city. But we also tried to focus on what we could do to change and better our city because we knew a lot of people were in crisis.

So we were talking with minority support groups—and this is before I went to jail for arson. Before the Storm, we had started the Gorilla Academy. This was GO-REAL-LA, Go Real Louisiana. That's when we were still fist-fighting on the back streets for money. But Goreala Academy was basically a way for some of us to show people what *real* is. Being real means being honest, being truthful about oneself. It was a push toward righteousness in my sense of the word. It was to create a sense of honesty within the self. But we wanted to work with minority support groups. I still had the influence over the kids and was part of the arson and burglary run. And I go to jail, and within this nine- to ten-month span, I had people call me Black Jesus. Gorealla Academy is still part of me, alive and well in a lot of us.

When I went to prison, I did what they call "rattled the cage." From the bottom, from being incarcerated and in bondage, I was able to shake up the people that were in office, the people who were behind the desk, to the point that they knew I was there. And they didn't like it that I was there. I met up with a spiritual advisor that was a Muslim. He used to come there and bring me Korans, letters, magazines. So I told him I was an artist and asked him if he could bring me some drawing material.

And he told me that he could do that, but then asked if I could do a favor in return. With the drawing material he provided me, he wanted me to draw what I felt, what I lived. So I drew it. I drew editorial cartoons, I drew comic strips. I drew sports. I drew the process in which the inmates make their plea. I drew all these things. I drew the conditions in which we were being housed: asbestos on the walls and toilets leaking non-stop. I drew people fighting over one working shower, in a facility that housed ninety-five men. Not only that, but all the toilets were overflowing, to the point that you had to put paper bags over them to keep the insects from coming out of them. People would walk around with abscesses in their mouth and cysts and knots on their eyes, even spider bites. I actually got bit by a spider when I was incarcerated. And I drew all of this.

As a result of these drawings on top of grievances and grievances, after complaints of different styles, the Consent Decree was formed. The same decree we're under today in New Orleans.[2]

The prison authorities didn't like the fact that I was in this facility and drawing pictures of what they were not doing right. They claimed to be doing one thing, but the pictures I drew showed clearer than a photograph. The people on the committee would say, "Oh yeah, this inmate drew these pictures, and he's currently in here now. You can look up his DOC (Department of Corrections) number. So these pictures can't be a lie because he's living in it right now." As a direct result of that, people were fired. Everybody had to be moved out of the prison tent 'cause they'd be talking about it, the stuff we painted, the events we done—the showers were reworked. We'd get an entire new facility.

You were learning a lot about yourself by explaining things and drawing?

The power was art. See everything is artful. Whether it be comic art, literary art, visual art, musical art, martial arts, it's all an art form. Therefore, if you use the power of creation—you have got to think about it. The power of creation is the essence of God. Love and creation is the divine power. That's the Most High. As you grow into using art, you got to take that into other parts of your life. It's powerful. You could change the world with art. It's a universal language. So while I was incarcerated, I did all these things, and the Most High showed me that I can do more than what my situation allows. Once I got out, I had a clear plan of what I wanted to do. I learned more in prison than I did at Delgado Community College. I had been there for business management and music, and Louisiana Tech for carpentering. I was in school by the time I went to jail. So it was like I wasn't able to finish it because of my incarceration. But what prison did was enhance my understanding of life because it forced me to implement my understanding of the self.

I now had a clear blueprint of how I wanted to run a business. I had time to write it out. So when I did get out, I started to hit the music a little more, hitting the open mic. And I was just spitting, spitting (rapping). And as I'm rapping, everybody's like, oh, this guy is deep. Something serious is going on. So it got to the point where I was offered to host my own event, because I was doing open mic things so much, and everybody was familiar with me spitting and knew I was a good rapper, a good MC. They're like well, you know, would you

---

2. The Federal Consent Decree is a much publicized and controversial ruling, demanding significant changes in the way Orleans Parish Prison operates.

want to put together your own event, your own showcase? And I'm like yeah. So I started doing it in 2010.

I was literally given the opportunity to do open mic events over at the Hangar 13 (a concert hall). So I started doing that in early 2011. And as I was doing these events, I started to see the diversity in our own city. There was diversity in an educational and intellectual way. Some people thought like this way, and others thought like another way. So like physically there were two different crowds. There were the college crowds and the convict crowds. People that were on the street who wanted to be on the street. People who were of the books, of the schools, who wanted to be in the schools.

And most of these were African Americans, but two different groups within them?

Exactly. And they kept away from each other, because one preyed on the other one and the other one exploited the other one. And they were kind of like playing on each other. And that was the vision. So I developed a showcase called "Rap Versus Poetry." It was a project that I created myself to basically support the diversity between the local spitters and the local book people in the city. But I also didn't want to exclude anybody. So I implemented different ways of including different genres. I performed at a lot of different churches, but I used to do these showcases at clubs. When I went to the church, it was more of a solo thing that people invited me to because they heard one of my songs.

You sang about the Most High in the churches?

Yeah. You see, my music is somewhat universal. I perform in churches as well as clubs with people on the street. I had ministers bobbing their heads, just like I had murderers bobbing their heads. So it's like many people like what I'm saying, because what I'm saying is true to life. It's true to my reality—that's why it's Gorealla. That's the philosophy I live by. Gorealla means be a truer person than you were yesterday and means go real with yourself, go toward truth, go more toward truth. Every single day. Be more and more truth. Be more and more honest with yourself as well as with other people. So as time went on, I did these showcases. And it was actually getting quite big because I was using the music in order to promote positivity. I was trying to go against the mainstream media and combat the negative effects of that by pushing positive, live music throughout the city.

Not only that, but I wanted to focus on local productivity by linking up with local vendors and local business owners in order to produce promotion and productivity in bringing local artists into a showcase, in their production. It was like a way to rebuild the city, because I felt the city was being taken away. You know, after Katrina, a lot of people were moving into the city who weren't native, and they were trying to take what they could out of the city without giving back. And that's the kind of state that we're in now. So when I was doing showcases, it led me to the Healing Center (where the Icons meet now). It is a well-run, large community center with a restaurant, a grocery store, yoga, performances, rap, with various community groups meeting there.

I developed a close relationship with Chuck Perkins, the owner of Café Istanbul in the Healing Center. He is a real good community activist himself. And you know, it was him who led me to Sergeant John Johnson. 'Cause I went over to Café Istanbul one day, me and my brother, David, to book another event. David says, "Oh, I've never been upstairs and I want to see the rest of this building. So we go upstairs through the art gallery, and we see the Icons for Peace office. This was 2015, the beginning of this year. So as I walk into the office, I see Sarge sitting there. And he's putting stuff on the walls. He's this old military sergeant. He's got this old GI-issued T-shirt with camouflage pants and no shoes on. He's a very big guy.

So he's like hey, how you all boys doing? And we're like, hey, trying to find out what he's doing. We saw the banner for Icons for Peace and ask, "What's the Icons for Peace?" And he says. "I'll tell you all about it but first things first, are ya hungry?" And me and David look at each other like, yeah. And Sarge says, "Well let's sit down in Café Istanbul and eat and have a minute to talk about it." And he was telling us more about Icons for Peace and what the purpose of the organization was, which was to organize young people.

So I'm telling him like, man this is ideal to what I been working on with the Gorealla faction. (A lot of my friends were incarcerated and when I got out, I was the only one that was pioneering toward this digression.) So when I meet Sarge, I'm like this is what I was dreaming of. This is what the Most High led me to do. So I actually fit right into Icons for Peace. And I brought the Rap Versus Poetry initiative into the organization (the street people and the book people). And I started to use the showcases as organizational meetings for artists throughout the city.

And many, many people started to take a liking to the showcases, and not only that, but they started to join Icons for Peace because they wanted to be part of the movement. You know, they've seen that Gorealla was more than just music. They started to understand it, now. Even when I was younger, I was an Icon though I didn't know it.

I was forced to be a leader because in childhood I was ostracized. Because I was poor, because I got a lot of scars on my body, because I had a lot of burns. And kids can be cruel, they didn't want to play with me. So the only person I had when I was growing up was my brother David. As I got older, it wasn't until I entered middle and high school until I developed my own group. But I was this standoffish type of dude that everyone kind of admired secretly. Because I was always focused and driven on to the next step. So as I got into Icons for Peace, I'd seen this was the minority support group that we'd talked about, back when I was with my Gorealla Academy members, when Earl got killed.

You know, I felt like everything happened for a reason. Divine intervention, belief, walk by faith, not by sight. I was going off of what I could see around me, not in front of me. If I just keep going forward then I know that even in the midst of the shadows, I will find the light. So, this Icons for Peace organization that's supported by the Isaiah Institute, Catholic Charities, Justice and Beyond, and Heart of Justice—all these organizations mean to me that people want to help other people.

And you learned that the hard way, but you learned that.

And this is what I've been feeling my entire life, that I was put on the planet to do for others, instead of myself. I never seek selfish gain. I seek what I can change.

Derrick, I especially appreciate that you're bringing people together. Those who you call the convicts and those who are more school, more intellectually oriented. They really aren't very much in touch with each other. But through your musical events and your artwork, you're bringing those groups together. And most of this is within the African American community. I hope more and more of us whites join in.

Exactly, even before Icons for Peace, I had a lot of mixed-race friends. I got a white friend of mine that we went to high school with, and ten or eleven years down the line, we're still friends. And there are a lot of different other people that I've worked with, all different types of ethnicities. I never was one to be like, oh, I don't like this type of person or that type of person, but when I was younger, we used to prey on tourists simply because they were the ones who had the money, not because they were white. Locals didn't have any money. Someone from California or Wisconsin would have a whole bunch of money in their pocket, coming down here just to blow money. As I got older, I started to see the error of my ways, and that there's more to life than just selfish gain. So I tried to seek what I could change in myself in order to promote change within the world.

Let me ask you this: Can you think of a special wilderness experience where angels have ministered to you? I think you've been telling me your whole life has been a wilderness experience; different people and the Most High have ministered to you, but has there been a special time?

There was a time, in high school, I was still trying to figure out what I was going to be, all the way. All the way a demon *or* all the way a saint, an angel. This was in high school when I was about fourteen. I had a strong spiritual battle I was fighting as an adolescent. There was a certain teacher, when I was in John McDonogh, Brother Rob we used to call him. He was a black history teacher and—like I said—I knew I wasn't the type of person to seek out friends. I was a standoffish person, even in high school, and people wanted to either be my friend or pick on me.

So I used to fight a lot, and collect trophies. And the trophies were when I would fight somebody, I would intentionally make them bleed, so they would get blood on my shirt, and that was the trophy. And I used to hang the shirt on the wall, as a little violence medal. I'd write that person's name on the shirt. So this violent way of thinking was going to be the end of me, until I met this teacher, who was teaching me more about seeking understanding. More about knowledge and such.

He didn't know how influential he was. I actually saw him, Brother Rob, a couple of months ago this year and I was telling him how influential he was to me, and he was shocked—when I told him how much he meant to me. Basically, Brother Rob instilled in me to seek more in life. Seek more education, seek more. Because what I was basically doing was trying to fight into the in-crowd, which itself was divided, as opposed to what I really wanted to do in life. And I was still trying to discover what I was really trying to do. So definitely, he was trying to tell me to seek more now, seek more understanding. "You have greater potential than what you think," he'd say. And when I remember Brother Rob, I try to be more than what I am.

And by me being a known good fighter, people always wanted to see me fight. They used to try to provoke stuff, or try to send people at me so they could provoke stuff or antagonize me, you know, but this teacher taught me to be more humble within myself. He was African American. When I ran into him a couple months ago, he told me that after Katrina a lot of the old public school teachers lost their jobs, including him.

When I told him what he had done for me, he had no idea he was my angel. "Brother Rob," I said, "you were the most influential teacher in high school, you were the teacher I remember the most. Because you showed me what it was to seek understanding and truth. You showed me that you cared as a teacher." And he said that he felt like he didn't make any impression on anyone's life. He felt like all of his teaching was really in vain. So I told him, and I gave him a new sense of reassurance. He was my angel in the wilderness.

And I told him how successful I was in life, and even though I had many pitfalls. It says in James, "Consider it pure joy whenever you go through trial and tribulation. Because at the completion of these trials, you are blessed with an abundance of endurance, so that you may be mature and complete, lacking in nothing" (James 1:2-4). That's what I told Brother Rob he had done for me, and that's what I live by.

Reaction:

I have many responses to Derrick's story. Here are some of them. *First*, I become more convinced than ever that if we middle class whites *and* blacks in New Orleans are going to successfully connect with young people like Derrick—often known as "street people"—we need to *partner* with them, often letting them take the lead as we move toward justice and peace in our violent city. Icon advisor Sarge Johnson speaks convincingly about this when he tells of how the Icons formed and how they make their decisions. Through his music and his art, Derrick and fellow Icons can inspire and lead many of their generation that we of the middle class—black and white—cannot. Who among us knows that the popular street name for rappers is "spitters"? Who among us knows the difference between "the book people" and the "rappers"? More importantly, who among us can get a big turnout of the young and black for our concerts, our church services, our grassroots efforts?

Second, as Derrick told his story, I realized that he joined street gangs because of his need for what we in the church tirelessly call "support groups." His awakening came in Mississippi after Hurricane Katrina, where he met new friends, and in Orleans Parish Prison, where he became known as Black Jesus. He discovered there that, with the help of the Most High, he could find positive-seeking friends—a support group!—not directed by greed, revenge, or the thrill of violence. If only the Icons could multiply themselves throughout our violent city and beyond.

Third, I was moved by the gift Brother Rob made to Derrick in high school, even though Brother Rob did not know it and, in fact, thought his teaching career had been a complete failure. I very much appreciate the fact that Derrick was able to thank him many years later.

Fourth, I marvel at the way prison inmates of different faiths often get along so well, a model for all of us. Though known as the Black Jesus, Derrick was befriended in prison by an older Muslim, Donald Chopin, one of the key members of Justice and Beyond, the program that meets every Monday evening at Christian Unity (described in chapter 4). And Derrick uses a customary Islamic name for God—Most High

Just recently when I was part of a long Kairos Prison Ministry weekend—this time not at Angola but at Dixon Correctional Institute—I came to know two Muslim inmates as my "brothers"—one from my family table of nine, the other as my special "guest." Both loved the three-day, twelve-hour-a day broadly Christian program and easily brought all of the Jesus talk into their Islamic faith. As always, at the end of the weekend, we placed Kairos cross-necklaces on all who chose to wear them. All thirty inmates received them. As each man received his cross from the three clergy volunteers, he would say, "I am counting on Christ." As we bestowed the crosses, we would say, "And Christ is counting on you." Of course, when I put the crosses on my new Muslim friends, I said, "Christ *and* Allah are counting on you."

As I write this, I am thinking of all the terrible mass killings in the U.S. and beyond in the last year. If only we, *all* the people of the world, could learn from Derrick, Donald Chopin, my Kairos Muslim friends in prison, and the Most High! As one inmate, a Muslim imam said, at the end of a previous

Kairos weekend, "The Qur'an says that Christians and Muslims should be friends. I am as much a Muslim as ever, but after this weekend I have new Christian friends; no, new Christian brothers."

Fifth and maybe most important, as I listened to Derrick's story, I couldn't help but think of the men I've gotten to know through the Kairos Prison Ministry. So many of the Icons from the gangs they talk about could have been in prison for long sentences if they had made just a particularly harmful misstep. I meet the Kairos participants after they have been in prison five, ten, twenty, or even thirty years—and they are different people. All the more reason for all who can, to support the Icons and programs like the Icons for Peace. As I keep saying, instead of us whites always trying to recruit African Americans, like the Icons, to join our groups, it would be great if we joined theirs.

An Update:

In October of 2016, Derrick was shot nine times in a drive-by, but is doing amazingly well although he is often in much pain. He does not need his crutches most of the time, and is still performing and taking his art and love of the Most High just as far as it will go. And for me and a lot of others, he is a black Jesus.

- -

Yahmel Bey: Love Rising from Who I Am

Yahmel is one of the first Icons I got to know well at our weekly gatherings. He is twenty-four.

When he told me he was living in his car as his way to bring peace to the world, I knew I had to have a conversation. I explained my "angels" project to him. I asked him first to tell me what he wants people to know about his growing up here in New Orleans and then to talk about his hopes for himself and for the Icons.

> **Yahmel:** Well, I want people to know about the hard times I've been experiencing, but also my accomplishments after the downfalls. I want people to know about love rising from who I am. You have a great dream, but then the world outside the doors where I stay does not want that dream to prosper. Especially if it's about peace, love, and unity. Because outside of the car doors where I stay, it's separation. It's cold outside. It's disappointing.
>
> Part of my hard times growing up was my dad made decisions that hurt me even though I wasn't really being raised by him, but being raised by my grandmother. I am just coming to the realization that everything happens for a reason. If I put myself in my dad's shoes and see what I would do when he was at the age of twenty-one, messing around with a sixteen, seventeen-year-old girl, then pop comes the baby, me. Then, his mom's telling him to join the Army

or Air Force.

My birth mother has never really been in my life, and still to this day, not that much, though I can see that she tries. I still have the love inside me from my birth mother, and I'll always be open to it. I have the memories of her calling on the phone saying she would come get me, and still her not being there. Like, we would talk on the phone, and she would tell me that she would come get me on the weekend. I would have packed my bags and I would be very happy that I was going with my mom instead of staying at my grandmother's house. And I would just sit in the chair next to the door, waiting. You know, I'm a little kid, only five swinging my feet on the chair, happy like I'm on the swings. Then I'd fall asleep. I'd wake up the next day and I'd still be in the same chair by the door. Nobody came. At that time I was staying with my grandmother, my father's mom.

I knew that, even as a kid, that my mother was supposed to be around. I could just feel it. My mom was supposed to be with me. You know, my grandmother raised me, and so when she would take me to school and we'd have days where parents were supposed to come on campus, I would see everybody sitting with their mom and their dad. But my mom wasn't there. My dad wasn't there. My grandma came when possible.

I did receive a lot of love from my grandmother, my father's mom. And that's why my music is so powerful. That's why I express love so much in it. Think about it. Any lady who has raised three kids and put them through college, now has a grandson, me, and put him through high school and two colleges. My father was not in the picture very much. I can't say he didn't try. Like I said, I have to put myself in his shoes. I have to think of what I would have done if I were him.

My grandmother told me the story all the time of how she came in the room and gave him an ultimatum about the different military branches to go to. And she let him know like, you can do that, and I'll take care of your son. But there is a deep yearning inside that will always come back to me like, why didn't my mother or father come get me?

I feel like I'm lucky to still be here alive; I'm lucky to not be in jail. I feel like the devil was definitely touching me, trying to make me go in another direction to where I will be enslaved. 'Cause I really truly feel free. I've been tempted to break in houses. I've been tempted to going into the Quarter and snatch somebody's phones, just to pawn it. I've been tempted to . . . hmm . . . there were a lot of things. I have done drugs. smoked marijuana. I've done shrooms (psychedelic mushrooms). I've done acid, LSD.

Like I said, it's the upbringing and my grandmother's voice in the back of my head that helps me come back. She's a master teacher. She retired after teaching over thirty-two years at Sarah T. Reed High School in New Orleans. She taught gifted math, remedial, really all levels of math at the school. And she was also an organizer in that school. I remember she used to bring me to her classes when I was a little kid. And people that graduated from that high school still ask me, "Is your grandma still alive?" I remember how she used to bring me everywhere with her. She never left me alone. And I find it amazing when I walk around how many people know her, and know me, because of her. And it's like, that's one of the many things that keeps me out of trouble, 'cause I don't want to disgrace her name.

I graduated from Warren Easton High School, the real purple and gold. Then I went to Southern University in Baton Rouge. I went to business marketing, then that later changed to business administration, then that changed to engineering. Because I was there still not knowing what to do. I felt like high school didn't fully prep me or teach me what I needed. High school didn't guide me in a free direction. It was stagnant. Everybody wanted to be a fashion designer in high school, or a football player or great athlete. They didn't promote being a doctor or lawyer. They didn't promote owning your own business, they didn't promote being an advocate for justice or a philanthropist. They didn't promote any of that.

Instead, they promoted Nikes, drugs. They promoted being the popular one. They promoted being the one with the biggest house at the end of life's game. The expressions at high school are cruel. They're real cruel. I can remember not wanting to fit in. It's not a specific crowd that I hung with. I was a very quiet person. I kept my thoughts in my head. Because I knew what I was saying might offend people because it was truthful. If I told somebody how I really felt about a situation or about them in New Orleans, it would be chaos, it would be a fight. Simply because all the males want to be Mr. Macho and all the girls want to be, the It Girl. They want to be the one with all them dudes running behind. Like, everybody wants to pick her first.

I was fourteen during Katrina, and we went to Alabama. My grandmother never thought she was going to be able to come back. And that was the first time I'd really seen her really cry. I'd seen her cry at funerals. But not like when Katrina took her home. Me and my grandmother were together during Katrina, and my mother wasn't looking for me and didn't know where we were.

I see people with their mom, dad, sister and stuff like that. If I turn around and see them smile, I feel the love they have for each other. I know it's real, but it can be hard on me. I'm supposed to appreciate that love, smile back, even though I didn't have it from my own parents. It's a test of my love and faith if I can love back. Every time I pass that test, my love gets greater. And when I'm faced with a harder test, I try to show as much love as I can keep dishing out, no matter the obstacle. Like every time I get punched in the face, or every time I make a mistake, my grandmother's love still helps me. "You never stop teaching and you never stop learning," she said.

She's in Arizona now because of her health. My uncle is watching over her, so I'm happy with that. But when she was very sick, and I saw her in the hospital bed—that was when I got back from Southern University and I couldn't find no jobs. I had sent in applications, but I really could find no jobs. I saw her in the hospital bed, and I just broke out in tears. 'Cause I'm sitting there like man . . . I can't find no job and if she goes, what am I going to do? Because all of a sudden, she had a tumor on her kidney. And then she was the only one from that side of the family, my dad's side, that lives in New Orleans, Louisiana.

She's sick, then she gets out of the hospital and moves to Arizona, and I still have no job. That's when I went into survival mode. Like Marshawn Lynch, beast mode.[3] You have to get. You have to hustle. You have to grind, fill out applications, fill out more applications. When you sink down to a certain level, you attract people of that same lack of energy, you attract people on that same thought pattern. And that's not healthy. There are a lot of things that I've done on this planet, on this Earth. You could measure or weigh me, and my heart would still be as light as a feather, up in the sky. 'Cause I would never do things to be spiteful. There is always a reason. You know it's a very good thing if your heart is as light as a feather. Nothing can beat you down if your heart is up there.

Right now, I'm sleeping in my car, chasing *my* dreams. My uncle offered to buy me an apartment in Arizona, my auntie offered me a place to stay in Virginia. But to me, fighting for my freedom and my dreams, I've chosen to sleep in the back of this car so no one can interfere with my dreams. I still do job applications . . . it's just a hard time.

Let me ask you this, Yahmel, why haven't you been hired? You seem like a good person and you have a good record.

I don't know. I've never been to jail; I do have a clean record. And then I got a background check that came back clean. I was shocked that it came back clean, 'cause I thought people were trying to arrest me. But it just goes to show you, just keep the faith, and don't do anything irrational. Like when I was hungry, I would walk around Walmart, eating their grapes or bananas and then leave. And I got to the point where I was like I don't want to do that anymore. I worked at Home Depot about eleven months. I am not sorry I left Home Depot . . . well, sometimes I am, but it was very wishy-washy because of the situation I was in. I was working very hard, but they were not supporting me there.

Then I connected with the Icons for Peace when I met a couple of family members of mine—Kush, Damo, and Jardan. When I met them, my life was already changing because of the choices I was making—to better myself, with or without a good job, to express what I feel inside. They brought me to the New Orleans Healing Center on St. Claude Street. And when I went in there, there was an Icons for Peace meeting going on. That's when I started to see that they were doing things. They wanted to do things in the community. And most of them were artists, music artists, like me. When Sarge was saying this was a place where we can put people to work together and bring together common interests, I saw an opportunity. I saw an opportunity to take my gifts

---

3. A nickname used for a particularly aggressive football playing style coined by the Seattle Seahawk running back Marshawn Lynch.

and at least try to get something to do that was fulfilling with my gift of music and poetry. It all stems from poetry.

I am going to offer my art at the next Rap Versus Poetry session this coming Thursday and every Thursday. [Derrick explains this in his story.] We encourage people always to come out. We've been to an open mic at this restaurant called Buckner's. And there were a lot of European people in there. And we went in there and sat down and people turned around and said, "Oh my God, it's these dark men, black men, what's going on?" And they saw us sit down and first listen to their music. Then once we finished our thing at the open mic, we invited them to come out to our event. It's open to everyone. It's open to guitarists. It's open to singers. It's open to people who play ukulele, it's open to people who play the harmonica, it's open to people who sing opera. Every Thursday at the Healing Center, at 9 o'clock. Some came.

People in New Orleans need to know this is going on. Most don't. But here you are with the Icons and other people. Through your music and your poetry, you're trying to spread the love of Christ. Call it what you want, but that's what I think. Bringing people peace and healing through your music.

I feel like that's my mission. And that's my intention. My intention is to take my gift with words and my power with words and use it to heal people. That's why I'm sleeping in my car, because I know it's coming. We go to open mics, and we perform, then we try to encourage people at those open mics to come to ours. Derrick also does poetry. He is actually the one who started Rap Versus Poetry. My relationship with him has been getting greater and greater. Because he is a reflection of me, and I'm a reflection of him.

And really that's how it is around the world. We're all reflections of each other, no matter what skin pigmentation, but you have to be open to see that. And a lot of people don't see that because they are really self-centered. I let people know that I'm always there to listen. I'm always there to listen. And I want people to listen to me because I am on the edge myself. Because of how many of applications I've been sending in for jobs with no success.

Let me change the subject a little bit. What are the underlying problems in New Orleans? How much does racism have to contribute to the problems in New Orleans? People like you should be able to get jobs and be able to live the kind of lives that they want to. But what's going on?

The air has no such thing as racism. You have to give things life, and that's what people are doing. They are giving racism life. They are giving it the breath to live. Because of the media, specifically because of the media. If you take a kid and you put a coloring box in front of him. And you put some people of different colors in front of that coloring box, and ask if that coloring box is related to those people, the kid's going to say "No" because kids are only going to see them as a person, as a human being with a heart. He's not going to sit that person next to a red crayon or a black crayon, or a white crayon. That's what I mean. You see, you have to birth racism. Kids aren't born with racism. Kids are born not knowing anything about racism so imagine if the world didn't know about racism.

People see television and see dark-skinned people shoot each other, or rob each other or shoot at Europeans or rob them, but they don't see the flip side of the coin, Europeans committing crimes. There was a case I knew about where a kid in Mandeville[4] was a arrested with a whole bunch of cocaine. And he was going to Mandeville High School. And they didn't put that on the news. And that's why I said racism is birthed, because they show black violence but not European violence. Racism is something that has to be programmed into someone's mind. It has to be shown to you over and over again. It has to show certain people doing something that would make you harmed. Make you scared and back off from black people. But then they see you with so much love, to where it spurns the hate, makes it go away. If you don't show love, it makes you hate, and you get that hateful energy back.

So, there seems to be a lot of racism. How do we undo racism in New Orleans?

What I would do really, if I had money and, well, really, I don't need money, I just need the right people, I would throw a respect rally. 'Cause respect is peace. So if you had a respect rally you would have the younger generation partnering with the older generation. It would bring the whole culture together. Because it's common issues that are going around. You have people who care about the Louisiana wetlands that we're losing and so much poverty in the city. You have people who do care about what's going on in the lower communities, the so-called "hoods." I have European friends that if I needed it, they would let me sleep on their couch. But some of them are in a house where they can't offer me that.

You said we need to bring people together to have conversations and treat each other as fellow people and realize we have a lot in common and how we can support each other. And I don't think that's happening very much in New Orleans.

Right. We're not learning how to tolerate or accept each other. We're not learning how to accept each other for who we are. And I feel like a lot of people don't accept themselves for who they truly are. Also, speaking from experi-

4. Mandeville is located across Lake Pontchartrain from New Orleans.

ence, when you don't do anything, you find that the idle mind is the devil's workshop. When you don't have anything, you don't have anything to eat, you don't have nobody to talk to, you resort to survival. You resort to taking. You tap into that animalistic mind, the cruel part of yourself. All of us have that part. A lion, if it's hungry enough, it will eat another lion.

So what's the answer? Here in New Orleans.

The jobs situation. If you're not giving people jobs, they are going to resort to taking. And that's what's happening. There are not enough jobs for people to survive. There are not enough opportunities for people to even work for themselves. Because people are too scared to hire blacks. They watch TV, and it is always a black person committing a crime. You rarely hear about white-on-white crime. So Europeans get scared of blacks, all blacks.

Yahmel, tell me about a wilderness experience you've had and who were the angels?

I am in the wilderness right now because I have been chased by the wild beasts, being refused for a job, sleeping in a car. One of my angels is my auntie. You, right now, listening to my story. My auntie, my father's sister. When I was sixteen or seventeen, she always took me everywhere. She's always been there to support me. Sarge Johnson, at Icons, is Arch (an archangel). If I hadn't gone to Icons for Peace, I wouldn't have met you. I wouldn't have met people from Justice and Beyond [their conversations are in chapter 4] or my new friends at SUNO (Southern University of New Orleans), like at the peace rally we had there. I have performed there. These are bridges that have helped me meet people. I have learned from Sarge that everything is not what you see. People misuse our love. I can prove to my Most High that I can do what the Most High wants me to do. I researched the word boss in the dictionary. I know whose I am. Not that person at Home Depot who made things hard for me. My boss is Most High. The Most High wants me to find love in everyone. My grandmother also taught me that.

What's good for me may not be good for someone else, may not be better for them. Like if I am begging on the street and someone gives me a dollar to get something to eat, but that person can't feed his own children. Good for me but not for them. We have to figure things like that out and how we can best love.

The last thing I want to say: I want people to look at my story and not judge it. And listen to my music and bear witness to the love that's being expressed, bear witness to how anybody can take anger and channel it. Anything that causes agony to people, that's what causes them to be uneasy and to act mean to other people. So I try to remove the agony.

Keep telling your story. . . .

Reaction:

First, I appreciate how Yahmel keeps questioning himself so that he can love more. It broke his heart when his mother and father abandoned him. Still, he tries to put himself in their place asking himself if he would have done better when he was nineteen. When he sees families showing love for each other, he tries to take that love into himself instead of being jealous. When he is able to love despite many obstacles, it makes his heart as "light as a feather" floating up there, and nothing can bring it down. He and I have that inherited love in common: Yahmel from his grandmother, me from my Old Charleston family, racist maybe but full of unconditional love for me even when I began to work on the edge of the civil rights movement.

I also appreciate Yahmel's thoughts on how racism works against him, his family, and his friends. You have to "birth racism" he says. He believes that most of the racism in our society comes from television—people seeing black on black violence, and black on white violence, but not white violence. I wish racism was as easy to overcome as Yahmel imagines. As a one-time proud son of the Deep South, I know too much—those endless racist jokes, those protests against integrating busses, schools, even churches—those things that helped shape an entire culture, those things that still live on in various ways. I'm afraid I agree with Michelle Alexander, who in her book *The New Jim Crow,* says that it will take something equivalent to the civil rights movement to significantly reform massive incarceration in this country, much of which is an attack on African Americans. She points out that there are more black males in prison now than there were male slaves in 1850.

But however Yahmel understands racism, he is for sure one of the angels who will help all of us overcome it. He is going to bring people together through his poetry and his music, he is going to organize "respect rallies," and help all of us love those different from us. So determined is he not to see black and white, to him people like me (pale white) aren't even white—we are Europeans! Actually, my Old Charleston family would like that.

Here is something else. When Yahmel was talking about his angels, he named *me*, a new friend, as one of them. I was indeed surprised when he said that and I began thinking of this project in a different way. It is not going to be just writing a book about young and black in New Orleans. It is going to be even more about building relationships, like the one I am developing with Yahmel. So, I find myself rising to a new level of commitment.

Now a downer: Late one afternoon shortly after I had met with Yahmel the second time to go over our conversation—and had written out my response—I was waiting in front of the Healing Center to meet with another Icon, Torry. When Yahmel strolled in, I said, "Hello Torry, good to see you." "Don't you know who I am?" Yahmel said as gently as he could. Another Ralph Ellison *Invisible Man* moment! When will I—we—ever learn? Torry never showed up. I try to convince myself that often I am not able to recognize people because of what psychologists call prosopagnosia, or "face blindness."

═══════════════════════════════

Jonathan Lewis: My Father Lives On In My Purpose

Jonathan, age twenty-three, met with me in our home on December 5, 2015. Perhaps the tallest person I know, he is also a loving husband and devoted member of the Icons. He spoke of his deceased father being an "angel" before I even told him about my "angels in the wilderness" writing project. He also told of his getting to know Sarge Johnson, the advisor to the Icons. I began our conversation, as I often do, by asking Jonathan what he wants people to know about him.

Jonathan: I would like people to know that while my name is Jonathan Lewis, I share common traits and conditions with everybody else on Earth. And that I desire to know more about myself. I plan on learning that through knowing more about other people. I want everyone to know about how I really care about other people. 'Cause, I realize how necessary others are, to really know about myself.

I think that in the face of any kind of suppression or oppression, the expression of self through the arts is necessary. Even if you're not widely distributing your art, if you create something that's fully you—something that's not put into any box—not only does it let people truly know who you are, but it also releases in you any kind of blockage you may have in expressing yourself in other avenues in your life, be it through your pains and /or your actions. I can express myself fully in the Icons.

I write. I'm a poet; I started out as a poet. And now I'm getting into music production 'cause I really love music. I make music to create something that could be an enzyme . . . that can catalyze a reaction between different people. I want to be that receptive person that receives from everybody and thus fosters a connection from everybody I receive from. You know, I'm a very easy person to get along with.

Just like everybody else, sometimes my feelings can be kind of strong. At times I can be polarizing, but for the most part I'm a very receptive person because I like people. And I understand that all of our conditions are symptomatic of our environments. So if you are mad at another person, you need to address the environment that the person comes from. You should try to find a common ground. Everybody is nice to somebody, you know. And even the guy

Jonathan Lewis, Icons for Peace, making his long-deceased father proud

who you think is mean and a complete horrible person, there's somebody in the world that he's nice to. And I think that capacity of being nice is indicative of the capacity that we all have to connect to other people. That's natural. And when you can't, it's only because you're having trouble connecting to yourself.

And how do you connect to yourself?

Honestly, being married is helping me out a lot. My wife is named Anastasia Ebel. We met each other randomly at the Boot three and a half years ago.[5] I was with some friends, we went in, and me and her locked eyes, and we connected. And we started talking. And we've been inseparable ever since. Now we've got difficulties, but the reasons I said my wife helped me out a lot with connecting to myself was that we can always relate and we can all compromise. If we're all mentally healthy and stable, we can compromise.

Let me ask you, where does this come from in your growing up years, your desire to see what's good in other people?

Well . . . man, I think . . . I'm not really sure where. But for starters, I was raised religiously. I was raised in the church. I went to Philadelphia Apostol-

---

5. It is a hangout right around the corner from us, where mostly Tulane students drink beer and meet new people.

ic Church, part of APMI (Apostolic Prophetic Ministries International). It is here in New Orleans, across the canal. You know, over the Industrial Canal. But it was destroyed in the Katrina flood. But I went there, and I didn't understand fully why . . . I didn't understand the intricacies of what God actually is and the details of the God to be praised. But I did learn the stories of the Bible, and I felt like the stories and the ancient texts are so important. Those stories are the meat of it. They are the symbolic flag of everything we need to know.

You know, Jesus's favorite way of teaching was telling stories. Parables. So what's a story from your younger life that stands out.

Man . . . when people experience trauma they do a good job of blocking things out. And I found that when I think about my life pre-Katrina, there are a lot of things I don't remember until I walk past anything that was there before Katrina or see the place where my church was. My church was destroyed during the Storm. And that's not saying that I won't be able to remember any stories, but as I start to tell my stories there are parts that I remember that I couldn't remember before.

My father was a fireman and an EMT. He was also with the Harbor Police. He did a lot of things. And he was a really valiant dude. He always did a lot for other people, and it was evident in the line of work he decided to go into. He was actually a fireman for eight years and was about to make captain before he died. I was just a baby.

I found this out later that he had taken the test to become a fire department captain, then he passed away as a hero fighting a fire. My mom found out he had passed the test after he died. Having no dad, I was raised by my mom. And I think not having a father is a highly determinate factor in mental health and mental stability. But, as far as maintaining yourself and having some kind of emotional homeostasis, it is hard if you are only raised by a female. It's very lopsided and can lead you toward emotional excitability.[6]

And how does that play out in your life?

Having no dad played out a long time in my life with my emotions being exaggerated. And I see this in a lot of people who come from the same background. Emotions, exaggerated both positively and negatively. It almost creates like a bi-polar wave. And I'm not saying that women are not consistent, but even in the hormones and the fact that their emotions can be tied to their body signals and hormones and things like that. And if you're a child and don't under-

---

6. I admit I had to look up the meaning of homeostasis—being consistently stable no matter what is going on outside—like keeping a temperature of 98.6 wherever you are.

stand these things, you just wonder why your mother is really upset sometimes and why your mother is really happy sometimes. And why she's prone to bursts of anger. You don't understand, you just think that's how people are.

I'm positive about my mother; she was a victim of trauma. Definitely, growing up in the housing projects in the day in New Orleans. Growing up in her economic situation, she exhibited a lot of traits of somebody who had post-traumatic stress disorder. She was prone to outbursts of anger. She had an "exaggerated startle response."[7]

An example, you ever been in a store and you see a mother with a child and that child picks up something that it shouldn't have picked up and the mother goes above and beyond being upset? It's like a startled response, I think my mom rationalized it as "I'm their mother and father. So I have to not only nurture but I have to discipline too." And when you have both aspects coming from the same vessel, it forces you to have to kind of create a boundary that you have to dig yourself out of at all times. And I think that affected me.

But to get back to my father, I combined his death with being raised by my mother, and it formed the idea (or image) of my father in my head as an angel that made me, and it still kind of permeates me today. I found that I have a purpose now, and I have to feel that purpose before I can go anywhere, but my father made me a lot like a martyr. But not just religious, but behind any good cause. Whenever I give myself to something, I give myself to it heart and soul like my father would. In a way it is a gift not having an alive father. Since he was a hero, I only have positive thoughts, no bad thoughts as I may have it if he had lived. I think my father has done for me in death that some people's fathers have done for them in life. He helps me be the caring person I am and helps me keep going no matter what happens.

Because he passed away in such a valiant way, I never thought of him negatively. It gives me pride to know I come from the stock of somebody who would be willing to do that, be a brave fireman. Also because he worked for the city, he left behind a trust fund. And I got $20,000 when I was eighteen, way too young to get $20,000. I totally spent it on things, none of which I have now. He also gave me a scholarship, ten-semester scholarship to any public university in Louisiana.

Changing the subject a little—you try to live in the moment, right?

No, I don't live in the moment. I live in the purpose. I believe the Holy Spirit is not some little voice that you literally hear. I think it's a misconception when people teach that Holy Spirit is gonna be some words that you hear in the back of your brain that's going to tell you to do something. I think that's just a setup for mind control. Like the government can just beam some radio waves at you.

---

7. A common symptom of PTSD, defined as "a hyper-defensive response to sudden or threatening stimuli that is likely connected to the traumatic event of that person's past."

I feel like the Holy Spirit comes out in the nature of the creation, as if we can look at the world around us and look at the way things coincide and the way people interact and the way things react and see the Holy Spirit around us, subtly screaming this gospel to us. You know? Screaming it at us. And people are so busy that they don't hear it. And we don't hear it.

And what's screaming out at us, Jonathan?

Oh man, from what I've seen, homeostasis is real. As in, everything would right itself if people listened to their purpose. *Everybody.* As in, things would play out the way that they are supposed to play out. Just have faith that things that are supposed to happen will happen. You know, that's not a hands-off faith where you're just kind of like "whatever will be, will be" and you're just shuffling through life. No, you have to listen to your purpose!

You're trying to help yourself find your purpose and help others find their purpose.

Exactly, if I can use a puzzle as an analogy, don't worry about placing other people in their spot on the puzzle, you find your spot. And somebody else will. You know, we achieve our self-consciousness through projecting it onto the world around us. You know, there is this guy named Georg Friedrich Hegel and he has this concept called the "Master-Slave Dialectic," where he states that when two people meet or see each other, that in that moment, they project themselves onto that other person. They are mesmerized by the mirror image of themselves. So initially instead of seeing that person as their own person, they see that person as an extension of themselves. At which point Hegel says that a struggle begins, as I try to enact my will on a self-conscious person that is also trying to enact his will on me. And eventually somebody wins, and that's when you have the slave and master relationship that begins. And at this point, Hegel says that the slave's fear of death is what resigns him to that position while the master feels that his consciousness is not dependent upon the slave's life.

So the conclusion is that when the slave is put to work to create things (from nature) for the master, he starts to see himself in his creation, this helps the slave achieve his self-consciousness. Meanwhile, the master has no relationship with nature because the master never actually has to make anything himself. He just manipulates the person to make the object. So in effect, the master becomes a slave to the labor of the slave.

Wow! Now, let me move on, if we can, to how you got to know Sarge. Through basketball?

I met him through my wife's mom, and honestly I was blown away by the life he leads. I was blown away by his lifestyle because I feel like, like I said, the

Holy Spirit is in the workings of the creator. So I can see what kind of person you are by what you do, and from what I saw and from what he was doing I was really impressed. The self-control he displayed in his life, the set values he displayed in his life.

And then we became friends, at that basketball game for young black men that organizer Joe Givens set up in July of 2014. Sarge and Joe Givens had known each other for a while and came together and concocted that they would be the advisors for an organization that would start out to help young people, first by playing basketball. It grew into the Icons. I hope that the Icons for Peace can be a tool to fulfill a myriad of an individual's purposes. I think that the Icons for Peace could be the prototype of little organizations all over the country and the world of people who are in similar economy situations or in similar geographic situations (live in the same place) that want to come together and try to right what has been wronged by having a society based on love and caring.

What about racism?

Well, I honestly think . . . you know, Sarge has an interesting view on racism. And I've kind of adopted it because it makes sense. Sarge believes racism is an exaggerated camaraderie at the expense of the outlier, at the expense of the minority—of any society. White folks tend to be comrades and preclude people on the outside. Racism becomes a problem when the people who are being excluded don't have any camaraderie with the other people who are being excluded. And I think racism is running as rampantly as it is because the people who are being racist are the ones who have the economic power to take advantage of minorities, who lack discipline because often they are just trying to survive. We can't successfully fight racism until we develop camaraderie in our own community, maybe like the Latinos.

If there are two groups of people who don't like each other, it's not a big deal with them not liking each other because you can live where you live and I can live where I live. But, instead of us being able to live separately, you try to live on top of me. I don't think there's anything wrong with me looking at a white skin baby and a dark skin baby and prefer holding the dark skin baby. That's just camaraderie. God created us in his image, that's why he loves us. It's only natural for me to love my image. I don't think we should try to fight that. I think if you try to fight that, you're just trying to skew the natural order of things and get them to want something that's foreign to them.

For example, in America the dark-skinned person has been systematically programmed to not want to produce more of itself. If you're from the black community, you know this to be true, that lighter-skinned women are favored more than dark-skinned women. But what happens essentially, in reality, is that you have less babies that have dark skin. And these babies have the same programing and indoctrination. And when they chose a mate they are going to choose a mate with fairer skin than they have. It's like genocide produced from an anti-dark skinned pathology. As you can see, I'm pretty dark skinned.

Let me see if I'm understanding this. Black folks need to develop a camaraderie among themselves and also there needs to be this crossover so that black folks and white folks become comrades. Both of those things need to happen.

I think that crossover camaraderie will happen when we all respect each other. 'Cause you know, I don't have to prefer you to my people, but when I respect how well you take care of your people and you respect how well I take care of my people and we see that common ground, the love that we express, then we'll achieve the camaraderie. It starts in the home. And if I don't see you loving people in your home then I don't expect you to love people outside of your home.

Let me ask you this and make sure I understand it. As an Icon and as an individual you are trying to develop that camaraderie within the black community and then in the larger community. And you and the Icons are doing this in part through your art and your music, and your singing. Do you sing or play an instrument?

I play the trombone. I've played for almost six years. I sing, well, I mean, as my confidence grows I start singing more. I'm a poet, and I rap. I think music is super powerful. I'm a student of the school of hip hop. I believe hip hop is so important because I feel like it happened for a reason. Honestly, hip hop was just an embodiment of black people's inherit ability to make lemonade out of lemons. Or just a way to practice their religion. A way to . . . it's hard to explain. Hip hop for a young tribe of people, when it first came out, was the main export.

You know, our black culture is the main export of America. That's documented. Everybody in the world kind of follows our lead, musically, culturally, and hip hop is an embodiment of that. And it didn't just happen for no reason. Hip hop is the enzyme that I was talking about earlier, and everybody can connect through hip hop and see the likeness within each other. I can support that in my concerts and contacts. I'd like people to see that we can operate in love and still get ahead. The world has people confused that you really need to operate in selfishness and hatred in order to really succeed. You can teach everybody to respect others, even those people who don't deserve that respect.

I hope we can find something in everyone to respect. I want to find something, like the fact that they have gone through hardship and haven't killed themselves is something. And I mean having that stance, you know, some people would say that it always puts you in a vulnerable position because you're always looking for the good in people while they're always looking at ways to exploit you.

Let me stop you there and just ask you this question: What is the wilderness that you are still worrying about?

Man, the wilderness experience for me was when the hurricane happened. I was about thirteen. And I had just started off in my ninth-grade year at McMain. I had worked all summer at a shoe warehouse to buy this really nice pair of shoes. And it was the first time I learned a lesson about the cost of things. I felt like my wilderness experience extended from the hurricane ten years ago to when I met my wife two-and-a half years ago.

During Katrina, we first went to northern Louisiana. It was the first time I saw seriously segregated neighborhoods. These were the blacks who were like, "Oh don't go over there!" That was the first time I had seen that because I'm from New Orleans and it's not like that here. After that we moved up north to Raytown, Missouri, and that was also when I first started smoking weed. And I feel like weed is way more dangerous than anybody will give it credit for. Because *time* is the most important thing that you have. And anything that can take that time from you and anything that takes that motivation from you . . . it basically renders you useless. Someone like me believes that God wants you to fulfill the purpose of your creation. And anything that stops that is inherently evil. You lose *time* while you're under the influence. You lose that time while you're pursuing and trying to go get some more weed. You lose your time in jail if they catch you with it.

Now I have to admit, I don't feel like I can be completely down on weed, because I've had some of the most amazing trains of thought while I was under the influence of marijuana. And had things put in perspective for me in a lot of different ways. I was able to bond with people that I never would have bonded with before. It's brought a lot of people together.

Let me ask you this: Who were those angels who helped you move forward from the time of Katrina to the time you met your wife? That's a good stretch of time.

It is lots of people. I'm going to say my mom helped me out a lot. She was really good. And she just helped me out by being patient with me. She didn't put me out, though she could have put me out. Because once I made eighteen or nineteen and I got a car, and I got this money after my father's death, I should have moved out. I really should have. She almost didn't help me by not putting me out because instead of spending money on the things we needed, I was just spending money on frivolous things. She's always had patience with my development. My mom never was a very affectionate person. She raised three kids, she worked three jobs her whole life. So she was never around, and when she was around she was sleeping. But she gave us as much opportunity as she could.

My mom taught me how to be selfless. And I think my selflessness is going to push my soul where it needs to be. She taught me by example. My mom is the queen of giving what little she had. She was always doing that, her whole life, even though she grew up in poverty and in New Orleans.

And she kept going even when your father died.

Yeah, but my father wasn't the only one of her children's fathers who died. You know my older sister, her dad died from a cocaine overdose. Then my mom met my dad, and he died in a fire. Then she met my younger sister's dad and he beat on her. And then going through that while taking care of kids. I know it's trying and I know it's stressful, but she still did it. She did it. She's a soldier for that.

But another angel I'd say, in school, there was always one teacher. At least one teacher. At McMain, his name was Mr. Schneider. He had a mullet hairstyle, an exaggerated mullet. He was really passionate about what he taught. And he was really passionate about history. The scope and way in which he taught really captured and enamored me. Man, it inspired me. My sisters were amazing angels. I mean, in my mother's absence with her three jobs, my older sister really raised me. Some angels would be the people around me who were going through what I was going through and gave me something to focus on outside of myself and my own thoughts.

Were you ever part of a gang?

Well, it wasn't a gang. Before Katrina, New Orleans was separated into areas. So it was like you were with people from your area. So, say, I'm from the Eighth Ward. He's from Downtown. So if somebody else was from Downtown, it's like: "Hey, you from Downtown too?" They'd get that comradery going on. I was never part of a gang, but I was proud of where I lived. The neighborhood belonged to us and not to the dudes who lived in another part of the city, unless we welcomed them.

My mom had kept me as sheltered as possible. One of the side effects of her working all the time was that she gave us things to keep us inside our home too. Because she knew *what* was on the other side of the door, she didn't want us to leave. She always made sure we had books. She always made sure, like if a videogame came out that I wanted, I got it.

I hear a lot of anger from most of the African Americans I know about racism. They often say it is as bad as it was before the civil rights movement. How would you respond to that?

I think that people should, number one, control their emotions better. I think that once you give someone else control of your emotions you give them control of your mind. If I'm basing my emotions on what you're doing to me and not looking at the facts, that doesn't help. Our population in the country is a minority, so it's going to be really hard to rally a majority to try to pass the things that you want passed. We have to think analytically about the situation, rather than having this outburst of anger and exaggerated startled response. 'Cause we all experience trauma. And that brings me back to what I think is the solution, which I think is to govern ourselves. The people who are being oppressed need to first master themselves.

Before you can make a move outside your community, you need to move *within* the community. And that's exactly what I'm doing. And I feel like one of the first steps is to address the trauma that people have and help them find healing. People need to live in an environment where they feel safety, security, and freedom

A lot of people with trauma express it as cannon fodder. It just comes with the territory. And I believe it really affects people. And when you know the symptoms of the disorder, you start to catch them better and ask, "Wait, why am I doing this? Why am I getting mad so quickly? Why do I not think about my future? Why am I worried about the things that I'm worried about?" Young black males of this period of history, we see other young black males as a threat rather than a brother. I think once you alleviate these things within the demographic, you can take the solidarity that you gained and the camaraderie that you gained—like we talked about earlier, people have to have camaraderie within themselves first. Then I think it will be easier to mobilize people to create a change.

I know that this kind of dialogue is necessary because there is honestly no other place to have that dialogue but on the street, where you feel accosted. And at that moment, that's not the place to have that conversation.

Before we end this, one more question: what else do you want people to know from your story or your beliefs that we haven't covered?

I want people to know that to live is to grow. If you ever stop growing you're not living. Don't be so rigid in your prejudices that you can't witness a paradigm shift in others. Don't hold so staunchly onto antiquated beliefs. People are moving forward. The American psyche isn't as dark as people around the world think. We really do love life and liberty, and we are all pursuing happiness.

And I hope you keep that optimism and that way of bringing people together not just in the black community but for all of us.

Yeah, I mean, I can't stop. As long as I'm alive, I got to do it.

Reaction:

Throughout our engaging conversation, I was trying to get Jonathan to talk less about theory and philosophy (as much as I appreciate his thoughts) and more about action. I had to remind myself that this was, after all, his story, and his understanding of God and humankind was what he wanted to talk about most of all. Somewhat to my surprise, when he did talk about action, he talked about the necessity of helping "his people" come together—finding "comradery with themselves"—before trying to solve the great problem of racism in the country. Building that comradery is exactly what he and the Icons are trying to do.

I have some difference with Jonathan here, as I do with Yahmel. I believe fighting a common war, like fighting racism, *can* be the best way to bring people together. But what we probably need are both the strong and angry advocates for racial justice—like the hundred plus people I meet with every Monday night at Justice and Beyond—*and* the "comradery" builders. That's the Episcopal way after all—both-and.

When I met with Jonathan to go over our conversation, I told him about my own father—not a strong man, a long way from believing in integration, pretty much stuck in old white Charleston culture. "But Jonathan," I said, "the Old Man gave me a lot of love when I was growing up and almost, almost went bankrupt when he sent me to a private college, Sewanee, in Tennessee. He wanted for me what he didn't have for himself." Of course, Jonathan, who thinks in dialectical terms—good and bad influencing each other—understood. And that meant a lot to me. I don't easily tell African Americans of my racist background and my slave-owning ancestors.

My last response to the three young Icons I interviewed has to do with the centrality of music in their lives and in their stories. As much as I love all kinds of music, I am such a music outsider that I can't really explain why music is so life-giving to the young people I am getting to know, not just to the Icons but the other groups as well, especially the Mardi Gras Indians. They sing and dance for hours on their "walks." Well, one thing is for sure: Music is the universal language and understanding and appreciating the music of one group of people goes a long way toward understanding and appreciating *them* and their culture.

Chapter Four

Justice and Beyond

Justice and Beyond is a coalition of African American clergy, union organizers, political office holders, community leaders, and those whose families are affected by lingering racism in New Orleans. Justice and Beyond meets each Monday afternoon from 4:45 till 7:00 at Christian Unity Baptist Church with a New Orleans supper of baked chicken and red beans and rice. Reverend Dr. Dwight Webster, pastor of Christian Unity since 1988, and Mr. Pat Bryant, longtime civil rights leader in the city, are the co-facilitators. Each Monday, well over a hundred people discuss topics particularly important to New Orleans's black communities. I am one of ten or so white people who attend regularly. Formed in 2012, Justice and Beyond is becoming the most important voice of black New Orleans. It focuses on righteousness ("right relationships") as well as justice. Some of us say that the "righteousness" we pursue is another way to talk about love in action.

I believe that Justice and Beyond is a good model for African Americans seeking racial justice in all of our cities. When I served as a clergyman in South Carolina, Boston, and Washington, D.C., I knew of no organization comparable to Justice and Beyond in New Orleans, and I did spend much of my time getting to know and supporting grassroots black organizations.

Since the early 1980s, Pat Bryant has pushed hard against racism in the city and in the Gulf region. He is recognized as one of our most important leaders. I have known Pastor Webster since 1990 when he invited Trinity Episcopal Church, where I was serving, to be part of Jeremiah, a local Industrial Area Foundation chapter. Founded in the 1940s by labor organizer Saul Alinsky, Jeremiah, like other IAF organizations, gathers low-income people and helps them identify the most important issues to their communities in order to change oppressive conditions. Some IAF members still represent labor unions, but now most come from faith communities. IAF prides itself on a bottom-up approach.

Pat tells his story first, and then three of the younger leaders of Justice and Beyond tell theirs: Kristen Rome, Steven Kennedy, and Nakita Shavers.

Pat Bryant: A Christian Faith of Liberation

Because I asked Pastor Webster to introduce Christian Unity Baptist Church in chapter 7, for this chapter I asked Pat Bryant to talk about how Justice and Beyond began, what it is doing now, and what his hopes are for the future. Then I asked Pat to tell some of his story and who were his angels. We talked in our home on May 16, 2016.

Pat: Justice and Beyond is a coalition of individuals and organizations that unite around two things: justice and righteousness. And that means right-re-latedness. We began about four years ago, when Justice Bernette Johnson, who was a Louisiana Supreme Court Justice, was about to be overlooked as Chief Justice because she was black. She was the longest serving member on the Court. The law practiced then and now was that the longest serving justice would become the Chief Justice when that position became vacant. And she was being overlooked. She called me one day and asked if I could help her do some organizing to help receive the position she deserved.

Yeah, I told her, but I was kind of ill. About a year before I'd had a stroke and still wasn't comfortable in what I could or could not do. But she urged me to help, and I did. In four or five days, we called a meeting in one of her conference rooms. And there were about thirty-five leaders from around the state. A justice from Shreveport, a white male, had been favored by white jurists to take her place. The other justices discussed it, and they were going to pass over her. Justice Johnson said she wanted to fight that decision and she asked for our assistance.

What sort of leaders did you bring to that first gathering?

The NAACP, labor, senior-citizen groups in Baton Rouge, faith leaders, women's rights leaders. It was a good mix of white and black. And after the meeting, people went back and started organizing locally. And Houma, of all places, had the largest gathering. Houma had about 1,200 people come out at a rally organized by the NAACP.[1] They honored Justice Johnson with a big banquet and awarded her something, an eagle or something. A lot of black judges from around the state came. It was quite an event, and we had several events here in New Orleans, too. We started meeting locally.

The momentum was picking up. And we were holding meetings every week in New Orleans. Our numbers had grown from twenty to something like thirty, forty, or fifty. We were making plans to purchase ads statewide to push our cause for Justice Johnson to the newspapers. There was a federal court hearing where the judge ruled against the State and in our favor. Justice John-

---

1. Houma, in southern Louisiana, has a population of about 33,000, about a fourth of which is African American.

Pat Bryant, co-moderator of Justice and Beyond, longtime civil rights leader

son began to be seen in a favorable light. And then the Supreme Court came out and said, "We're going to choose Bernette Johnson as our Supreme Court Chief Justice!" And that was great. We had a big victory celebration. In the process of our organizing, several other issues came up. So we would not be a one-issue coalition. Issues related to education, employment, housing, police behavior, and other things came up. We consciously decided who we were and what we were doing. And we moved from being "Justice for Johnson," which is what we were first called, to "Justice and Beyond." And that's pretty much the die that's been cast for us.

And you were bringing together people who hadn't come together before on these issues?

You know, our understanding of the way that community power works is that none of us are strong enough in ourselves and in our own organizations to make the change that we want. So we have to work with others who are like-minded and try to get the broadest strategy that can involve the broadest amount of people. And that's been the driving ideal. When we were first beginning, our group was mostly older leaders. And we were very conscious that we could not have the force and power we desired if we did not bring young people into our ranks.

Young people would come in as issues affected them, like charter school issues, but they would only come in for particular issues. In terms of consistency, they would not be there regularly. When their organizing spirit was subdued, they weren't there. So we were, and still are, strategizing and thinking about how to bring in more young people. It's hard to do when most of the organizers are older, and we've had some tensions about multi-racial organizing.

Talk about that if you will.

We've always had a multi-racial focus. There are whites who want justice as much as African Americans, and we need to work with them, as well as Latinos and Asians. You know, the hardest groups to work with are the Asians and Latinos. Harder in the sense of spatial distance between our organizations. And we're not really working on the same issues. Not like the whites and blacks are.

So the tension came from those who wanted it to be an all-black effort?

Well . . . yeah. There has always been this underlying tension that somehow we can't do what we want to do with white people in here. But we've committed to multi-racial organizing. But black control of the leadership is a must. I've discovered in my years of organizing that white leadership domination will not work on issues of social justice.

I think that's so important. I try to preach that to the white groups I work with, but not many of them listen. Keep going.

One of my mentors, Anne Braden, preached it all the time. She'd say to the white folks, "Now, we're not going to lead black struggles. The best we can do is help move the system in whatever way we can." And you know, most of my adult life, I've held on to that jewel. And I always saw that white support had to be strategic in the sense that it didn't dominate.[2]

From the beginning, we were committed to both multi-racial and multi-generational organizing. Those two things are very important. But there is a style by which you have to accomplish that. And we're still working on that style, but it's unequivocal that blacks be in leadership roles. Members of Justice and Beyond must be able to articulate their wants and desires, and folks then decide either to support them or not support them. For example, Daphne Cross with Lots Academy Community Resources has been working on juvenile justice issues and recently was well received.

For your piece on Justice and Beyond, I don't remember exactly when Nakita Shavers and Steven Kennedy became part of Justice and Beyond. But we

---

2. Anne Braden, a well-known white civil rights leader, was the subject of a recent documentary film, *Southern Patriot: Anne Braden, 1924-2006.*

saw how sharp they were, and they almost immediately came up to sit at the head table. They were focused, they'd prepared themselves in their studies, and they were committed. People who want to make a change, particularly young people, will dry up on the vine if there is not something they can attach to that can sustain them. And that has been the primary focus of Justice and Beyond: to be a place where people who have progressive ideas can link up with others who share like-minded ideas.

It's tempting for young people, as well as us older people, to feel like they can do it on their own, or with just a few other people. But you need that community to work with.

Yeah. There is an organizing moment, when the conditions bring people to resolve that something has to change. I call that an organizing moment. And that moment has to be seized within a certain timeframe. It doesn't stay there for long periods. But you have to come and help those who need help. We're like doctors ready to work on patients and give them assistance and support whenever it is. And sometimes the biggest support you can give them is listening. Listening is very important.

You know, our weakest point is to talk about our vision. We don't do much on the vision side. Anne Braden used to say that you have to know what cathedral you are placing your stones in. Because many people, for years, might be on a course trying to reform this or that and then end up one day realizing that with all their work they've wasted their time—the cathedral never gets built. It's very important to know where you are going.

That's a good analogy. I used to work for the Washington National Cathedral so I know what you mean. You build it a stone at a time, but you need to build the same cathedral.

Right. It might be a stone at a time, but we need to have a shared vision of what this cathedral is going to be. Let's take an example. In education, we're agitating about getting the schools back here in New Orleans like they were before Katrina. And having a school board that has power over the schools with local control. But I think we also need to talk about what we want in education.

Right. I hear a lot of that from parents and grandparents at our Monday meetings.

Yes. We need to talk about the failures of education. Not just in New Orleans but the failure of education period. What forces are driving education today? Are we moving away from an education where people truly know the world in which they're living? Or do we have an education system which is set up that drives people to work certain jobs? Or no jobs at all? It seems that only a small percentage of the available workers are actually needed in the production process. It seems that decisions have been made *not* to educate surplus workers.

Can't you do both—educate our young people so they understand the world they live in and at the same time educate them for important vocations?

I think you have to. And I saw this successfully done in Cuba on my recent trip. Even in elementary schools, they start very early in giving people a very broad base in arts, sciences, humanities. But, at the same time, they focus on occupations. I mean, I looked at one school where they had electricians come and teach. Then in that same school, there was also a dental chair. Children were being trained to be dental hygienists! At seventeen years old, you've got kids going off to medical school. They turn out some of the sharpest and best doctors in the world. One doctor per 770 people. They are lifting the value of human beings beyond which we have not seen in the world. It's amazing. We have to look at what our resources are being used for. Are our resources benefitting only the 1 percent and not the 99 percent?

What I'm hearing is that we in Justice and Beyond must develop a vision for what we want to see happen in the classrooms. That's the cathedral. Then we can have strategy arguments. When we are talking about strategies to meet a common goal, we don't have to kill each other because basically we are on the same side.

And that needs to happen in education, housing, employment, medical care, recreation, law enforcement, incarceration, and anti-racism. Our focus has to be on anti-racism. Racism colors everything. You can't talk about employment unless you talk about racism. You can't talk about incarceration unless you talk about racism. You can't talk about housing unless you talk about racism. We have come to be a neo-colonialist society, one in which the first colonial masters have faded into the background, but now the neo-colonist masters have come center stage; they manage the systems of government and industry much in the same ways they were managed under the colonial system. So we have not come a long way.

Now back to Kristen Rome. I didn't know her until a year ago. But I knew of her because I knew her uncle and her father. Her uncle and her father Joe were leaders in the Youth Chapter of the NAACP back in the sixties. They were very active, and her uncle and I grew to be very good friends. So when I met her, it was like I knew her. She had the same stride and aspirations as the two gentlemen I knew. And I'd like to read her story for your book when she approves it. I like her spirit. She's her uncle's niece and her father's child!

She's one of those who needs that wider support you're talking about. It gets pretty lonely going back and forth to criminal courts to defend black people who cannot pay their bond that can be more than they make in a lifetime. And she and others are finding support in Justice and Beyond. Another question: How did the organization grow from twenty or twenty-five people to hundreds, thousands?

There are at least twenty-three thousand people in the city who see themselves as a part of Justice and Beyond. When people have issues that concern them, they come to Justice and Beyond if they are ready to work with others on those issues. Justice and Beyond has been ready to deal with people struggling and fighting over issues wherever and whenever they came up. You have to be ready with the right material and proper research and community support for people and leaders when they need it. And that has been such a beauty. I believe we may have tapped into the surplus pool that government and industry have discarded.

I think this works two ways. One, you give people community support to move forward in their efforts. But Justice and Beyond is also finding ways to take action as a coalition. Would you talk about that for a moment?

We've always been focused on actions in our forums, describing issues through a quantitative and qualitative analysis that lends itself to action. What can you do, and what can we do together? And that moves away from just talk. Sometimes, the action we take is simply writing the letter. Writing letters is very important. Speaking before City Council, showing up in court. Showing up in court is a missile, a very large missile, right into the heart of racism. Racism, neo-colonialism doesn't work when people stand up against it. Because it doesn't make sense. "Why did you make this decision?" we keep asking. The person who made the decisions or policies now has to defend them, and they don't make sense. Racist policies just don't make sense. So you get people talking about policies and questioning them, and things begin to change. You know, you have to engage people in steps. When we write a letter, everybody who is present at the meeting has an opportunity to say something and then we put it all together.

You and Pastor Webster manage the meetings very well. You must get a lot of positive feedback about that. A lot of people with different understandings on what needs to be done get very angry, I think, because many city policies damage them and their families. A lot of the talk can fall into what one member called "Ain't it awful," and not get beyond that. But you and Pastor Webster try to find ways to bring people together and to move forward.

You know, it's a hard job. I probably wouldn't do this without Pastor Webster. He's a very special person. He's been in the trenches a long time, and he has many different skills. And if I'm in a foxhole, I want to be in there with people who are both skilled and know how to fight. And Pastor Webster is definitely that. I've learned a lot from him. [He tells some of his story in chapter 7.]

What are some high points in your background that led you into this civil rights work?

As a young boy, I saw, in very rural places, slavery-like conditions. The urban centers in North Carolina, where I grew up, were a little different. People weren't treated as poorly. My father was a preacher who had a couple of churches in rural areas. So two Sundays of the month we were in rural areas, and he and I would see all the problems black people had organizing against racism. People were afraid. In urban centers, people can coalesce more. In rural centers, it's pretty much "hang on!" Families come together, but that is basically it. Some of the rural areas didn't have an NAACP nearby. And in the rural settings, I saw some of the worst things that can happen to people. I saw, in Monroe, North Carolina—I lived not too far from Monroe—the Klan mobilizing on the weekends. Hundreds of cars driving through neighborhoods, with KKK on the sides of the cars. I remember hearing how they were assaulting people and the like. That kind of white terror drove me to fight against racism everywhere I could.

I moved to New Orleans in 1980 and soon got to know Jim Dombrowski and Avery Alexander and several people like that. I met Jim after I got here, but already knew who he was. And we'd worked with Anne Braden. Jim had been in declining health. But I could not, at a point when lots of people were leaving the fight against racism, go and do other things, change my focus.[3]

I think that's an interesting point. I think people were moving away from black community activism to a lot of other things, but you were driven to keep your focus?

What meant so much to Dr. King and the movement in the mid-to-late sixties was that the poor workers and the poor people were so dedicated and so important in bringing change. It was the poor people's movement that was his focus when he was assassinated. I settled in the tenant movement, where people were being governed under the same rules that governed the sharecroppers in the South and the serfs in the Middle Ages. It was clear that there

---

3. Both Dombrowski (1897-1983), a white Presbyterian minister, and Alexander (1910-1999), a black Baptist minister, were key leaders in the civil rights movement throughout the South but especially in New Orleans. I knew Jim in his later years; he was one of my mentors too.

were certain places where people could be organized better than other places.

As a youngster in Raleigh, I went down in the housing projects to get kids involved in the movement. And when we marched from my high school to downtown, it was mostly kids from the projects. So, I began to focus, in my early years as an organizer, on the housing projects in support of people fighting against Urban Renewal because it was destroying black neighborhoods. And those were struggles I cut my teeth on. And I became a tenant organizer. It was a several-year process getting to that. And we organized against small and large landlords. In the eighties, I was up and down the Gulf Coast. We had, at times, about forty-seven communities connected from Birmingham to Baton Rouge. Kept me in a vehicle a lot.

When did you join Christian Unity Church? And what brought you there as a singer and occasional preacher?

Three or four years ago. And you know, Pastor Webster has a keen sense of justice and fighting for justice. He and I struggled together. Before, I couldn't see being a member of a church. I had looked for a church home for a long time. I had joined a couple churches, but none of them were my cup of tea. You know, everyone needs something different from their religious practices. And for me, I need a God that liberates me. I need a God that liberates workers and the poor, a God that fights in battle and leads my sword. I've been an itinerate preacher. I've preached wherever I go.

Now, to your angels. Sounds like Pastor Webster is one of your angels. Any others? Your family?

Oh, all of them definitely. My father was a pastor, and he didn't turn away from these very hard struggles in North Carolina, so he was a good model. You know, my father always carried a .45 in the seat of his car. He never had to use it, though there were times when he'd be stopped by the cops and they'd say "What's that?" and he'd say "It's a .45." And they'd say, "Can we see it?" And he'd say, "No." And that was it.

So, the other Angels?

I've mentioned Anne Braden. Also, C.T. Vivian and Reverend Fred Shuttlesworth stand out. I worked with them for twenty-five years. And these were people of action and great love. They taught me so much. C.T. is still living. We used to talk all the time. He is in Atlanta now, and we still talk.[4]

4. Vivian and Shuttlesworth were key leaders in the great civil rights struggles of the sixties and seventies, working closely with Dr. King and preaching a Christian faith of liberation. Recently, President Obama said that C.T. (as he likes to be called) is

More and more I appreciate that Justice and Beyond is all about both action and love, like your angels. How do you express what they taught you?

I do a lot of things I saw them do. Fred was a guy who, if you sat around and talked with, would say, "Okay, what are we going to do?" And I look at every dialogue now and try to figure out what can we get out of this in terms of action.

And that's such an important question for Justice and Beyond to keep asking. You give people support and give others a chance to express anger, those who need to express it, but finally you and Justice and Beyond talk about what we can do. So you write letters and show up in court and whatever else. Go on a demonstration where two hundred people are arrested, that time you told me about. . . . Well, you've got a lot of angels. I bet Judge Clare Jupiter (Pat's wife) is a big influence too. (Judge Jupiter was first elected to Orleans Parish Civil District Court in 2011.)

Oh yeah, she is not only my number one angel but the best wife, mother, and grandmother judge that I could share with the New Orleans community. She understands me and supports me with all these things going on. I'm a very complex person. I have a big need to chip away as much as I can against racism while I'm alive. And I work hard to make sure that I'm in great health so I can be around for a longer time. There is a lot to do. And she and I don't agree on everything. But she tolerates me. And to tolerate me is a massive job! I mean, there are some times that I'm so focused on the fight I'm engaged in, that I'm not present. I may be physically present, but not mentally so. And she understands that. And I'll confide with her about the problems I'm working on, and sometimes she gives me her advice that I don't always take. And it's remarkable how we've been able to stay together. She comes to Christian Unity sometimes. And I come to her church sometimes too. She goes to New Life Ministries. And we enjoyed raising our children, now thirty-one and twenty-eight, and we have four grandchildren.[5]

Pat, we want you around for a long time. Are you taking care of yourself physically? I didn't know you'd had a stroke.

"the greatest preacher who ever lived"; he is ninety-one. Rev. Shuttlesworth (1922-2011) was a cofounder of the Southern Christian Leadership Conference (SCLC).

5. New Life is a non-denominational church that strives to "transform lives through God's truth by reaching out with compassion to those who seek healing and restoration."

As much as I can. I take a little bit out of each day to relax. I'm in the furnace. I put myself in the furnace. In the heat you know. Organizing is in the
furnace, and you're going to get kicked around, no matter what you do. And
you have to care for the people you often times might get kicked by.

Reaction:
I so appreciate Anne Braden's and Pat's image of the cathedral—the kind
of society Pat wants Justice and Beyond to build, a stone at a time. Participants though get caught up so quickly on particular issues that there's little
time to talk about "the cathedral." When we do agree on what the cathedral
should look like, our differences become more about strategy—how to get
there—and tend not to be divisive. Pat is certainly right that the chief archi-
tects for his cathedral must be African Americans. People like me can design
parts of it, like, say, the gargoyles, and we can certainly help add stones. (I
have planned several forums for Justice and Beyond that were well received:
two on re-entry from prison, one on HIV-AIDS prevention, one on the cruelty of a large punishment prison within Louisiana's huge maximum security
penitentiary, known as Angola.)

The Pat I know now is one of *my* angels. I will keep asking him about his
health and whether he is doing those things that help him relax and if he remembers to *enjoy* life as well as fighting the wrongs of society. And that day,
if it ever comes, when he has plenty of time, I am going to insist that he write
his memoir. Maybe this conversation will get him started.

Kristen Rome: Claiming Who I Am

Kristen is a young criminal defense attorney, whom I met recently at Justice and Beyond. She is also a good friend of Jerome Morgan, whom Justice
and Beyond is supporting. He had spent twenty years in prison for a crime
we in Justice and Beyond believe he did not commit. The District Attorney
was trying to send Jerome back to prison even though the two witnesses who
sent him to prison in 1993 have recanted. Jerome is living a productive life
now, after being released nearly two years ago. Kristen is one of the young
people who, I am sure, will continue to grow as an angel for peace and justice
in New Orleans, where she grew up and now works in her family's law firm.

On December 12, 2015, Kristen led a protest of seventy or so supporters
of Jerome Morgan—many from Justice and Beyond—as we sat silently in
one of the criminal courtrooms. A judge was deciding whether to continue
Jerome's new trial. He set January 6th as the date he would finally decide the
case. When the hearing was over, Kristen rallied us on the criminal court

steps for our next action. (Jerome's case was finally dropped in June of 2016.)

She met with Corinne and me in our home on December 8th to tell some of her story. In an earlier conversation she had told me of her teaching law at the University of Shanghai. When I asked her how she happened to teach there, she said she had learned of a job opening online and simply applied. As I often do, I asked Kristen what she would like people to know about her most of all.

Kristen: I am not my best self every day, so I am a work in progress. I get frustrated or impatient sometimes. My dream is to create a space for myself and people I come into contact with, that will allow us to be happy and free from oppression and sexism, where we can feel free and able to be our best selves.

I started journaling in 2014. It gives me time to reflect on my days—good days, and days I mess up. I try to be conscious of the good things I do, the small victories in my life. Journaling has been a way to be a little easier on myself. For example, we were speaking earlier about my experience in China. I started journaling when I began teaching law that June at Shanghai University. It was a very lonely place for me at first. People just showed me the neighborhood—this is the university, this is where you will live. For several weeks I was in a very local area among all Chinese people—none of whom spoke any English. I couldn't identify foods, I couldn't communicate.

When I went to Shanghai University and started teaching American Constitutional Law, the cold was a big problem. Conserving energy over there is important. So my classrooms did not have heat. And it rained my first day of teaching! I had no umbrella. So I was soaked and freezing in the classroom. This went on for a week. Then a student, Beatrice, e-mailed me a message about how comfortable I made her feel. She told me she felt as though I were her big sister! So many people in her family and town had warned her not to study law—lawyers were corrupt and evil people. She should go into medicine (both her parents were doctors). How grateful she felt to be in my course. The lectures were interesting. My journal entries had been about how lonely I was, that my classrooms were cold, I didn't have much to eat in my apartment. Then, hearing from a student that our connection really changed the trajectory of her education lifted my spirits.

In the midst of these things that my superficial self was concerned with, my Chinese experience helped me realize how grateful I should be to be twenty-eight, living in Shanghai, and connecting with people across the world in a non-judgmental way. Even if my purpose there was only to reach Beatrice, my purpose was being fulfilled. My entire time there I had to remind myself to be grateful. That has helped me find, even on days when everything's bad, that I can find one thing to be grateful for to the Creator God.

Also, a huge thing I learned was that no experience is the same. The way we react is directly related to our lived experiences. Sharing things with Chinese students—we talked about many things, such as the death penalty,

"Mr. Ed" Buckner, founder and coach of the Red Flame Hunters

"Big Chief" Tugga Cloud, longtime leader of the Red Flame Hunters

Robert Burnside, proud member of College Track

Tia Cage, College Track member, now "differently abled"

Troy Simon, from tapping in the
French Quarter to winning a scholarship at Yale Divinity School

Derrick Strong, from prison to serving as a leader in Icons for Peace

Jonathan Lewis, Icons for Peace, making his long-deceased father proud

Pat Bryant, co-moderator of Justice and Beyond, longtime civil rights leader

Steven Kennedy and William Barnwell, Justice and Beyond

Nakita Shavers, a leader in Justice and Beyond
and founder of various community services

Lindsey Ardrey, school chaplain and co-chair of the Racial
Reconciliation Commission for the Episcopal Church in Louisiana

William Gillespie, Tulane scholar and budding writer

Nancy Hampton, librarian and member of St. Luke's Historic Episcopal Church

Kelly Harris DeBerry, singing poet and
active member of Christian Unity Baptist Church

Ashleigh Gardere, senior staff member for the mayor of New Orleans
and member of Christian Unity Baptist Church

Sister Maryam Henderson-Uloho,
formerly incarcerated, founder of Sister Hearts in New Orleans

wrongful incarceration, gay marriage, health care, and, of course, the tradition-al constitutional rights, our Bill of Rights, and so on.

Typically people like to think that Asian students are smarter than others. My experience has been with my students, and talking with foreign teachers who are working in China. Chinese students are very good at memorizing. It's their meticulous culture. In Mandarin characters, if you miss one little tic mark in a word it's a whole different word. That's how their education works. If I give a student a packet, he or she will memorize the entire packet. But they were not used to reflecting on issues. It frustrated me—"These students don't know how to think; they just repeat back to me what they've learned," I would say to myself at first, but I became more patient with the students and encouraged them to think critically.

Back here, doing criminal law, that experience changed my approach. Of course if you murder, rape, or rob someone, it's morally wrong. But there has to be a way to reconcile defending an individual client but feeling that we shouldn't take another person's life. I recognize now that a person cannot be reduced to an act. So I don't look at someone who has committed murder and define that person as a murderer. That person is several other things as well, just like my Chinese students were who they were in part because of their lived experience, but they had other interests as well. The acts that people commit—there's always a reason. So a large part of resolving issues is understanding the "why."

What in your growing-up years led you into this profession and your viewpoints?

My father was a criminal defense lawyer. I have vivid memories of my father's clients, of my father and mother going up to Angola Penitentiary. We had a family friend (like an uncle to me) who was convicted of armed robbery and kidnapping in the 1990s. His daughter is my parents' goddaughter—like a little sister to me. He was sentenced to 160 years in prison and was paroled in 2012—one of the fortunate ones. I can remember my mother and father going to visit him. However, I never visited Angola until I was in law school.

My dad and I have an office now, but when we were growing up his office was in our home. I never felt that his work was separate from our lives. Clients came to our home all the time. I saw that while they had committed offens-es, they were still full human beings. They asked for a Coke; they had grand-mothers, mothers, and aunts who would come with them; they were always nice to us, bringing us things. In some ways those unconscious experiences added to my viewpoint: we always knew, "They are no different from me. They are part of that family as well." Our "uncle" called from Angola all the time. With anyone else, I knew to ask if we should accept the call. But we always took his calls. And then we attended his first parole hearing together—myself, my dad, and my mom. We never saw my dad's work as "work," but as his life; an intimate part of who he is.

Now, my hope—along with Mosi Makori and other friends—is to help young people here support changes that need to happen, especially now that Hurricane Katrina has forced many African Americans out of the city. Those of us who grew up here are feeling that we are being pushed out, even out of our homes, out of the narrative, because of Katrina. We are now dealing with disaster capitalism in our city. People come and seek to benefit from the disaster. I got an invitation on Facebook two days ago—to tour the "smallest house." It is in the Irish Channel. I live in the Irish Channel, in a house I bought in 2012. I was interested in this new container home, on a lot which was about one-third the width of a normal lot. A shipping container has been built into a house by an architect—from outside New Orleans—and a developer, also from outside New Orleans.

I had made renovations to my house in that neighborhood, and I had had a difficult time because we live in a historic district so that I had to obtain approval for each change. Well, this group had built a house that was completely unlike any other house in the historic district. The house is less than one thousand square feet. And it was offered for $380,000 or something like that! That is a great example of disaster capitalism. People had left that neighborhood after Katrina, ten years ago, and were not able to come back. People from away bought the property and changed the character of the community.

The University Medical Center is another example of disaster capitalism. That entire land where the hospital was constructed was previously a neighborhood of houses owned by black families. All those houses were taken so the medical complex could be built. As you know Charity Hospital was closed.

Charity Hospital was closed permanently after the Storm; it had been important for low-income people for many years. Charity was crowded but usually provided excellent medical services. At least that is what I understand. Is this your understanding?

Absolutely. Most of my friends were born at Charity. Another huge example is the charter school system. We no longer have a local school system. Charters are businesses, run by CEOs. Their goal is profits rather than helping the children. They have their own boards, and they focus on good test scores. They are taking out students who are not doing well in order to only keep the students who are "teachable." Many students can no longer attend a neighborhood school. We don't have strong PTAs or strong communities that support schools any more. The kids are all spread around. Some kids have to get on busses in the dark, before dawn, to commute to a school far away.

And schools are related to the growth of the criminal justice system. Schools are structured in a way such that the focus is not on helping an individual student. The focus is on discipline. If students do something minor, the solution is to suspend or expel them. If a student has too many suspensions or expulsions, the student may be brought to court for a hearing to see what is happening. This is not nurturing. The schools are becoming institutionalized. If students can't cooperate, then we push them into the criminal justice system.

How are you working with young people to try and overcome these problems?

Well, when I finished Spelman College in Atlanta, I began to work here with youth. It helps *me*! It keeps me in touch with what is going on in the lives of these young people. I worked for a while with the Urban League. I also tutored at Booker T. Washington High School on Earhart Boulevard once it became an "alternative" school. I then moved on to the College Track afterschool program; I worked there about three semesters. I began as an English and Social Studies tutor, and then I transitioned into teaching an enrichment course, talking with the students about getting college applications ready, their taking the ACT, and other college directed activities.

I now co-facilitate a class with Mosi Makori and Jerome Morgan at Mc-Donogh 35 through the program Students at the Center (SAC). Mosi and Ashley Jones co-direct Students at the Center. It was founded by students in 1996 and has been directed by Jim Randels and Kwame Ya Salaam for nearly twenty years. We worked with students on a campaign to bring attention to the cases of juvenile lifers and, in particular, Shon Williams's case, teaching them to organize in the community. Now Students at the Center program is only at McDonogh 35.

We're organizing around Jerome Morgan's case. Jerome was sentenced to prison for murder in 1993 and was released a couple of years ago when two key witnesses recanted, but the DA is still trying to send him back to prison. The witnesses that sent him to prison now face perjury charges. Jerome himself helps facilitate the class at Students at the Center. We focus our class on English studies. Mosi and Jerome work with Ashley Jones's (SAC co-director) freshman English class and an African American Studies class.

You're preparing young people for the world they're going to be part of. You're passing on your drive for social and economic justice through your legal work among other things. Tell me about a wilderness experience in your life recently.

It has been an overall . . . well, part of why I wanted to leave and go to China for a while was that I'd been growing frustrated in my work. I'm at Tulane and Broad, at Criminal Court, all the time. It's tough. I cannot go in without seeing a black man in shackles. It's difficult for everybody, but particularly for me. I hope I never get used to it. Every time it's a heavy thing for me to see—judges berating young women and men, because they are black. It's difficult for me to see people going to prison for drug habits. The overwhelming problems of my clients have been drug issues. So it weighed heavily on me. I thought a change would help. I should try to teach. And I wanted to get away from the United States for a bit of time.

When I came back from the other side of the world, I came back with no money and had to start working immediately. Nothing in my practice had changed. I was even more frustrated—it was the same thing every day. Then I started to build a relationship with Jerome. Through our relationship, I started to realize that I had no right to be tired or frustrated, compared with Jerome. He'd been locked up since 1993, when he was a teenager. He always had such a positive, tireless attitude. There's no time that you'll call him when he won't come out to talk about justice. And meanwhile he'll listen to all your personal problems. So, for me I started to recognize—the building of our friendship helped me recognize that I cannot get tired.

We don't have the luxury of getting tired, because there are so many people who need us. People like Jerome fight on. They don't get tired. So we don't have the luxury of getting tired. Jerome helped me see the work not as work but as part of who I am. We hate what we have to deal with, but we find such meaning in relationships, not just with Jerome, but others as well. I'm thinking of John Thompson (J.T.) and my friendship with him. He was exonerated in 2003 after eighteen years—fourteen years on death row. These are such amazingly generous, nice, positive people. To think that they can live in this space, in this city. When I think about it, I think, "If I spent twenty years in prison for a crime I did not commit and finally got out—don't talk with me about courts or prison. I'd just want to make up for the time lost." People like Jerome and J.T.—they haven't gotten tired. They're still committed to the fight. Even after being locked up so many years.

Also Calvin Duncan, who was exonerated after spending twenty-eight years at Angola for a crime he did not commit; Norris Henderson (out of prison after over thirty years) a prison reformer while at Angola Penitentiary; George Toca (freed after thirty years at Angola; he had been incarcerated since he was sixteen)—meeting all those men has meant so much to me, on the days that I feel hopeless or frustrated. I recognize that I cannot get everyone out of prison. I cannot keep everyone from going to prison. But even one person may have a huge impact on so many others. Hopefully I will have an impact on others one day.

Reaction:

The New Orleans district attorney, Leon Cannizzaro, despised by most members of Justice and Beyond because of the charges he brings against mostly black people, dropped all charges on Jerome Morgan on May 27. The court decision followed. I had been to three of his six court hearings along with some seventy members of Justice and Beyond. We wanted to let the judge know of our full support of Jerome.

I told Kristen that I appreciated her creativity in finding that teaching job in Shanghai online. Anyone else I know would have applied through some well-known program. As she talked on I realized just how creative she is about her work and her determination to bring some justice to New Orleans.

When we talked I had not yet heard the term "disaster capitalism" to describe how well-off people have taken advantage of so many African Americans who, after Katrina, could not come back to their now too-expensive gentrified neighborhoods. As Kristen talked about post-Katrina New Orleans, I realized that the problems she brought up were the very ones we have been discussing in Justice and Beyond, even though she is new in the coalition: the gentrification, the disaster of closing Charity Hospital, the charter schools that are not working, the young people who move from school to prisons. So many of those problems arise when high-level policy makers make key decisions for those who are supposedly helped, giving them little or no voice in the decisions.

But what I appreciate most is Kristen's ability to see the strength and love in those that society has abandoned as throwaways, those like Jerome Morgan, John Thompson, and Calvin Duncan. (I had officiated with Calvin at a wedding a few years ago). They are, in fact, her models for endurance in such difficult and often thankless justice work. She reminded me of one long-term Angola inmate I know; he makes guitars out of the good wood "hidden beneath the surface" of throwaway pianos. He speaks of his redemptive change this way: "I find my work incredibly fulfilling," he says. "I see myself in every piano, discarded by society but redeemed and put to use in a new way."

Kristen says she cannot get tired. I am probably not facing reality, but even at seventy-seven, I am learning from Kristen and others that I cannot get tired either. There's just too much work to do.

— —

Steven Kennedy:
The Light Shines in the Darkness

Steven Kennedy, age thirty-five, met with me in our home on January 7, 2016. He is probably the most active young person in Justice and Beyond and seemed eager to tell some of his story. He is presently a real estate salesman and a volunteer urban planner. Recently, he became a licensed lobbyist; frequently at Justice and Beyond, he talks about legislative issues, especially as they relate to public education and incarceration. I explained my "angels" project and began our conversation by asking Steven to talk about his growing up.

> **Steven:** I had a harsh experience growing up because of my mother's use of narcotics. The earliest understanding I had of my mother's drug usage: We were staying on the third floor of the St. Bernard apartments, a housing project—we lived in a one-bedroom apartment at that time—my mother and two children. One day I walked into the restroom and saw a syringe in my mother's arm—that memory is still with me to this day. It had a huge impact on me.
>
> I went to Medard H. Nelson Elementary School. Even though my home was troublesome, I was on the honor roll my entire life, even in college. I was

Steven Kennedy and William Barnwell, Justice and Beyond

always intellectually curious. In 1994 my mother was incarcerated. I was about thirteen. My aunt met this guy named Father Robert Allach at Boys Hope, at Jesuit High School here. He had a close relationship with the executive director of Boys Town in Omaha, Nebraska. Boys Town was started in 1902 by Father Edward Flanagan. There was a famous movie about Boys Town that featured Mickey Rooney as a teenager.

I wound up going to Boys Town in 1994 for three years. I was kind of scared. I thought Nebraska was outside of the country. Nebraska was a super rural area. Omaha had maybe 100,000 residents. I got there and I still had a lot of anger in my heart. I felt that nobody cared about me. No matter how smart I was, no matter how hard I tried, nobody cared. Before I went to Boys Town, I didn't expect to finish high school. Maybe I would have been murdered or would spend the rest of my life in prison if I hadn't gone to Boys Town. Growing up in a tough way, you really do become a product of your environment.

I was at Boys Town until 1997. We used to come home for visits—for Christmas holidays, for Easter. It was a great experience for me to be out there. Prior to that, I'd never encountered white people. In that environment we had white Family Teachers—our "parents." They had eight kids to look after, with an assistant family teacher. A few homes had girls also. There were numerous homes—a city within a city. We had our own high school. There may have been three thousand youth there.

Now they call it Boys and Girls Town. They taught us a lot of social skills; for example, how do you exactly accept feedback? If you don't agree with a person you can still dialogue with him. We lived on a point system. There were points for doing chores on time, or you could lose points. It allowed us to gain enough points to go into the pantry or commissary; or you could get to go to the movie theater, or go out and have fun with your friends.

When I graduated in 1997. I had scholarship offers from several colleges, and chose to go to Grambling State University in Louisiana because a friend of mine (my best friend from Chicago, Harry Moore) had chosen that college.

I'm reading a book right now, *The Richest Man in Babylon* by George Clason. They talk about the thinking of a free man faced with obstacles; the free man figures out how to solve problems as they come up. The thinking of a slave is "I'm just a slave; things are just going to be the way they are." So how do you break that slave thinking? Here is how I do it. If there's an obstacle in my life, I try to get over it, get around it, or I'm going to bust through it. No matter how difficult, I'm going to persevere. I am also going to pray. Patience, perseverance, and prayer—that's what's gotten me through life, the three P's.

I stayed at Grambling almost two years; I was about nineteen, still on the honor roll, but still didn't know what I wanted to do with my life. I moved back to New Orleans because I didn't see what was going to be the significance of my being in college. When I came back, I couldn't find a job, so I started doing some bad things. I started selling narcotics—instant gratification, and also to support myself, keep a roof over my head, pay some bills.

That led to my being incarcerated for almost five years. I was in a federal facility in Beaumont, Texas. That's when a light went off in my head! "I can make amends: I can go back and instead of destroying communities, I can rebuild communities." More and more as I read—I read between one thousand and two thousand books while in prison—I read *The Wealth of Nations,* by Adam Smith, and began to understand economics. I read *The Intelligent Investor*, by Benjamin Graham. I read *Native Son* by Richard Wright. I read everything I could get my hands on. I read about African American culture, but I also read about world culture, including African culture.

I had a better perspective. I was angry at being in prison, but that was a double-edge sword as well. I hated being in prison; however that gave me time to understand who Steven Kennedy is as a man, as a human being. That gave me a lot of time to think; I didn't have letters that I was receiving, people who were reaching out to me.

Now I always open the letters with "I hope this finds you in the best of health . . ." because I didn't get letters like that. Only when my mother was confined did I get letters like that. My mother's a stewardship kind of person. She would send me Bible scripts. I understood my mother's heart and what she stood for—it was just drugs that put barriers around her heart that kept her from loving her children as she should. Still, I love my mother dearly—more than anything in the world.

She was in and out of prison many times. She might have spent five years or more incarcerated. In August 2015, my mother came home from being incarcerated. My mother lost my sister and lost two of her sisters and a cousin; some died while she was in prison. It was very hard on her coming back home from prison to my sister's funeral wearing shackles.

What was that light that went off for you when you were in prison?

I had a cellmate—he'd been in prison twenty-five years at that time (he'd gotten a life sentence). He got a PhD while he was in prison—President Bill Clinton had permitted inmates to receive Pell Grants. A lot of prisoners educated themselves! He said to me, "Young man, why are you in prison? There's no reason for you to be confined within these walls." He helped wake me up.

I was also a tutor while I was in prison—I helped other guys get their GEDs. I used to help them write letters—even poetry (since I write poetry)—I helped them write poetry to their girlfriends. Even though the poems were my intellectual property, I let them have the poems. They would hear back from their significant others. I became a kind of go-to guy. Whenever guys had problems with the institution, I would organize; we'd arrange a meeting with the warden to try and work problems out—to have an environment that was more conducive to living in a penal system, as comfortably as possible. As I was reading a lot of books, I said to myself, "Oh, man, I don't need to be living like this anymore."

This cellmate was one of your angels.

Yes, he was. And I have a lot of life advisors (even though they don't know they're my life advisors). Every individual at Justice and Beyond has been important to me. They've talked to me about their problems. I see a man every day at the corner of Baronne and Girod streets in downtown New Orleans—a homeless guy. Every day he asks me for money. I never give him any, but I always walk into a store to buy him something to eat. Even if I don't have the money. I made that promise to myself—every time I see him. I see other people who he asks for money—they jump inside so he won't touch them. I ask myself, "How can they consider themselves God-fearing people, but they won't help a hungry person?" That was always touching to me—knowing what it's like to be hungry. Knowing what it's like when people don't care about you. I keep that on my mind as I walk around.

You did five years in prison, and then in 2005 you came home?

I went to Los Angeles—lived there for roughly two years. My cousin Bryan's father had some property. I helped him with that. In 2007 I came back to New Orleans for good. I got involved in the planning process, to help rebuild the city after Hurricane Katrina. We had all these planning meetings to give input on what should be in the master plan to restore New Orleans. I went to many meetings and spoke up, soon was recognized as a community leader. I didn't even know I was a planner.

A lot of the people who suffered during Katrina—trapped on their rooftops as everyone saw on TV—were people I was highly involved with. Most of the people in my life were highly impacted by the hurricane. After the Storm, they found places to stay with other families in crowded houses or apartments. Some stayed in hotels. Many never came back. I was giving a lot of input for the Master Plan even before I understood what urban planning was all about. I started taking planning courses at UNO (the University of New Orleans) and took my undergraduate degree in Urban and Regional Planning. I began to realize that everything had to do with policy and the law.

I started a job at Sherman-Williams paint store, but after two weeks I got fired, because I had left the "box" empty when I filled out their application. I knew if I checked "yes" in the box, showing I had been convicted of a felony, that I would be fired. So I worked at least for two weeks, to get some money before they did a background check. I came back from making a delivery of five gallons of paint in New Orleans East and was informed that they could not have a convicted person on their payroll. It broke my heart. I was at an impasse.

That's when I went back to school to get my degree. After UNO I enrolled at Tulane to get a real estate development master's degree. I have finished all the graduate work except my master's thesis. That was a challenge—the Tulane program was in the daytime, but I didn't have enough money to sustain myself. I had jobs here and there. So I stopped going to Tulane and worked for PSI–Professional Service Industries consulting engineers. They then gave me an ultimatum: work, or school. So I chose school. I picked up part-time jobs wherever I could. I had to pay Tulane at one point about $9,000 for tuition. My back was against the wall.

Catch me up on what you've been doing in the last two or three years.

I was trying to build a business. I started a company when I was in graduate school called REO, an acronym that means "Real Estate Owned." I just love the urban environment, real estate. I hope to do community development not just in terms of building capacity of citizens, but also to work for all kinds of justice as we do in Justice and Beyond.

Tell me about your younger sister who was murdered.

She was shot in a drive-by shooting. She was not the target. It was in the "Back'a Town" area. I had always been telling her, "You've got to be careful. You've got to know who's around you." So when my other sisters began arriving at the scene of the shooting, we took her to University Hospital. But the doctor came in right away from the examination room, and told us she didn't make it.

My sister was a really friendly person. She'd talk to anybody on the street. She was naïve. That day she was talking with someone who'd been arrested several times for armed robberies in New Orleans East. So I guess one of the guys he'd robbed was driving around looking for him. When he did spot him, that driver got out of the car and started shooting at him. The man on the street ran away, but my innocent sister was killed. We never heard back from the police about any follow-up. The victims' families are just ignored.

You said last Monday night at the Justice and Beyond group when you were giving a talk, that Pastor Dwight Webster who'd been talking with you about your activism said to you, "Steven, how are you doing?" He was asking you about not just your work but about yourself. When we are working so hard at organizing, it's easy to forget about ourselves, our own health. So, Steven, how are you doing?

I guess Pastor Webster sees the material I've been posting on Facebook and other social media. I wrote that I still have faith to turn away "shadows and rain," to quote from the song. I feel that in my life I've been surrounded by shadows and rains. That kind of weather makes people feel and act down and depressed. Sometimes I feel down—but when I think of my blessings, it is different.

Dr. Chandler at Xavier University of New Orleans asked me, "What does it take to make a seed to grow?" I answered, "Well, sunlight, soil, water. . . ." She said, "It also takes manure to fertilize it. You've got to go through some of that in your life, let yourself be fertilized, in order to let some beautiful sprouts grow." I have had plenty of that manure.

And Bill Gilchrist, the chief city planner for the City of New Orleans, is another one of my life advisors. He worked as a deputy mayor for Mayor Mitch Landrieu. He suggested that I read *Reflections* by Marcus Aurelius. A lot of people have been my life advisors, pointing me in different directions. I'm grateful.

People give me bits and pieces of knowledge and inspiration. They tell me how they got through situations in their lives.

You have an ability to not just listen but to make these suggestions your own. Like those one thousand books you read while you were in prison.

In Proverbs the Bible says "The glory of young men is their strength; gray hair the splendor of the old." (20:29) I think about the thirty-one chapters of Proverbs a lot, and I try to think about what I'm about to say before I speak.

What haven't we talked about?

Well, I love the U.S. Constitution—particularly the Fourteenth Amendment. "No state shall deprive any person of life, liberty of property without due process of law or equal protection of the law." Life: How can I take care of myself? Liberty: How can I have some type of freedom to go about doing what I choose to do? And Property: How can I have some place I can call my own, and that I can leave to someone else. What is life if you can only live on the cusp of starvation? Which leads to not having liberty; without economic stability you can't take your family on vacation. You can't even go out to have a nice dinner at a restaurant. And you certainly can't acquire property. All those things are inter-joined.

In America with the civil rights movement and the Voting Rights Act, we've been allowed to be integrated socially. But we still have those economic injustices. The injustices in the courts—everything's tied to economic inequality in America. I hope we can wrap our head around these problems. I think Bernie Sanders has been doing an excellent job in speaking to the hearts and minds and souls of the people. I love everything that he stands for. It's unfortunate—an old friend of mine says that he won't win in 2016 because he suffers from OJS (Old, Jewish, and Socialist syndrome).

One last question: how do you think we're doing on race relations in New Orleans?

I think we have a far way to go. We have some progression, but we still have a lot of problems that prohibit us from having good relationships. The economic challenges are the biggest. At a football game or second line event, those barriers come down. When people are partying it seems that most racial tensions are quelled.

I really appreciate your talking with me today, Steven. You are moving toward being one of these angels I write about. When he introduced you last Monday night, Pastor made it clear that you are an emerging leader in the community.

I just feel that during this time I am borrowing from the Higher Power, I am just trying to do my small part in the world.

Reaction:

When Steven talked about the "light that went off in his head," I thought of one of my favorite images. In his Prologue, John speaks of "the light that shines in the darkness, and the darkness has not overcome it" (1:5). When I quote this passage, I always think of Victor Frankl in his *Man's Search for Meaning.* A Jewish psychiatrist, Frankl was sent to one of the terrible Nazi prison camps in World War II. He describes the suffering, the evil that pervaded the place. About to give up, early one morning before the sun had begun to rise, he saw a light go on in a distant farmhouse, and John's words came back to him. He realized that if he couldn't find light and life—that is, meaning—inside the barbed wire, he wouldn't find it outside either. That experience led Frankl to give of himself, what little he had, what little food he had, to the other prisoners. After the war when he was set free, he began his practice as a psychiatrist and developed what he called "logotherapy"—his word for helping any one of us find meaning in life. He spent the rest of his life doing just that. The logo comes from John's Prologue; *Logos* is the Greek word for "God's *Word* that became flesh."

The light that went off in Steven's head was the same "light" that Victor Frankl saw—the light that gave Steven hope and inspired him to spread it just as far as he can, first in prison and now among us here in New Orleans.

It turns out that Steven is the older brother of Kareem Kennedy, whom I knew personally. A few years ago, he wrote a popular memoir: *Aunt Alice Versus Bob Marley,* which is used in college writing classes. Until Steven and I talked, I did not know of the family connection. More reason that all of us in New Orleans need to keep talking—and listening!

■ ■ ■ ■ ■ ■ ■ ■ ■ ■ ■ ■ ■ ■ ■ ■ ■ ■ ■ ■

Nakita Shavers: Everything I Am Is Everything I Do

Nakita and I met at our home on March 20, 2016. A nice surprise, she brought her mother, Ms. Yolanda Adams, with her. Nakita is one of the leaders of Justice and Beyond and sits up front with Pastor Webster and Pat Bryant, our co-facilitators. Growing up and now as an adult, she has had a strong drive for justice and works in several areas. In March of 2015, her career was interrupted when she had a heart attack brought on by Discoid Lupus. I asked her to begin our conversation by telling me about her present work in light of her illness.

Nakita Shavers, a leader in Justice and Beyond
and founder of various community services

Nakita: Until last year I was able to run my own non-profit because I had a lot of outside assistance. It is the Dinerral Shavers Educational Fund (DSEF), named for my brother who was murdered in 2006. DSEF has provided programs and initiatives to promote youth empowerment, community development, and enhanced educational opportunities in New Orleans.

Tell me about your early life, Nakita, and what seemed to be important in making you so ready for your ministry today.

I'm here this afternoon with my mother—she was a single mother, raising my brother, my sisters, and me in the Lower Ninth Ward. We were a family of strong Baptist faith. That's been the foundation of our strength, perseverance. I had an amazing grandmother and other relatives who built our family home pre-Katrina.

I would say I didn't have everything I wanted as I was growing up, but I had everything I needed. We attended Mercy Seat Congregational Baptist in the Lower Ninth Ward. It was right around the corner from my home. That was when New Orleans was a community-based city, and every community had its churches and schools and bars and everything else it needed. We were very territorial, so we kind of stayed in our communities. But now we (the church) are right up here on Second and Daneel in Uptown New Orleans at Pressing Onward Baptist Church.

Coming through Hurricane Katrina, we lost everything. My entire family lived within a four-block radius in the Lower Ninth Ward. During the Storm everyone lost everything—photos and all. The following year my brother was murdered. That's when it hit me the hardest—we didn't have any pictures or anything to remember him by, to have at the funeral.

In 2005 I graduated from McDonogh 35 and the New Orleans Center for Science and Math at the same time. I was always an over-achiever. My mom had just driven me to college when the hurricane hit New Orleans. I was at Florida A&M University in Tallahassee. I had left most of my belongings behind—they wouldn't all fit in the car. I remember being up all night watching the Storm and flood hit my home; then I ran to class, and went quickly back to my dorm room to watch TV again—watching the levees break. It was devastating. My mom didn't leave. I knew my brother was in the city—he was staying in the same hotel where the media was so I knew he was OK.

Growing up we always knew when it rained hard, our neighborhood would have flooding. We knew to get to the part of the city west of the Industrial Canal, if it started flooding. We feared the levees would fail or be blown. My family was at my sister's house, on Audubon Street, uptown [that's also our street]. At the time I didn't know if they were still in the city or not. As I am watching TV, I was extremely worried. For weeks telephone service was unavailable. Facebook and other social media weren't yet available. I went through classes at Florida A&M like a zombie, without any news of my extended family.

After weeks my mom called me up. We cried for a minute straight. I told her I wanted to come wherever she was; but she said, "No, New Orleans needs you once you've gotten your college education. You have to stay where you are. Later you can come back to help save this city." We cried for another minute, and then the phone went dead.

That was in 2005. My family was displaced all over Louisiana. The very next year when I was home at Christmas, my brother, Dinerral Shavers, was murdered. He was a fine musician. He founded a marching band and taught at Rabouin High School and was very well known around the city and was a member of the Hot 8 Brass Band. His murder sparked massive marches and protests. Thousands of residents—of every background and race—came together to march to protest the lack of leadership and safety in New Orleans.

The CBS television program *48 Hours Mystery* did a program about his murder; and *Tremé* on HBO incorporated a segment about his death into that series. Season 2 episode 5 is when they re-enacted his death; I also played myself in that segment.

Dinerral was very well known around town. He was finishing a gig downtown the day it happened; he was picking up his fifteen-year-old stepson and a friend from another friend's house in the Sixth Ward. The stepson was involved in a beef with another boy from John McDonogh School. When they got into the Sixth Ward, an altercation broke out. Dinerral didn't know about all this. He picked up his stepson, and at that moment the other boy stepped out from the crowd and fired into the car. Everybody else ducked, but Dinerral was shot twice in the head and died. It sparked outrage in the community.

A week later a white filmmaker, Helen Hill, was killed in that same neighborhood. The murders angered everybody, across the city, leading to a protest march and movement; it got into the national press. I actually went back to college the very next day after the march, a Saturday, and I received calls every day to come back home and help organize the new group, called Silence Is Violence. I told them, "I can't leave school! I can't go back home now." They were telling me that this was a pivotal moment in history. (The day of the march for Dinerral, I had been one of the speakers.) I was passionate, I was in pain. A lot of money had been raised. "We need you," they told me.

After a lot of praying, I decided to leave school for a while and come home in 2007 to help start Silence Is Violence with Baty Landis, a woman who was a professor at Tulane, and Ken Foster (an author and professor at Loyola at that time). We were confronting the politicians, the community, the police. We held press conferences on television every time a violent crime occurred. We met with District Attorney Eddie Jordan and Police Chief Warren Riley. We were fighting for a safer city. We began different programs; we began a music clinic—a program to have practicing musicians teach kids in the community. We had peace programs in the schools. We created a program proposal to use the arts to teach peaceful skills in order to overcome the students' tendency to react with anger and violence when things went wrong in their environments.

What kinds of arts were you using?

If you learn to write, or paint, or dance, you can express yourself without violence. At the time the New Orleans criminal justice system was in a shambles. We didn't have a crime lab, for example. And yet we were dealing with "701 Releases"—the revolving door; suspected criminals were being arrested, but then not charged within the prescribed forty-two hours. Then under Section 701, they'd be let go to go back into the community. They would repeat their offenses, and be arrested and jailed once more. The DA's department didn't cooperate with the police because they said the police wrote the reports incorrectly. That kind of thing.

Serious crimes were continually being committed. We had lost so many assistant district attorneys (ADAs) and police officers because of the Storm. In our case—my brother's death—we must have had six ADAs—they kept switching the setup; it was too hard for a new ADA to figure the case out in a hurry. The system wasn't working for our family, or for other families. Eventually, the case against my brother's murderer was dismissed; the key witnesses were three young girls who were in the house where the boy with the gun was. Getting ready to testify, they were threatened, their houses were shot into. Then my brother's wife and his stepson refused to testify. For a time the charges were dropped.

But we kept the pressure on the case. I made sure that the people were subpoenaed, and eventually the case was reopened. We kept the spotlight on Eddie Jordan and eventually the case was reopened. I made sure that the wife, stepson, and everyone I could name was subpoenaed, and ultimately we were able to get the three girls to come back and take the stand. In the courtroom on the day of the trial, however, the girls were threatened again. The man who had been charged flicked rubber bands at the girl while she was on the stand and was making gun gestures at her. Both our and his attorneys saw it, but his attorneys denied it. The judge was asleep. He had retired, and they brought him back. So he was dazed out.

That little girl ended up retracting her testimony. And then the murderer was acquitted. Then, maybe two weeks later, he shot up somebody on Canal Street, in downtown New Orleans, and now he's in jail for fifty years. My brother's stepson actually ended up in jail for life too. It was for an unrelated case, but my brother died innocently for something he had nothing to do with. That situation in itself played a tremendous role in who I am today and what I try to do.

Right before my brother passed, he was in the documentary *When the Levees Broke* by Spike Lee. And after Katrina, Spike Lee took the New Orleans Hot 8 Brass Band with him on tour all across the nation as they responded to the Katrina disaster. Spike Lee had hung with my brother for a year, and they got really, really close. So when Dinerral passed, it took a lot out of him. Spike Lee has in a sense adopted our family: whatever our family needs, Spike Lee's been there.

We had a lot of resources coming in and were trying to think of a way to put some of those resources directly back into the community. And that's when we created the Dinerral Shavers Educational Fund. It allowed me to create an outlet where I could focus on educational opportunities. Silence Is Violence tends to focus on anti-violence initiatives and DSEF allowed me to focus on more educational initiatives.

So I had done this while I was home in New Orleans, but eventually I went back to school in August. And I had a lot of catching up to do, but I was able to graduate on time and with honors. I got to graduate with all my friends. I would come home when I could and would help support post-Katrina from Florida. We would add on different programs every year, but it wasn't until later that I got grants. After I finished at FAMU, I came back home and did my grad school online at Walden University. I got a Masters in Non-profit Management and Leadership. Then I completed the Institute of Politics at Loyola University, and then I completed the Harvard Kennedy School of Government while I was sick. I wanted to go to the Harvard program physically, but unfortunately my Lupus sickness prevented it. So I would be in bed, dressed from my head to waist, like in the classroom on my computer.

Eventually I want to go into politics. And my Institute of Politics programs (at Loyola University in New Orleans) have really shaped my political ideology and the work I want to do politically. When I was in the tenth grade, back in 2001, I was chosen by both McDonogh 35 and New Orleans Science and Math

High School to represent New Orleans students in introducing First Lady Laura Bush at the University of New Orleans, so I was in the spotlight for the evening.

And I remember the big climax was when I said that I wanted to be the first African American female president of the United States and the whole crowd just went wild. I lost all of my pictures and souvenirs from the event during Katrina, but after writing the First Lady she went through the White House archives and resent me everything. So, even as a young girl from the hood in the Ninth Ward, it was very ambitious for me to say that I wanted to be the first black female president, and when I said it everybody just erupted in applause. It was a room full of conservative Republicans—and they all were for it!

Then, fast forward a few years later, and I remember a speech I did with the Silence Is Violence after my brother passed. I remember the climax of that speech. I said, "I want to finish school and I want to come back and help save my city by becoming the first female, African American mayor. But I'm worried that I won't have a city to come back to." And then, when the speech ended, people were yelling and cheering because they realized that I had to be a politician, eventually to become mayor of New Orleans.

You know, that's my goal, so when women run for mayor here, I cringe. I say, "No, that's supposed to be me!" But that is my goal. I want to start as a state rep, and then I really think I could run for mayor. I think I could do it. The problem with our politicians: Nine times out of ten, they are not connected with the base or with the community. And those who are tend to lose focus. That passion just goes away.

It is clear to me that, having gone through everything I've been through, every issue I fight for, I'm passionate about it. I'm an overly passionate human being. Everything that I am is everything that I do. I just made that phrase up, so I don't know if it even makes sense. I just get so caught up and passionate about so many things, but that passion initially came from the things that I've been through. And I feel like I have this fight and I have this passion that everybody doesn't really have. And I think: Why not help causes that mean something? I mean, I try not to lose focus or stretch myself too thin, but I do.

Now, let me ask your mother, "Is Nakita taking care of herself in all this?"

Ms. Adams: Well, Mr. Barnwell, I have to still fuss at her. She don't go to bed when she's supposed to. She stays awake so long that she'll pass out from exhaustion. She's a night owl, so she'll stay awake until two or three in the morning working. Since she's been sick I've been trying to put her on a schedule to try and put all electronics away and have her go to bed at like 10 or 11 o'clock. But she can't help it; she's still awake and she do things at night. She's got to get her rest in. She's definitely a workaholic.

Now, you should listen to your mother, Nakita. We want you to be around a long time. Your passion is a strength, but you have to be careful with it.

Nakita: Yeah, that's true. That's probably my biggest downfall. I will say that this past year I've done better than I've ever done health wise and with rest and knowing when to stop. When I come home I try not to do anything, I like to chill. It now feels awkward and bad when I have to take out my computer at home, but I do. So, I work with a nonprofit in mid-city. Working there is really cool because it allows me to work with underserved populations, like sex workers and drug users—the marginalized that nobody is really fighting for. At the end of the day, we're all human, and their rights are constantly violated in our community. We live in a community that makes it very hard to earn a livelihood for African Americans.

What would you say is the reason for that? I mean, if you had to guess.

Just look at the jobs situation. I have two degrees and then some, and still can't get certain jobs. The implants from out of town who came here after Katrina [just about all white]—they are taking the jobs from young people like myself. My friends and I can't go out and get jobs, and we all have degrees and want to make our city a better place. So think about all those people out here in our community who don't have degrees or a high school diploma because they were faced with other circumstances in life and were dealt different hands. How can they get jobs? People resort to certain catastrophic situations and livelihoods (like sex work and drug use/selling). These people should not be judged for trying to put food on the table. They shouldn't be violated like they are; at the end of the day, they still have rights.

I know you're asking the question: What would Jesus do? And these are God's children too—the least of these, our sisters and brothers. And they need support and they aren't getting it.

Right. We have several communities that are marginalized. We have our LGBT community that everyone judges on a constant basis. And we look down on our transgender community. But you have a white transgender woman, like Caitlyn Jenner, the TV star, being praised; whereas we have transgender women and men in our community who we neglect. The question really *is*: What would Jesus do? And it feels good and liberating to be fighting for those communities who don't have people fighting for them. Nobody wants to hire a transgender man or women, so they're resorting to sex work. Who's fighting for these people? It is not my business how they pay their bills, but it is also not your business as an NOPD (New Orleans Police Department) officer to have sex with them and then arrest them (the prostitutes).

So it is just a lot of injustices, and I try to work on the criminalization side and to be able to work with these people and fighting for their rights. And giving them the resources they need. We believe in prevention and safety. I can't tell you to sober up overnight, but if I give you the tools and information you need to be safe while you're doing it, then I've done my job. And that's what we try to do: educate women about their bodies, educate everyone about HIV, and give them the tools they need. And hopefully they'll make better decisions. But it is not my job to judge them and chastise them for the life that they've chosen or been forced into.

So, just to be able to work in these different capacities is very fulfilling for me. Then on my end, with my non-profit, named for my brother, I've been able to work with New Orleans youth. One of our newest initiatives, GIRLS NOLA, is a girls' mentorship and empowerment program, which uses integrative arts technique to teach young girls sexual reproductive health. They're between seven and sixteen. My friends and I have taught them everything from reproductive health to etiquette to how to keep up their hair and nails. These girls come from all over the city. We've worked on a pilot program these last couple months, and we have about eleven girls that we started with. This coming school year we'll be developing that curriculum into an in-school program, so we'll be working with girls inside of one school.

You hope this program is going to spread through other schools. You'll set up a model that works, and then you can transfer that into various schools.

Exactly, we have a model. Before it was an afterschool program, and we had a lot of trouble with transportation and parents still at work and trying to get parents to the location and bring the kids. And that happened a lot. And so, I think it will be most impactful to combine resources with the schools. We have had requests from certain schools. I don't think we have enough resources to spread out too far too fast. But by fall, we'll definitely be in one school.

And then we are working on our music and culture education program for this summer. I did a lot of research on integrative arts and making art and history fun. And what better history to tell than New Orleans history, right? So I am helping to create this program, which is a two-sided coin. It will allow us to employ musicians and cultural icons to lead the program and at the same time to educate the kids in our community. Last summer, we had Mardi Gras Indians that came in and taught the kids about the history of Mardi Gras Indians and how to sew, sketch, and design costumes.

(Of course I told Nakita about the Red Flame Hunters.)

I have yet another program proposal for the schools. I spent about a year working on it. Normally it doesn't take me that long to write a program proposal. Like, I write these proposals in my sleep! But I wanted to do something that was sustainable and something that's different from what's normally done because we have a lot of music programs and a lot of cultural programs. But the history and culture of New Orleans is just so unique. If I gather a hundred people and ask them the difference between a "first line" and a "second line," maybe two can tell you what they are and how to distinguish between them.

So, tell me.

In a jazz funeral, the first line is the family and the band, and the second line is everyone else (guests, extended family) that follow. And at the many other second line events, a band like that of the Social and Pleasure Club is the first line, and then everybody else that follows is the second line. Always all kinds of people show up. You never know who's going to be in the second line. To teach that history is really important. You know, this idea of teaching New Orleans history came to me from the 2012 Mother's Day shooting at a second line event. And I remember the memorials and seeing all of the politicians and community members galvanized in the face of tragedy, like they were going to unite and change things—when in reality in the next two weeks no one would care about the violence that plagues our city.

I was feeling some kind of way about it, then I checked myself and said, "Nakita, what are you doing to better the community? Yeah you do a few things, give school supplies, help some kids and the like. But what could you be doing to make this situation better." And I challenged myself. While everybody was talking about what they were hoping to do with this, that, and the other, I'm just talking to myself in the corner in the back, and I'm just like, "This is what I am going to do."

The thing is, if we actually knew our history and understood the sacredness of our traditions, we would value that history. If we knew the meaning of our celebrations, we would not bring guns to Saint Joseph Night or Super Sunday (the closest Sunday to Saint Joseph's Day). If we knew how much of a diamond we were, we would learn to appreciate that diamond.

And you want young people to cherish our culture!

Yes. Young people don't know. It's not something that's been taught. African American history: we've been stripped of it. We've been taught not to pass it down and not to be proud of who we are. And that is still in effect today with the lack of respect and moral judgment we show toward one another. And I just feel like that is my part to help create particular programs on our history and traditions. So, I take life situations and try to do my best.

The book I'm writing is called Angels in the Wilderness, and your mother and I have an angel right here in our living room! She is one too.

My middle name is actually Angelle. When my mom was pregnant with me, they discovered that she had thyroid cancer, so she had to have her thyroid removed right after I was born. The doctors were like, this baby saved your life! As we wouldn't have known about the cancer. And so, I was her angel in that. She wanted to name me Angelle. My grandmother was like, no, she's Nakita. They compromised—my middle name became Angelle.

We can learn so much from telling each other our stories, and you, Nakita, are a storyteller as well as an angel in the New Orleans wilderness. (Nakita then went on to tell me of various angels in her life, and we would still be talking if the tape hadn't run out.)

Reaction:

Since I am always trying to connect people I listen to in my writing projects with sayings and themes in the Bible, I knew right away who the prophet Micah was talking about when he said: "What does the Lord require of you but to do justice, love kindness, and walk humbly with your God?" (6:8) Thank you Nakita, for showing the way.

I'm no one to talk about how wild it sounds to set up impossible goals for yourself, trying to do just what Jesus would do serving the least of these. But still I wanted to say, "Come on, Nakita, you can't do all those things you are trying to do! You make me look like an armchair liberal. Your mother and I want you to slow up. Your mother sounds just like Corinne, my wife, whom you'll meet. She says that I often get God and me mixed up."

When I have another conversation with Nakita, I will pass on my two kinds of goals—long-term and short-term. My long-term goals sound a lot like Nakita's, though I have never thought of myself as the president or even the mayor of New Orleans. But I do imagine and strive for a New Orleans where not just the white "implants" get decent jobs, but everyone.

For short-term, "achievable" goals, I write them in my Episcopal desk calendar each day with circles beside each one, and when I've completed the goal, I write a smiley face inside the circle if successful and an X if not. Now here's the really crazy part. If I think some task I did that day was worthwhile but not written as an achievable goal, I write it down as if it were and draw my circle with, of course, the smiley face inside.

But I also want Nakita to keep those long-term goals right up there with those things she does day-by-day. After all, both Moses and Dr. King helped us to visualize that Promise Land, out there on the horizon. They didn't get there and neither will we, but they helped us know what it looks like and showed us which way to walk.

Chapter Five

Four Different Styles of Working for Racial Change

In this chapter, young people from three organizations and one who is a recent graduate from Tulane University tell their stories, about themselves and how they hope to bring in change.

- Derek Rankins from the People's Institute for Survival and Beyond is a recent graduate of Tulane. The People's Institute, with headquarters in New Orleans, offers about 150 two-to-three day "undoing racism" workshops each year throughout the nation and beyond. It is arguably the most effective anti-racism organization in the country.
- Lindsey Ardrey is a co-chair of the Episcopal Racial Reconciliation Commission of the Diocese of Louisiana and a teacher/chaplain at St. George's Episcopal Church and School.
- Mark Walters is a community organizer with Micah (the local taskforce of the million-strong national PICO grassroots organization, inspired by the founder of the Industrial Areas Foundation, labor leader Saul Alinsky. PICO stands for People Improving Communities Through Organizing.
- Like Derek, William Gillespie is also a recent graduate of Tulane and has transcribed most of the stories in this book. He approaches race and racism from an historical perspective. He sees his future as both teacher and writer.

- -

Derek Rankins: "Truth Seeker" with The People's Institute for Survival and Beyond

Derek Rankins Jr. is a native of New Orleans. He is an anti-racist organizer with the training team of the People's Institute for Survival and Beyond (PISAB). He is a graduate of Tulane with a bachelor's degree in African American Studies and Sociology. He is a Secular Friar in the Order of the Franciscan Friars of the Holy Family. In high school he attended his first Undoing Racism workshop with the People's Institute, and now he dedicates much time both learning and practicing anti-racism organizing principles.

He has been in several different organizing roles on a local and national

121

level. Some of that work includes: being a co-convener of Students Organizing Against Racism at Tulane (SOAR), providing leadership to young Leaders of New Orleans's Freedom Library, and working with the People's Institute Youth Agenda and their Kwanzaa Freedom School. Currently, he works at College Track New Orleans (see chapter 2) as a Student Life Mentor and teaches a workshop where the students and instructor become partners on a journey through history to understand the evolving relationship between African people and education. I met with Derek in April of 2016 at College Track, where we both tutor regularly, and began by asking Derek what he wanted people to know about him most of all.

> **Derek:** I've found myself under the title of organizer these days. If I went back in time, I don't think I ever would have said I'd be an organizer. I am an organizer because of the impact of the levee failure and Hurricane Katrina. And it was through that time and work that I had really begun to start asking the questions that led me to begin the work of undoing racism and regaining my humanity.

What happened exactly?

> I would say this in two parts. One would be what happened with my thoughts, in one part of my life. When I was young and in elementary school, I went to a Catholic school. And every morning we prayed the prayer of St. Francis of Assisi—for two straight years. If I understood St. Francis at all, he was saying: "Let's see where this [being an instrument of God's peace] really goes." So I've been pushed and nudged to find inequality when other people often *will not* see it. Not saying they didn't see it, but at the time, nobody ever grieved to me that it was inequity and inequality. Then Katrina happens (2005), and we see inequity in a new way, and that's the second part.
>
> I was in ninth grade so I was roughly fourteen years old when the Storm hit. During that time, just watching on the news, my whole life had stopped and was gone. The idea that I would never re-enter my home or my city really did something to me in a way that I and many others probably will never understand. But I am clear about one aspect. In this terrible moment, President Bush is in a conversation on the news. And people are asking questions: "Well, why haven't you dropped water, why haven't you dropped resources for the people of New Orleans?" And what I remember—I may be a little off with the language—he said it would be hostile for him to do that. It was too hostile . . . to drop water in a city with paved streets and people who pay taxes and are a part of this community.
>
> Yet I remember clearly seeing people dropping water after 9-11 and having water and stuff together after many other disasters. We even had supplies ready for Iraq, where we dropped supplies and food, but we could not do anything for New Orleans. And it became a question for me. Why? How? What *is*

this thing going on, how does it work? And it put me on an alternative path. I think my life may have had several options, and I was in a place, New Orleans, where I got to choose. And so I chose this route and it chose me.

Right, you had a choice to do something about the government neglecting our city or not. And you chose to do something.

Right, so yeah, that happens, and life fast forwards itself to 2010, when I went to the United States Social Forum with the Greater New Orleans Organizers Roundtable (GNOORT). The United States Social Forum is a gathering of organizers, community activists, and anyone who wants to see positive change in our communities. This one was in Atlanta and I was seventeen, a junior in high school. And there I met myself in a new way.

That's a nice way to put it. How did you meet yourself again?

I met myself again talking, researching, connecting to people, and trying to figure out answers to big questions. I found myself in a different place from the traditional, normal, quiet, reticent Derek. It was a new Derek and a new dawn. And it was through that process in that time that I met PISAB. When the Social Forum took place in 2010, I reconnected with Dr. Kimberly Richards [a lead trainer with PISAB]. I had known her since 2007. She invited me over to the People's Institute office in New Orleans and then to GNOORT. Kimberly has been one of my angels ever since. It's been a challenging and a growing process these past seven years of committing myself to undoing racism with young people and people across the country and world to reach a place where they have a sense of their own power.

How do you hope the People's Institute can really change society?

I think the Institute has changed and can continue to change the way in which society works by giving us an *analysis* and a language to see things in a way we have been socialized not to see. And I think one of them is the way we treat each other, the way we treat ourselves, the way we treat family, the way we treat strangers, all the way up to how do we hold government accountable for government failures. We are quick to punish the person, but we are never in a position to have a conversation about the impact of systems and institutions on people's lives. And I think the People's Institute gives us an opportunity, if we take it, to find ourselves in deeper relationships with each other and the Creator. I think that's one piece of the impact of the Institute's organizing and workshops.

Derrek, talk about how these relationships grow, across race lines or within race lines or however you want to speak to that.

I would say that these relationships are across race lines, but I'm more speaking to the humanness of the relationships. Think of how often we have conversations with people that are not really real. For instance, if somebody asks how you're doing and you say "Okay" when in reality, you're having a real shitty day. But we'll say "okay." And we'll just keep on the routine because we checked the box—maybe we said "Good morning." But we need to realize that part of our work is being able to sit down and really listen to someone, and then being able to move forward.

And I think a big part of it is telling each other our stories. Does the Institute still do the Culture Sharing?

Yeah, telling people your stories is an important part. Culture Sharing, it's a key part of undoing racism organizing. Culture Sharing is our process of regaining our humanity and sharing culture with one another. And we do that by telling stories or cooking special food or dancing or sharing pictures. Cultural Sharing takes many forms.

Changing the subject some: What were you majoring in at Tulane?

I have been studying Sociology and African Studies. And I am proud to say I have an unofficial degree in "white supremacy" from Tulane.

And what is that?

It's a degree that proves I know how to work with white people. I learned that they "is" crazy as hell! [Huh?] Too many people think that African American men don't work hard, that we're thugs, that we're gangsters. There is so much that we *are* that nobody really knows *who* we are. And being a black man going to an all-white institution does not honor the way that I even learn. So when they give me a grade, I really have to wonder if they understand how I learn. And they are not teaching about my people. We have incidents where frats display insensitivity over the years. We've had groups push for more police presence on campus (because of us), we who are a very small part of the student make up. We've had reason to believe that there are people who intentionally make sure that it's a hostile environment for people of color on that campus. Yet there are many white people who will walk around and say they do not know what we are talking about.

I think you're exactly right, and that's one reason I want to hear these stories so white people like me and others can hear what you think. Why do you think that's the case with us white people? Are we blind or do we stop up our ears to not hear what's really going on?

The reason I shy away from those questions is that the answers come from a source external to myself. And I've learned from the Institute that in a way of love, honor, and respect in my work, in my colleagues' work those questions should really be left for the Institute's workshop. I would not want this interview to take away from the experience of an Undoing Racism workshop.

I'm afraid you've got a great insight there, Derek. But why exactly should more people come to the workshop?

I think it would benefit for people to take the understanding from the Undoing Racism through Community Organizing Workshop to become more effective in their work and life.

How do you plan to push forward in your own life now that you have graduated from Tulane?

That is an evolving question. It is in the unknown. There are many paths that have been identified and revealed themselves, but there are many paths that have still not revealed themselves. So patience is where I'm at. And seeking balance. My family house is now my full responsibility. And I'm re-rebirthing it in a spirit of growth. I am being carried by a spirit of elevation and black *amazingness*. So there are pictures of black folks some people would not know that are on the walls of my house. All the magnets on the refrigerator are black folks who have contributed to this world in ways that we do not properly honor. So they get to be seen the most because where do we go the most—the refrigerator! So creating a space that nurtures and allows for mind growth of the African people is where I am.

I've been reshaping my home. I have a library, a meditation space, and soon I'll have a garden in the backyard. It's about creating those types of spaces for me and my friends who want to go on those types of journeys—those journeys of self-explorations or learning about black amazingness. Some of my friends don't want to go there.

I appreciate that term you're using, "black amazingness."

You know, I just came up with it talking about it here! We really don't talk about how amazing black people are. That's not to say we do it properly for any people of color. But I think there is something about ignoring black culture. For as long as I have been in New Orleans, we African Americans have been the majority of the people here. However, our accomplishments are not ever the things that are lifted up.

You know, everybody honors and respects the work of Louis Armstrong, for instance. But we don't talk about the first black mayor (Dutch Morial), the first black woman legislator (Dorothy Mae Taylor). We don't talk about the invention of the beignet. You know, the beignet comes from a Black-French slave, who sold them in front of the St. Louis Cathedral in the French Quarter. The Café du Monde bought the recipe from her. And now that's the main thing they sell. A black person came up with that. When you look at the architecture of a city and the shotgun house, it comes from West Africa. We don't honor the work of black people.

I don't think we really honor the old neighborhoods where jazz came from. We know that Louis Armstrong came from Storyville; it wasn't just him but there were several other prominent amazing black artists who had to leave the United States and go to other countries to be properly honored. That level of black amazingness, if shared with people, can make a difference—for those who are descended from that black lineage, who carry that blood. When we learn about our black lineage, it helps us to have a purpose and a place and a space to see how we fit in this whole scheme of things.

I also think we white people need to understand that too, and also see our part in a lot of problems today. My ancestors were slave owners in South Carolina. It took me a while to understand just how demonic that was and how easy it was for supposedly good people not to pay attention.

Now remember, slavery was the business of the time. I have a historian friend who says to me all the time: Think of slavery as the people in modern day who all day are picking fruits or vegetables, or farm work or a lot of plant work or assembly line work. (Assembly lines are pretty much exclusively a post-emancipation phenomenon.) Enslaved people were investments of their owners. It was a part of the business culture. I and many others get tired of being stuck on the idea of white people being mean. It's really a conversation about responsibility. How do we have a conversation about fixing the bad things that are occurring?

You're talking about a responsibility of African Americans?

No, I'm talking about how white people need to take a responsibility for their actions across the world. There is no other race on Earth that has touched every continent and has done something to throw it out of whack. The United States was, in the distant past, an enormous mass of amazing, wonderful forests, wild beasts, amazing people, and an amazing way of life. And it has been destroyed to what we have now: kinda, sorta trees, kinda, sorta water, even though most waterways have been contaminated.

It's time to come and take responsibility for those actions. Now does responsibility equal fixing? No. Does responsibility mean giving all your money away? No, of course not. Responsibility means stepping up and making sure that we won't do it again. You know, many of us in the black community get upset with those Americans who say, shout, "Take our country back and make America great again!" That's not a new concept. We know what it really means. The Democratic white supremacist leaders screamed it 150 years ago after the Civil War.

You are still quite young, Derek. What are your hopes for the future? When you get to be my age, what do you hope this culture that we live in is going to be like?

One of the things I envision is an anti-racist community that is comfortable with people of color. We can't *make* white folks understand. They have to have separate spaces to heal what needs to be healed. We can't do that healing for them. And this community would also have the knowledge of when and how to create mixed race spaces and how to create those spaces with the least amount of oppression as possible. I think that's where we're moving to. I think we're getting closer to that. I see the rise in conversations around organizing for that in New Orleans right now—that's where we're going.

And I hope to see New Orleans flourish once again with people living in every house on every block [with so many Katrina-destroyed houses still around]. I mean, I look forward to a community that's *back*, pre-Katrina. Right now New Orleans doesn't have a community that's back together. And I'm not saying that we won't have new people join us or new people with us or that everyone who was here should come back to New Orleans. What I'm saying is that we did not face the fact of the Katrina disaster and did not give people the proper tools necessary to reenter our city. If we had stepped up and given those people the tools, we would have a very different city and we would be able to move past the pain of Katrina.

You started to mention this: Can you talk about a wilderness experience in your life and the angels that ministered to you and helped you?

So, I actually wrote a list of folks and we would be here for years if I told you all the stories. But I would actually say that all of the people who I'm going to name have been angels who have come and aided in my decisions when I arrived at my crossroads between opportunity and selfishness. Every time, they have helped me to do what is right instead of what is easy. And they do that in a variety of ways, even in ways they may not know. Sometimes it's been as simple as having a conversation with me or checking in with me or encouraging me. Some of them include: Ms. Daisy Raymond, my second-grade teacher, Ms. Gwendoline Paine, my first computer teacher, Dr. Kimberly Richards of the People's Institute (I've already named her); Dr. Rosanne Adderley from Tulane University. Others include Ronald Chisom (co-founder and head of the People's Institute) and Norris Henderson (former inmate and leader in the Louisiana re-entry movement).

None of my angels were invasive. They all allowed me the space to see what they could bring to a relationship with me and said "Look, if you want it, go get it." And I think the majority of the time I said, "Let *me* go get this. This is something *I* need to learn or figure out."

Can you tell me a little bit about how Rosanne has been a special angel? She wouldn't mind my asking that. She has been the senior warden, head layperson, at an historically black church, St. Luke's, where I often serve and write about in the next chapter in my book.

I know she wouldn't. She was special because she was a Tulane professor who saw both my potential and my weaknesses, and she helped me discover those weaknesses and helped me come up with solutions for them. I submitted a paper to her once. It was horribly written and too few pages. But she didn't say to me, "You have horrible writing." She said, "Derek, this is where you did good. But this is what you need to work on." And sometimes it's just as simple as "just keep writing. Don't judge yourself before you write, just write. And later, do the editing."

And that may seem small to some people, but that really shifted the way I wrote throughout college and will in the post-college life. I still write that way. I've found myself writing about two single space pages of text a day. I'm writing on my relationship with God. Sometimes I'm writing papers and finishing up course work. In my current role, I'm really trying to figure out how to teach African history in higher education and what has been black people's experience in higher education. What does it look like?

One last thing, tell me about your family. Who raised you and where are they now?

So, my family. I grew up in a four-person home with my mom and dad and my little brother. My little brother is now in college and my mom and dad have now divorced, and they are both, in their respective lives, moving forward. I can say I was never discouraged from seeking truth. I think seeking truth has gotten me here. And a lot of that—seeking the truth—comes right from my family. You know, to seek truth and find who I am and understand what I'm going into and discover the world I'm living in, these are things my family gave me.

You know, Jesus says, "Seek the truth and the truth will make you free!" But there is another side to that and not just for us white folks: "Seek the truth and the truth will make you mad!"

Both are very true. . . .

Derek asked that I skip my usual "reaction" to the conversations, and of course I respect that. He's right, his story stands on its own. But one clarification for people who do not know New Orleans: When Derrick said of white people: "They is as crazy as hell," it took me a while to figure out that he was imitating whites who think they are imitating blacks. I should have known this right away as it's legendary in New Orleans parades that African Americans often wear black face, especially in the Mardi Gras Zulu Parade. They could "get back at whites" by wearing white face since whites used to wear black face in parades, but it is a lot more fun—if that's the right word—to imitate whites imitating blacks. Only in New Orleans.

Lindsey Ardrey:
Co-Chair of the Episcopal Commission on Racial Reconciliation, "I Didn't Have the Option Not to Care"

I met with Lindsey on May 12, 2016, at our home. Along with Trevor Bryan (who tells some of his story in chapter 6), she is the co-chair of the Racial Reconciliation Commission of the Episcopal Diocese of Louisiana. I helped initiate the Commission when I returned from my ministry in Boston, in 2002. Since then, it has grown in strength and popularity in our diocese, which includes both New Orleans and Baton Rouge. It has the full support of our bishop, the Rt. Rev. Morris Thompson, and most of the fifty-two churches in our diocese. Here is the mission statement, based largely on the great prayer of St. Francis of Assisi.

> Since racism works against our Baptismal Covenant, we are committed to promote racial reconciliation in our diocese. We seek God's help to work in healing our wounded-ness to forge a life together where unity overcomes estrangement, forgiveness heals guilt, and joy conquers despair. In our ongoing spiritual formation, we will use prayer, worship, advocacy, intentional action, and education to become the Beloved Community.

In our Baptismal Covenant, we say that with God's help, we will "strive for justice and peace among all people, and respect the dignity of every human being." Recently, the Commission brought together fifty or so people across race lines to visit the Whitney Plantation, about fifty miles west of New Orleans. In 2014 the plantation was restored as a slave museum. The visit helped those gathered talk in depth about slavery, an almost forbidden topic among many whites and blacks—we whites want to deny our history and for many African Americans the subject is just too painful. The commission sponsors educational programs, retreats, and worship services through-

Lindsey Ardrey, school chaplain and co-chair of the Racial
Reconciliation Commission for the Episcopal Church in Louisiana

out the year, including a large racial reconciliation service at our diocesan
cathedral, Christ Church, in New Orleans. In 2014, our presiding bishop,
The Most Reverend Katharine Jefferts-Schori spoke. While I rotated off the
Commission a few years ago, I have always supported it.

Lindsey's full-time work is Children's and Youth Minister at St. George's
Episcopal Church in New Orleans, an historically white church. She also
serves as chaplain at the St. George's Lower School, which is sponsored by
the church. I began our conversation asking Lindsey what she wants people
to know about her most of all.

Lindsey: Well, I was raised in Bowling Green, Kentucky, from the age of
three until it was time for me to leave for New Orleans. I was actually born in
Greenville, South Carolina. My mother was teaching at Furman University at
the time, where she was a budding new PhD professor in political science. So I
was raised in Bowling Green, and my mother was a professor there and my father was and is an emergency room physician. I spent a lot, in fact most, of my
time on campus at Western Kentucky University. My mother was also the head
of the African American studies program there. She used to have a "Feminist
Onboard" decal on her car. A lot of my early memories are going to protests,

holding up political campaign signs, and making phone calls to people's houses and knocking on their doors. So that was part of my formative years.

One of the early marches I remember was a "Take Back the Night" march. It's an international walk for women's rights and to help rape victims and victims of domestic violence. I was in the local newspaper. I was probably five or six when I first marched. That was my first exposure to that. I don't think I ever had the option to not care, if that makes sense. I feel like it was built into me and was put into my DNA.

Your family must have helped that along as well. Talk about that for a moment.

Oh, absolutely. My father, as an emergency physician, was always taking care of people, but he was also taking care of us. I think even more important was that I saw my mother as a teacher. Actually, both of my parents were teachers. I had this love of stories and books, and I was in a nurturing environment. I would go to the hospital sometimes and see my dad do his job, then go to the university and see my mother's students. She was always organizing something, taking students somewhere.

I know when I was really young, we went to Atlanta, to the Civil Rights Museum and the MLK house and the King Center. Early on we would follow the Underground Railroad from Bowling Green. We would go right over the line from Kentucky to Ohio. There was the Rankin House (an important stop for the Underground Railroad). After Ohio, my mother would take us to Canada, and I only have vague memories of that. As years went on, we started going South and following the civil rights trail down to Memphis and the Lorraine Motel (where Dr. King was assassinated, now a civil rights museum). Down to Birmingham, Montgomery, Selma, and going over the Pettus Bridge at Selma (known for the 1965 "Bloody Sunday"). We did this all through my growing up years.

Later, I spent one year at Winston-Salem State University in North Carolina, then I went back home to Bowling Green to finish up at Western Kentucky University. So that was different: to be able to be a student at this university that I pretty much grew up in. And it was special getting to help my mother plan things and be a part of the activities in a little different way. After I graduated, I started working first as an AmeriCorps Vista at Western, where I was active in the Institute for Citizenship and Social Responsibility (ICSR).

Was that Institute a part of AmeriCorps?

It actually wasn't. What you do is apply to AmeriCorps, then they send you to a place to work, based on the information you filled out. And that was my placement. It wasn't just a lucky placement, because my mother was one of the three co-directors there and asked for me. In the ICSR, she brought in the political science and Afro-American piece, then another co-director was a community organizer with a bit of a religious background, then the third co-chair was the chair of the religion department at the university.

The motto of the religion department at the university was "Let's Talk." It was really about getting students involved in community engagement, social justice, public works, public problem-solving, and things of that nature. So my position was to coordinate this student program called Public Achievement. The program was built to target young people: children and youth, starting from kindergarten all the way up through high school. So what I did was to coach the university students who would go into the schools and do this program. And the program was built loosely upon community organizing principles. So we talked about freedom and diversity, self-interest vs. public interest and all of those issues. And the kids would pick an issue that they would really explore.

The program wasn't just for African Americans but was across the board. I was actually part of the pilot of the program. We started small with one group in elementary and one group on the high school level. And it was good because it was the high school I went to and was part of the school system I was familiar with. So I had some connection there and some familiarity. We wanted the groups that we had to embody the principles of public achievement, so we tried to get the groups to be diverse, but we also wanted to give students who normally wouldn't be picked for special things a chance to be a part of this program and help improve their self-efficacy.

After working in AmeriCorps, I ended up in New Orleans. I came to the city because I needed a change. I had found what I needed in the ICSR. After those three years, my best friend, who had been here in New Orleans about five years, was in the city. And I needed some freshness, so I decided to go. I packed everything up and a month later, without a job, I move to New Orleans. My friend is in North Carolina now. She left me about a year and a half ago, coming up on almost two years now. But she got me here, and I ended up working as a staff person for Teach For America.

Now that you work for St. George's Episcopal Church and School, talk about your religious background if you will.

I've been a part of the Episcopal Church for most of my life. But it's actually a funny story; my mother was raised Episcopalian because my grandfather was a coach and a teacher at St. Augustine's in Raleigh, North Carolina. So, my mother was Episcopalian, but when we were in Bowling Green, we went to a black Baptist Church. And that lasted for a while, until I was about in fourth grade. Then my mother finally *had it* because you know, she had her feminist decal and couldn't quite keep her mouth shut and through her political science teaching and leadership was always doing campaigns.

She always had a problem that the men and women had to study separately in that church. And a man was teaching the women's class! And it didn't make sense to her. And she was always going back and forth arguing with the people of the church. So we eventually ended up at the one Episcopal Church in Bowling Green, and it was just down the hill. It was Christ Episcopal Church.[1] And I was very involved there. All the youth programming, acolyting, the choir. I did all of it. Then, when I was going to Western, I was one of the peer ministers. I worked alongside Jim Quigley, who became the rector while I was there. He then came to St. George's in New Orleans, where I am now. Later he moved on to St. Albans Episcopal Church in Washington, D.C. He was leaving New Orleans when I arrived.

When I was a peer minister my senior year in 2007, we came down to New Orleans for my spring break trip and helped in the Katrina rebuilding and cleaning. When I moved to New Orleans, I actually went to St. George's because I thought Jim Quigley was there, but then I found out he'd already left.

St. George's is an old and yet forward-thinking Episcopal church, yes?

Right. And that's also part of what attracted me to St. George's. I said, "Well, if Jim's not there, let me see who is there." And I read about Richard Easterling (the current rector), and it said that he lived there with his partner, David. And I thought this looks like a great place. Then I went there and started introducing myself and quickly ended up a member. It felt like I just fell into the position I have now at the church and school.

As I like to say: sounds like it was the Lord who led you there.

Yeah, I think so. I had wanted to help out with the children's ministry there. And so I got in with the person who was formerly in my current position and started talking to her, and unbeknownst to me she was planning her exit. I became the Children's and Youth Minister at the church, and I am a chaplain at St. George's Lower School. We have a lot of kids in the church, but our problem is we have trouble keeping them when they come of age. We end up losing them to other churches, like Trinity.

I'm at the school a lot. I see four different groups in pre-K and kindergarten, and two different groups of three-year-olds. Then I see first through fourth graders, which is a bit broader. The chapel service I lead is about thirty minutes long. We do a prayer the kids create and have the kids lead us, and then I'll do a short lesson, then we sing songs. I like it a lot and I've been doing it about two years.

So tell me about your connection with the Racial Reconciliation Commission. How did you become a part of it and how does it work for you?

1. A historically white church

Gosh, how did I become a part of it? You know, the real story is, when I first went to St. George's, I was dragging my best friend with me, who was not Episcopalian at all. But, after service, St. George's has Sunday treats as we call them, so after the service, everyone sits around for fellowship and food. And then sitting at my table was Lee Crean and his wife Lynn.[2] And so, Lee would just kind of keep me in the loop, sometimes via email, but it really wasn't until I started the job, which was several months down the road, and I think he just pulled me in little by little, in a caring way, but still pulling.

So he invited me to become a part of the Commission about January 2015, and then he transitioned off and I started taking a more active role in seeing how the Commission had been formerly operating. It's been a bit of a challenge being in a denomination that is largely white and is not largely of people of color, at least in this country.

Can you talk about wrestling with that? How that's worked or not worked for you?

I spent a lot of time after college exploring and deciding whether the Episcopal Church was right for me, because it felt so white to me. But I found it difficult to find another church that agreed with me ideologically and theologically in the black community. I felt myself in a weird place, because I love the Episcopal Church, but it is just *so* white. And Holy Spirit led me to St. George's and even when I came to St. George's I was like *"Really, God?* You want me in this Uptown, mostly white congregation?"

So, I've been working to understand my place in the Episcopal Church. My place has been to speak my truth. And not just be a mere presence, though I think that presence as a black female is significant. But what do I say? How do I speak my truth and what is my role in helping to move the church forward, especially for racial reconciliation? What does that mean? What does that look like? What are we ready for? So, my role or rather, my vision as co-chair for the Commission is to build us as a spiritual body, first and foremost.

How do you define building a spiritual body?

Well, starting with the Scriptures. And praying together. And starting with ourselves and our own stories. I started realizing that we didn't know each other at St. George's and in the diocese. And because we didn't know each other, we weren't able to trust each other. And no one really knew why another Commission member was doing the same work. Why they felt compelled to join the Commission: whether it was because the Bishop said so, or whether it was

2. An interracial couple and longtime leaders in the diocesan Racial Reconciliation Commission

because they had this long history of doing this sort of work. But I realized we didn't know each other's stories. And so, I'm hoping for us to connect to each other on that level, and then we can become the mirror for the rest of the Diocese to grow and develop. I just first want to talk about these things before anything else.

So back in December, we had a retreat. And I really wanted that to start bringing the Commission closer. And we ended up having Dr. Catherine Meeks, of the national church's racial reconciliation effort to facilitate the retreat. We built a new mission statement that was more reflective of what we cared about. We do really work through identifying what we care about because it wasn't known. We felt like we didn't really have an identity. So we started there and shared our stories and that was really great.

Tell me more about your vision. As people get to know others who care about these issues and learn each other's stories, what is the truth you want to emerge from that work? You talked about how you wanted to speak your truth and I praise you for that, but talk more about that truth for all of us in the diocese, if you will.

I think there is a lot of blissful unawareness going on! You know, one time, someone from the Commission, in a prayer, asked for the freedom from the bondage of privilege. And that has sat with me for a while. And I think because people, mostly white people. . . . Well let me put it this way. In the Episcopal Church, we have a lot of white people who think they get it, and are liberal and they probably are, but when it comes to race, it's "hands off" and post-racial and think we've moved past it. We've worked it all out, racial issues. Or so many think.

That's an interesting expression, "the bondage of privilege." That's the kind of thing I could speak about, that privilege may feel and seem great, but if it blinds you, it's bondage.

Morgan Guyton (who is white) of the Wesley Foundation said that, and it really struck me. Because privilege really is something that blinds you to the experiences of everyone else and being able to not see the homeless person on the neutral ground as you drive by. Or to not understand why our public school system in New Orleans is the way that it is. And why our private and Episcopal schools look the way they look. I think this is a really special time in the country because people now have to look at and face these things. And it's perplexing to white people who thought we were post-racial.

In all my roles, at the school and at the church, I'm trying to find what is the best way to speak my truth. You know, my history is rich with black stories, but also in knowing injustices and other issues.

Are you more and more able to practice your truths in your work?

More so in the church. I'm not sure the school is quite ready. I am finding ways to incorporate diverse stories in my teaching though, like telling the children about "Mufaro's Beautiful Daughters"—an African tale about a king and his beautiful daughters. And by just incorporating black faces and different sorts of histories into the lessons that I teach. I am now able to be a little more outspoken at church and with the Commission. I sense that our diocese is ready for that.

Tell me about the Whitney Plantation experience that the Racial Reconciliation Commission sponsored. (An hour or so west of New Orleans, the Whitney Plantation slave museum opened recently; it has become an important site nationally for African Americans and whites to better understand our slavery past.)

We had old and young people, from different churches, international students from the University of New Orleans. We had a large group of people from across the board. We had old, we had young people. One of the members brought her five-year-old and her eight-year-old children. It was truly experiential learning, not just sitting and discussing racism in a classroom. We also had a reflection afterwards. You're always afraid that people won't stick around for something like that or that they will participate in a half-hearted way. But our group was really into the discussion. They were sharing how they felt about their experience there. That was a spiritual component.

Right now, we are planning trainings—racial sensitivity, racial reconciliation. We're going to use the national church's "Seeing the Face of God in Each Other" workshop. Some of us went to Atlanta in February to see how that diocese did theirs. We have talked with the Rev. Jane Oasin,[3] and now Bishop Thompson is saying to us, "Now, go ahead!" So we are setting up our training schedule with clergy.

I know your mother and father were wonderful caring angels, but who have been your particular angels here in this community?

Well, I mentioned that it's been difficult to make connections in New Orleans. I find that problem slowly receding as I grow closer to the Episcopal Church. I think of the Episcopalians I have gotten to know well, like Mother Minka Sprague, Episcopal chaplain at Tulane and a mentor in the study program I am taking, and the people who work at St. George's school. I do have to say that the one person who stands out is DeAnna Arcement, former member at St. George's. She is black. She's a lawyer and works for the federal government. Her husband and her daughter were attending St. George's Church. Without her I wouldn't have made that real connection with St. George's, and I sure as heck would not have obtained the job I have. I am the youth minister

---

3. Formerly of the national Episcopal Church staff

at St. George's—at the church five days a week, and at the school two days a week. We're trying to make that relationship strong, between church and school, as relations between the two ministries can sometimes be iffy.

One of the things Bishop Thompson wants is a strong celebration for Blessed Frances Day.[4] This year, we want the Commission to get more young people involved. We need their voices. We need high school students particularly—at that age they can get into the conversation. Even at the middle-school level children are ready to notice the differences, listen to stories—and they *are* wanting to deal with race matters. But high schoolers are really able to go there, and act.

Reaction:

I love the way Lindsey stresses the importance of telling and listening to one another's stories. If you can build a kind of friendship through storytelling, you are in a much better position to discuss potentially divisive issues in depth, *and* learn from one another. That's, of course, how I spend much of my time now—listening to stories and sometimes telling my own, always looking for those angels in the wilderness. Already, Lindsey is one of those angels.

I hope those of us, white and black, learn to talk more and more about what Lindsey learned to call "the bondage of privilege." When Jesus confronted the scribes and Pharisees, the privileged in his community, he was confronting them in order to challenge the oppression they were causing, but *also* so that they would gain some humility, breaking away from their bondage of privilege and more fully joining the human race. At least that's what I've been preaching for decades.

▬ ▬ ▬ ▬ ▬ ▬ ▬ ▬ ▬ ▬ ▬ ▬ ▬ ▬ ▬ ▬ ▬ ▬ ▬ ▬

Mark Walters: Community Coordinator of the Grassroots Organization, Micah

Micah is the local chapter of the national People Improving Communities Organization (PICO), which is a million-strong with mostly low-income families coming together to set their own agenda for change in their geographical areas. PICO has its roots in Saul Alinsky's 1940s labor-led Industrial Areas Foundation. Like contemporary IAF organizations, PICO is now mostly driven by communities of faith.

Micah is non-denominational, working with sixteen member congregations "to create innovative solutions to the plethora of problems faced by

---

4. African American, Blessed Frances Gaudet is the only Episcopal "saint" from Louisiana. See chapter 6.

those living in the Greater New Orleans area. . . . Micah develops leaders, influences public policy, and increases civic engagement." At their various planning meetings, the members of Micah decided to make significant changes in Louisiana's system of massive incarceration their primary goal. (We have the highest number per capita of people incarcerated in the nation if not in the world.) A recent Micah success came when the state legislature agreed to "ban the box," to take away the box in employment applications that ask those seeking employment to check if they have been convicted of a felony. Micah gets its name from the Hebrew prophet, Micah, who said: "What does the Lord require of you, but to do justice, love kindness, and walk humbly with your God" (6:8).

It is one of the groups I worked with when I helped organize a 300-person strong gathering in May of 2015 to help change the culture formerly incarcerated persons (FIPs) come back to—from a culture of shame to a culture of welcome. We called our gathering "Welcome Home Sunday." Mark Walters is Micah's fulltime organizer supporting successful re-entry. We worked closely for "Welcome Home Sunday" and have been working together ever since on various re-entry strategies. We met at our home on May 16, 2016. I asked Mark to begin by telling me all about himself.

Mark: First, I want people to know about the call that I received to move back to New Orleans. It started in Houston, specifically after the last time I did time in prison. I used to get passes to go hear the religious groups who were visiting. There were a lot of people who came in to minister to us in prison, and in their talks with us they always seemed to have a message for me, even when I was trying to hide in the back. I've been incarcerated six times. The first time, I did five months in the Marine Corps brig for insubordination to my first sergeant and not going to work for two days. Shortly after my release from the brig I was arrested again—I arrived by bus in New Orleans, and I had a gun on me. I still don't know how the police knew that. After I was in jail in New Orleans the cycle continued, in part because of my rebellious nature. When I was a valet driver, I had a bad habit of taking people's cars. I have had the police plant drugs on me while I was at work.

After Hurricane Katrina I didn't evacuate right away. I was a chef on the Mississippi Queen steamboat, where I could live when the city was devastated. They stayed afloat a year after the Storm and then they went bankrupt. I left for Houston at that time, and ran into Hurricane Ike. That was the first time I went to jail in Houston; the rental car company refused to give me another car after the car I'd been renting had flooded out. We went back and forth, back and forth. The police were called in. That got me a year probation because I had a lawyer. The Houston court wanted to have me placed in prison for several years, but I had a paid lawyer and he got me a year on probation instead.

My record followed me, and I couldn't get a job. I ended up homeless. I couldn't find a place to sleep. I would use cocaine to keep going, to stay up all night. I'd be able to take a birdbath[5] at the Jack-In-The-Box restaurant across the street. I started selling drugs. The day I was supposed to get off probation I was arrested. I was about to be given additional years on top of the ten years on the original charge. But I ended up with six months in jail. I was blessed!

Later when I was caught by the police "Gang Task Force," I had a felony-amount of cocaine that I was holding. I was looking at twenty years. But one of the guys arrested with me—and he was not on probation like I was— he suggested, "Let's have a prayer circle." This was before the authorities were going to come in the court and hand down our sentences. Somehow—by God's grace—I received another six months in jail. The other man ended up with four years. That's when my walk with God started. I did my six months, read the Bible constantly, led a prayer circle. The day I was to leave the security guard in my unit looked me in the face and said, "I'll see you when you come back." For me—I was rebellious—I decided, I'm *not* coming back! I didn't sell drugs again.

I moved to Dallas because my daughter lives in Dallas, and I ended up sleeping in abandoned houses there. I would use cocaine to stay up all night, if I didn't have any place to go. Finally I found a job at a Chinese restaurant in Houston, part of a national chain, P.F. Chang's. I worked at that job for a while and was able to transfer to the same restaurant back in Dallas. I was still struggling with my addictions—marijuana, cocaine, pills.

On my way to work one day I felt that God was telling me to quit my job. I didn't understand. Now I see that God was preparing me to come back to New Orleans. By God telling me to quit—I knew that it didn't make any sense. But as the weeks went along I would get to work five minutes late. Then when I started work, I would want to leave as soon as I could. I finally went to the chef and told him I was giving him my two weeks' notice. I knew I was a valuable worker—I had been training other restaurant managers by this time. I knew the new menus. The chef said to me, "OK, Mark." I knew that this was coming from God because the company had up to that point been fighting to keep me.

So, I went to a homeless shelter in Dallas and went through a whole lot of things. One night I was laying in bed and I hear somebody calling loudly, "MG!" (Only my family calls me MG because my father and I have the same first and middle initials.) I knew it was a call from God because no one at the shelter would have known to call me MG. This was an audible voice! Like the voice of Sarah in the Bible where she was talking with God—she said, "If you give me a son, I will give him back to you." And God said he would, and her son was Isaac. (Genesis 18:1-18) And it was like God telling David to go back to the place he first heard God's call.

5. Washing yourself in a sink

I knew my call was leading me back to New Orleans, because that's where I had first heard God's call to me. It wasn't my decision to *not* go back to New Orleans. I left Texas the next day. When I drove into the city limits, I started feeling peace. I started working at P.F. Chang's on the Lake Front here. I remember hearing from God, "That's not what I wanted you to do, to go back to restaurant work." But I was staying with my dad, and I knew my dad wasn't going to want to hear that I was about to quit my job. But I did quit. I didn't tell my dad. I washed cars for a bit. I stumbled into one of the Micah Bible studies one evening at the Household of Faith, a church on Jackson Avenue.

Rosie Washington [current executive director of Micah] and Daniel Schwartz [former executive director of Micah] were there and I started to talk with them before the Bible study started—they told me about the work they were doing with Micah. I volunteered for a number of months doing criminal justice reform. In August of 2014 I was hired full time and I've been doing re-entry, criminal justice reform ever since. I am the community organizer.

How did Micah happen to make mass incarceration the center of their work?

I don't know. They started this before I arrived back in the city, following what the community was telling them was the biggest problem that the community faced. I will be in Baton Rouge tomorrow, when the Ban-The-Box bill gets taken up by the Louisiana Senate. I feel sure it will pass. It was defeated two years in a row. This year what made the difference was collaboration among the organizations, and being up there at the committee meetings when the representatives were supporting it. It has been a long, drawn-out process. But it started to move in the right direction. Governor John Bel Edwards already told us he will sign the bill into law.

What formerly incarcerated persons need most of all is a job! And the box was a huge obstacle.

I had spent months in Texas filling out job applications and had to check the box every time. I was turned down for those jobs. The only reason I was hired at P.F. Chang's restaurant is that I forgot to check the box on the application. They didn't ask me about it, and I didn't say anything. I was with them for three years—started out washing dishes and moved up to the chef position.

What other Micah projects are you involved with?

We are working with the U.S. Attorney and his efforts around reform—they are helping to fund the Peacekeepers Initiative.[6] It's a slow process. The

---

6. An effort to mediate street conflict before it erupts in violence

biggest challenge for their office is to get the young people involved. I actually have a fifteen-year-old I am mentoring. It's hard—the youth these days are involved in very different interests than we used to have. We also have a 30-2-2 initiative. That means that we have thirty employers who agree to hire two former inmates for their workplace and keep them employed for two years. Micah is beginning to be the community infrastructure for Kenneth Polite, the U.S. Attorney who is funding the work.

There's still some concern on the part of adults from our faith communities working with these 14-, 15-, and 16-year-olds, because the teenagers are coming from a different place from us. The individual I am working with—I have had to go to his school twice. The first time because he poured a Coke on a third-grade girl. The next time because he said, "I am just not going to class." Just sitting and talking to him—I was telling him, "This is something you just have to do. There's no way out of it."

As a former rebel, that put you in a different position!

(laughs) Yeah. When you are a rebellious young teen. His attitude is, "No one's going to tell me what to do." He's doing fairly well now. He's up and down. The set-up is usually two to three mentors per mentee. But it's only me. I try to engage him, and it's a struggle. What they have in their mindset is: "It has to go my way. I don't care what other people say." Patience helps. I think about myself at that age, and I also think about my own son. He's sixteen right now—makes seventeen in the fall. He's going to be a senior next year at Warren Easton High School. He's about to start driving! I know this because he contacted me about money for a driving class. He's in a trade preparation track to be an electrician. He wants to be a business owner. He goes to SUNO (Southern University of New Orleans) on the weekends for college preparation classes. My kids are a lot further along and more stable than I was at that age; I also have a daughter in Dallas, who is fourteen—she is in honors classes and plays the violin in the orchestra.

My intelligence I did pass along to them, but the difference between them and me is that they apply their intelligence. When I was at that age I didn't want to cooperate with what schools were making me do. It brings me a lot of joy to see how well they are doing. We still have challenges—children without their father—because I was absent from their lives somewhat. I keep in contact with them and let them know I'm always thinking of them.

I know from my pastoral experience—they need their father, you! ... How is the planning going for the next Welcome Home Sunday event?

We are still going to do it this fall. It depends on Dillard University's schedule. We'll also do it in Baton Rouge. In last year's terrible weather—we still had over three hundred people. If things work out we may have over five hundred people this year, at the Dillard chapel. I think the best thing is at the end of the day we need to provide people coming home from prison with opportunities. If there were just avenues directly for housing and employment, it would cut down on recidivism. In Micah, we are working with sixteen congregations, including several strong ones, like St. Peter Claver in the Roman Catholic community. It's a black church in a historically black community. Our largest congregation is Greater Saint Stephen's Baptist Church. The Household of Faith has not been around as long but it is predominantly black.

A related question: how well are we, whites and blacks, doing in terms of working together and being comfortable across race lines?

I think we have a very long way to go. We could say that there's no more racism in New Orleans but the numbers speak differently. Fifty-two of every hundred African American males in New Orleans ages sixteen to sixty-four are unemployed. Of that 52 percent, 43 percent have criminal histories. Ninety percent of inmates in Orleans Parish Prison are black. And 80 percent in jails and prisons in the rest of the state. There are feelings of depression in the black community, particularly because of the shortage of jobs and lack of wealth. The average African American here makes about $25,000 a year, while his white counterpart makes maybe over $50,000 per year. So it's come to a point where African Americans are feeling hopeless.

I would love to have Micah be the vehicle for making things more equitable in this city. We are not there yet. Starting in June we're going to do ten listening sessions in neighborhoods that range from the Lower Ninth Ward to Central City, Algiers, and so on. We hope to get twenty-five to fifty people together at a time to tell us what are the health impacts of incarceration and other needs in their communities. What do they want to see changed in their neighborhoods?[7]

We hope that will lead in to the Welcome Home Sunday. At the grassroots level neighbors aren't coming to meetings. The average people at barbershops and car washes may not be at church—it's hard to reach them to talk about neighborhood problems and what they need to bring change into their communities.

Tell me about your angels in the wilderness.

I think of my dad, he's been the most consistent from when I started getting into trouble as a teenager until now. When I was 16 and he saw I was running in the streets—he said to me, "Mark, I don't want to be searched [*at Central Lockup*] so that I can come and visit you after you get into trouble."

The funny thing is he was the only one who drove all the way to North Carolina, when I was in the brig, to see me. He's been my support, my consistent figure through all this, from the point of view of my family. He didn't look

---

7. Here Micah is using the bottom-up model of their "parent organization," PICO.

down on me because of this—he allowed me to have my learning experiences.

From a professional perspective, my angel would be Dr. Lue Russell, the state organizer for the Micah Project, of PICO's national network. She does a lot of work in Baton Rouge and has been my spiritual mother—keeping me grounded, giving me insight spiritually. When I'm dealing with certain challenges, she's always there to listen and offer advice.

Those are the main two—my mom, we have a relationship but it isn't the best. It's gotten a lot better over the years. I guess the break came when she saw me shackled and in an orange jumpsuit when I was incarcerated for the first time in New Orleans. It disappointed her and fractured our relationship. I'm a whole lot closer with my dad. Healing relations with my mother is a work in progress. We have had some intentional conversations about it.

What have we not talked about that we need to include in your story?

I guess it would be . . . I'm going to be involved in this work for a while. It is my calling. When people's lives are transformed long-term—that is satisfying to me. When I see people affected and engaged, to see things change, that is fulfilling.

There are about one million people in the U.S. involved in PICO. It also exists in Central America and also in Africa. The difference between PICO and other similar organizations is the faith component. PICO is open to all different faith denominations. We're predominantly Protestant and Catholic. We do have some Jewish congregations. The difference is that faith—our understanding of God—is always at the forefront of everything that we do. Faith is the center of our work. For me personally, I don't think there's a difference between church and state. As Scripture says, "The government is upon His shoulders" (Isaiah 9:6). God is the head. And we are the church body. So we have to be involved in what goes on in government and in communities. We remind the congregations that they are the pillars of the community. They are the jewels of the community. They are called to help rebuild the communities. So, the fact that we put God at the center of everything that we do—I think that gives us a distinct difference between us and other organizations. At the end of the day it's ministry. It gives to people—it becomes more welcoming to people. They see the church out in the community with them.

Do you attend one particular church?

Yes, I attend Greater Saint Stephen Baptist Church. It took me a while to settle into one church when I returned to New Orleans. When I was in Dallas I was part of The Potter's House run by T. D. Jakes. Coming from under that strong leadership it was hard. People tend to feel that you can get lost in a large congregation. It was a process of my trying to figure out where I belonged in New Orleans. I have great rapport with Pastor Debra Morton. Naturally I have rapport with the Micah leaders from that congregation.

Call on me if I can support any of your projects. And keep up the good work.

Reaction:

Mark writes about how, when he was younger, his stubbornness got him into more and more trouble. Then God spoke to him and showed him *how* he needed to change and move forward. As a traditional Episcopalian, I don't hear God speaking to me the way Mark does. But what we have in common is this: We won't know if are carrying out God's will until we see the results of our work: Have we or have we not effectively brought—what we both call—the love of Christ to others? Mark is bringing that love. In our many earlier meetings for the 2015 Welcome Home Sunday, Mark had never talked about his faith, thus confirming a belief in importance of telling and listening to personal stories if we really want to get to know one another.

He reminds me of what I know all too well though I like to forget—just how far we in New Orleans must go to build an environment where young African Americans have a real chance at a good and productive life. Our unemployment and under-employment rates are staggering. We imprison more young African Americans than anywhere else in the nation if not the world.

In listening to Mark, I think of Wilbert Rideau and his profoundly moving book, *In the Place of Justice*. In 2005, Rideau was briefly incarcerated in Louisiana's Calcasieu Parish Prison after serving forty years in prison, mostly at the Louisiana State Penitentiary at Angola. Himself African American, he was amazed, horrified—and heart-broken—at the level of hopelessness and destructiveness he encountered among his young and black temporary dorm mates, some headed for a life-time in prison, hurting many along the way. Things were bad enough when Rideau was first incarcerated, but are even worse now. He writes:

> My guess is that most of these youngsters never held a job. They are not part of the American economy and exist at the fringes of society.
>
> They display adult comprehension and abilities in only a few things. For example, one man I met in my dorm was expert at dope pushing and the economics attached to it, but was largely ignorant and inept at everything else. He planned on "getting some bitch pregnant" when he got out.
>
> I asked why, and he looked at me puzzled. "That's part of being a man. That's what you supposed to do, so your name lives on after you dead."
>
> Love and a relationship don't enter the picture, and he had no plans to care for the child.
>
> "That's on her," he said, then laughed. "If she don't want a baby, she shouldn't open her legs."
>
> It was painful for me to look at these street-raised weeds, these outcasts

and misfits. I know only too well that they do not care about a world that does not value them. This makes them walking time bombs.

These "outcasts and misfits" can change—I deeply believe that: That is the central theme of my last book: *Called to Heal the Brokenhearted: Stories from Kairos Prison Ministry International.* But it is going to take a lot of angels to show them the love they never had, to show them that they are *valued.* And they must have jobs and a place to live. I realize that I can help only in a marginal way. But I can do some things—as I am trying to do in this book—getting to know and gaining the trust of many of our young people: Mark and Lindsey, Derek, and the many others I have gotten to know in various groups—then passing on their stories so that fellow whites and also blacks will better know what is going on in our city and cities throughout the country. I hope these stories will help us know where at least some of our hope for the future lies—in our young angels and in those who have been angels to them.

William Gillespie:
Bringing Change By Knowing Our History

Unlike Derek, Lindsey, and Mark, William does not see himself as a social change organizer whose job it is to "undo racism"—the stated objective of the People's Institute for Survival and Beyond. His calling is more academic: What is the history behind slavery, Jim Crow, and today's racial disparities? In the long run, William's contributions will be as important as the contributions of the other young people who tell some of their stories in this chapter. It is so easy to ignore our history. Many African American leaders are appalled at how little young black children and teens know about such culture-changing events as the civil rights movement of the fifties, sixties, and seventies.

William just graduated from Tulane—in the same class as Derek Rankins—and has faithfully transcribed most of the recorded stories in this book. I met him through the Episcopal chaplain at Tulane, Mother Minka Sprague. I explained my project to Minka and asked if any Episcopal student might like to work on my angels project. She put me in touch with William, who proved to be just the right transcriber. She didn't tell me he is African American—a nice moment, as we are learning, ever so gradually, not to always identify people by race (making me question the overall theme in this book, not just "young" in New Orleans but "young and black").

Because William had moved home for summer vacation when it was time for him to tell his story, I asked him to interview himself and send me

William Gillespie, Tulane scholar and budding writer

the written story. He had a better idea. He asked his father to be the interviewer asking the kinds of questions I would have asked. William will be back in New Orleans in the late summer to pursue a master's degree in History at Tulane. (He, by the way, graduated from Tulane with a 3.9 GPA and won the Montgomery Award for the highest male GPA in the History Department.) His father's name is Eric Lynn Gillispie. He began by asking his son what he wanted people to know about him: the kind of person he is, his faith, his goals, how he sees race relations today.

William: I guess I want people to know that I'm dedicated to a true understanding of the historical past. I want people to know what happened to their ancestors and forefathers, and to the best of my ability I want it to be as honest and truthful as possible. I guess I'm a good person, or I try to be. I was born and raised in Indianapolis, as was my mother. I'm a Christian, I love God and fear God. To me, Jesus is an aspect of the big man. In my understanding, they are three parts (Father, Son, and Holy Spirit) of the same Being and so, praising one versus another doesn't hinder it in my understanding. I understand the importance of Jesus's actions and what he represents, but praying toward the Holy Spirit versus praying to Jesus versus praying toward God isn't a distinction I'm too worried about.

If somebody says they know William, what would they say? What would your best friend say about William? What would you want your family to say about you?

Uh . . . I don't know, that I'm friendly, intelligent. I'm also hard working, intellectually curious, gifted, and I hope that I make history interesting. I know my parents would say I'm the best child in the world. (laughs) Let's see . . . my family might say that I'm loving, clearly hard working, and dedicated to them. I guess I'm also working in the family's best interest, you know, towards its improvement, especially when it comes to keeping the family history. I'm also a writer. I write fiction.

I don't want to put words in your mouth, but a good way to wrap up or sum up what you are is to call you a scholar?

A scholar. I like that. That is a good way to wrap up what I said.

Okay, so let's move on. What have you learned in your studies at Tulane and in your life that influence you to work for or desire to work for racial justice?

Okay, so let me back up for a bit. When I was growing up in our well-to-do family on the north side of Indianapolis, I got everything I needed and most of what I wanted. But, always being around other African Americans, I started to see a disparity between the way they lived and the way we did. I wouldn't say my parents were radicals, but they didn't hide me from the truth about racism as a historical and real event. I really don't know when I was first introduced to poverty, maybe it was schoolmates. But at some point I started to notice others didn't live like we did. Both blacks and whites and other races were less well off than us, but especially blacks, who didn't have that same monetary freedom.

Then, in middle school, I switched from science, which I had wanted to do since I was very, very little, to history, in part because I hated math, but also because American History really interested me, including the parts about the black experience in America. And one of the things that I've come to see is that a lot of the problems that we face today are diminutive forms of the problems our black ancestors had. That is, a lot of the problems that the slaves and later the segregated African Americans fought against, argued against, struggled against are the same problems we have today just in a smaller form that affects fewer of us. Now, some of the problems still affect many of us, like our community's crisis with broken families. A lot of the things that were problems then, which clearly stemmed from segregation or slavery, are similar to or the same as the problems we face today. And gaining this understanding showed me how important working for racial justice is today.

So fast-forward to high school where it became clearer to me. Actually, in high school it was a class issue. The poor needed help and I keep seeing that over and over again. I think it stemmed from the Jesuit education, which is a lot about social justice and fairness. That showed me that the poor needed help from the better off. And you know, what else I saw was that even those who were better off would penny pinch, sometimes in a way that was almost offensive. And that showed me something about how the rich are taught, probably in the home, to hold their money tightly, and the poor are taught they can't survive without help from the rich, which is the harsh class divide that doesn't do anyone any good.

So, then, at Tulane, I saw the same thing I'd seen earlier, that the problems that we have today stem from segregation and slavery, but I could now put it in a more refined and logical form. Because, one of the big things I learned from studying history, which I think is super important, is that everything we experience and use today comes from somewhere. A lot of problems we have, not just racial problems, stem from our past. From knowing our history, you can see that the problems that strike African Americans today aren't twenty-first century problems. The racism that stems from our institutions clearly isn't gone. It can't be gone, because otherwise the problems wouldn't still be there. If racism was the source of these problems, and the problems continue, then it's not illogical to say that racism continues to fuel the problems, one way or another.

Now, let me make a side note here. I have to give credit to Americans versus Europeans. I think Americans are actually better at facing their racism head on. The Europeans act like it's over even more than we do. That was my experience when I was studying abroad in Italy. They are so convinced that they are the epitome of modernism that they completely ignore the racial issues they face, despite the fact that many of these countries are starting to have large African populations in their cities. So I give credit to Americans for that: at least some of us are trying to have the conversation. There are people here who say we don't have a racial conversation, and I would tell them to go to Europe and really experience not having a conversation.

All of this that I've talked about and explained has shown me that we need racial justice and that racism still exists. And we need to work toward changing that. And I think it comes down to two aspects of reform we need. The first is internal. It's about the black experience itself and how we talk about it and *how* African Americans consider themselves to be black. How they raise and talk to their children. All this is internal reform, and we need to work as African Americans toward improving the way we think about ourselves. What might help us, I could argue, is a period of High Culture, kind of like the Harlem Renaissance, Reconstruction after the Civil War, or the late sixties to early seventies. I think a period of High Culture like those times would be good for us. And that idea stems from my studies of history and looking at the world. Those periods of high cultural achievement really seem to be linked with the better periods for African Americans.[8]

---

8. High Culture is a term often used to describe the blossoming of African Ameri-

The second aspect of reform we really need is institutional. Look, if we went around, and tried to convince every single white person to not be a racist, we wouldn't ever get anywhere. That very slow-step process isn't viable. We can't convince every single white household to end racist practices or change how they feel. We're not in the days of segregation or slavery. A black person can walk down the street and doesn't have to step aside for white folks. Black people don't have to be employed as servants or laborers for white interests. Now, they may not be able to find better work, but they're not forced into that, as they were during segregation or slavery. So changing every white person's attitude about black people is not going to do what we need. What we need is to change the institutions that our problems stem from. We need to get the institutions to acknowledge how they have treated African Americans, then change how they treat African Americans now, and in the future work together with our community toward our improvement.

If the U.S. government was on our side, there would be no limit to what the African American community could get done. But, it's not on our side. One branch—or actually the head of one branch—seems to be on our side—the executive branch. Congress is not on our side. The Supreme Court has protected African Americans in the past, but recent decisions have not had our best interests at heart. But, if we can push the local systems, like the police, the city and state governments, the public and private organizations to work with us, instead of against us, we could really change our world. Because we, since the days of slavery and segregation, have been fighting to succeed in spite of these institutions, but *if* we were on the same side . . .

What would that look like?

Well, let's point to Affirmative Action. That's an example of trying to work with the community. It's giving poor African American a chance to get into hard colleges. If poorer, young African Americans are given an opportunity, offered by that government and supported by the African American community, to get into better high schools and colleges, that would be an example of the two of us working together. We would make sure that poor blacks are not limited by where they are from and that colleges that are mostly white can't continue to prevent African Americans from entering their schools just because it's the way it's always been. That's the government and the black communities working together. Another example of an institution working with the black community is when schools try to recruit and shepherd black children through magnet schools and other systems, into the colleges, and some of them do, though many are quite bad at it, if that makes sense. . . .

It is a long march. But I think that changing the board of directors at a school like Tulane is much easier and more significant than trying to change

can culture in the creative arts and literature, influencing generations of Americans.

the way every white person in New Orleans treats their black neighbors. The latter isn't going to achieve what we want.

What special contributions would you like to make toward racial justice/ reconciliation in the future?

So, first, let me say that I don't think I was born to be an organizer. I don't think you'll see me out protesting anywhere. What I would really like to do is spend time on that internal first aspect of reform. You know, large-scale community organizing is for the second, institutional aspects of reform, which are just as important as the internal reform, but the opposite is also true. And I want to work on the internal part, and see if we can't rewrite what it means to be an African American. One thing I really want to do is help the black community get its history straighter. And to create a sort of intellectual curiosity within these African Americans about their community and families' histories. Because a lot of African Americans end up bored out of their mind in their history classes at their bad, underfunded schools.

These kids are listening to dry history lectures about old, white men from Virginia who won wars against the British. That's stuff they can't relate to. But, if they hear instead about the black soldiers who fought in integrated armies in the American Revolution or how Thomas Jefferson struggled with questions of racism and racial prejudice himself, they would have a different view of what this country means. From the beginning, African Americans were in this country, were a part of it, and if the black students understood that and saw it in their history books, they would understand their country and their role in it differently.

One other thing I'd like to be a part of, though definitely not lead . . . If we could do some sort of really intense cultural reform movement somewhere in this country, I think it would do a lot of good. Let's say we got a lot of black music producers, black publishing companies, black artists, and made out a big call to try and pull all the black art, black music, black writings together. They could even have people respond to the callout by creating new things. We have cultural successes. We have artists, and musicians, and writers, but they are completely integrated in the wider world. We don't feel the *communal* cultural achievements as we did in the Harlem Renaissance or the late sixties or early seventies.

How do you do this while at the same time allowing or encouraging segregation as opposed to integrating African American successes in the wider world?

I think the risk of that is much less than the potential success our communal cultural achievements could bring. Once again, I have no desire whatsoever to spearhead this project and in the advisory committee meetings I would raise that same concern; however, I think we could come up with a way to make this what the black experience really is in the twenty-first century. This is what African Americans are today, this is what they believe and how they feel about themselves, and *this* is what we need to change. And I think you can do that without scaring away white people. And that in itself could make a big difference in the institutional reform as well. Because, if black people stop scaring white people, then the things that protect white people should stop attacking us. Like police . . . or the court system.

Hmm . . . Let me ask you this. How have you found Tulane to be in dealing with racial issues?

I think they recognize they have a problem. They were a southern school that only integrated in 1963. They know that one of the reasons they don't have a strong showing of non-athlete black students stems from the fact that they were segregated for much longer than they were ever integrated in a meaningful fashion. The other problem with Tulane is that it tries to draw its students from all around the country, a lot from the NYC area and California. That means it wants the best out of those areas, which usually means the wealthier, or better off students . . . not the poor or minorities. So Tulane has a race problem; it knows it has one, but it doesn't know what to do without redoing the whole way they get students.

How about the wider New Orleans areas? How have you seen or dealt with racism in New Orleans outside of Tulane?

You know, it's interesting because this is something I think Tulane actually does well. That is, show its students what New Orleans really is, outside of the Tulane or Uptown "bubble." Through our service learning, which is basically required community service, we have to go out and work with a local partner for a certain number of hours for free. There's no way to get out of it, and that makes these well-off, often upper-class students have to go out into the community and work toward social goals, often racial justice. I myself went to two different, very poor inner city schools. For the first I gave cello lessons, and in the second I tutored a few kids in social studies. And I saw how tough some of the school districts are, even with the new charter school system. They need help here in New Orleans.

All right, let's shift gears for a minute here. What else from your early life and teenage life helped you as you look toward your future?

Well, hmm . . . my parents and paternal grandmother were very important and were always super, super supportive. All three are angels in the wilderness for me, which we'll get to in a minute, and the way they raised me was a big aspect of being able to recognize racism and see the world for what it really is and get ideas on how to change it. One thing I'll say about my grandmother now is that she doesn't walk around with resentment despite the way she was mistreated for a lot of her life. She cooked and cleaned for white families all her life and that couldn't have been easy. She went to Dayton from rural Kentucky at age thirteen to work for a white family. I can't imagine that could have been fun. But she still carries a high degree of kindness and caring and a deep respect for life and other people's lives. What I could say I gained from that, when I really connected everything and learned about how my amazing and loving grandmother had a difficult life behind her, but still showed me that the solution to our problems can't be vengeance or retribution. It can't be punishment for white or anyone. It has to be peaceful coexistence. That's really what we're trying to get to, not resentment.

So, that showed you that violence is not the way.

Right. Violence and retribution are not the way. If, despite it all, you can be respectful and kind and caring, you can make a difference. I imagine my grandmother has changed more white people's minds than the aggressive and violent new Black Panthers.

Now, I'll say one other thing, which is a bit of a tangent, but I don't like looking for racism. I think there is enough that we can easily see. I don't like the idea of hunting down hidden racism. There are plenty of clear problems that are lying around that we need to deal with before we delve into micro-aggressions, where people do something small and don't mean it. One of your current favorite stories is that you were trying to sign up for a new Sam's Club card, and for it you had to put down your income range. And, being part of the well-off and very blessed family we are, you put $200,000 and above. And the lady at the desk said, "Now, you know that says $200,000 not $20,000 . . . " Now, that's a small thing, it may not even be intentional, and though it is racist, getting lost on that will prevent us from getting anything done. If we're stuck trying to fix that kind of thing and *not* the fact that young black male children have almost no chance of getting through college, we'll never get anything done. I think we have enough clear racism to deal with before we get to the small things.

Who are your angels in the wilderness throughout your life?

Okay, now let me preface this by saying that, while I have had tough experiences in my life, I don't know if I can say that I've had a true wilderness experience. It's probably coming, but I don't want to say I've done my share of wilderness wandering.

But, as I mentioned, both my parents were very important in making me who I am today. Your mother was essential as well. All three showed me love in its purest form. And, I know it's cliché, but that kind of pure love is powerful. And if we could really see each other as . . . you know, brother and sister, father and child, grandparent and grandchild, if we really thought about each other with a real, serious unconditional love, it would make the world a very different place. But it's hard. Jesus preached it, sometimes roughly to treat your neighbor as your brother, but nobody has really ever really succeeded at it throughout history. I mean, I'm not a dumb historian, conflict clearly continues and appears in new and different forms again and again.

And we may never reach the place called for by Jesus until God himself brings together Heaven and Earth at the end of everything, but undeniably, things are better than they were. I think we can improve our world. I really think we can. And, you know, sometimes we African Americans can't seem to accept that the world has improved. And that leads to confrontationalism. We have to give people the opportunity to be wrong, or they'll never know they're wrong. I mean look, I love my cousins, but some of the stuff they say about white people I think is crazy, but if I don't logically explain to them why I think they're wrong and what I view and think about it, then they'll never learn. And, another thing is, within the black community, just because it's more liberal or more "modern" doesn't mean it's right. You can be wrong as a liberal, and if somebody more conservative tells you you're wrong, you've got to actually think, do some research, find out if you're wrong or right before you decide that every conservative viewpoint is wrong.

Let me go back to angels. Outside of family, who else has been an angel for you?

Well, you know, I play cello. And I've had two fantastic orchestra directors. I had a guy named Ed Staubach and a guy named Steve Horneman for high school. And Mr. Staubach showed a sort of love for our learning and our growth that really affected me. He just loved to see us improve the way we played and sang our songs and was always so supportive of us in that process. And Mr. Horneman had to have a book-of-life advice. He always used to tell us to leave a place better than you found it. And I still hear that in my head all the time whenever I'm going places, I always think about it. He had lots and lots of life advice I still think about to this day. And, you know…both of my teachers just had joy, pure joy, when we succeeded. And it's the same joy God feels in us. And we can experience it and see it. I could go on forever talking about my angels, but those two in particular affected me.

Reaction:

As William talked, especially when he reflected on one of his grand-mothers, I thought of something Dr. Martin Luther King wrote in his 1967 book *Where Do We Go from Here: Chaos or Community*.

The ultimate weakness of violence is that it is a descending spiral, be-getting the very thing it seeks to destroy. Instead of diminishing evil, it mul-tiplies it. Through violence you may murder the liar, but you cannot murder the lie, nor establish the truth. Through violence you may murder the hater, but you do not murder the hate. In fact, violence merely increases the hate. So it goes. . . . Darkness cannot drive out darkness; only light can do that. Hate cannot drive out hate; only love can do that.

For William, it is love—like the love his grandmother showed to everyone— that will change the world. "Hate cannot drive out hate; only love can do that."

I appreciate how William as a recent college graduate is able to assimilate his past as he moves forward into the future. He realizes he is not an organizer but knows that he has a calling—he would say from God—to help all of us, but especially African Americans, understand and appreciate our history, especially black cultural history. As his father kind of forced him to say, he is, in the best sense of the word, a scholar.

William's many insights gave me a fresh understanding of who we are today: why there is often much brokenness within black families, our need for another High Culture among various black artists, musicians, and writers—and how this will not likely re-segregate the wider culture—and the importance of not focusing on the little things like the clerk asking his father to be sure he was checking the right blank for the family income. And, after reading William's story, I more fully appreciate the necessity of popularizing *historic* black culture.

As important as the Black Lives Matter movement may be today, William's contributions in the future along with other black scholars will make such a movement less and less necessary.

Chapter Six

St. Luke's, Historically Black and Historic Episcopal Church

According to a former rector of St. Luke's, the Rev. George Swallow (who served from1966 to 1973), "The Negro church in New Orleans was established in 1855 by the Right Reverend Leonidas Polk, the first bishop of Louisiana, for the provision for religious instruction of the colored race." Polk had met with several free people of color to organize the congregation, originally named St. Thomas. During and after the war, the church declined in membership as many African American Christians looked to churches like the African Methodist Episcopal (AME) Church to find their church home. Bishop Polk later became a Confederate general in the Civil War, defending slavery, and was killed in action.

In 1887, the church congregation was reorganized and the name changed to St. Luke's. In the early 1900s, Frances Joseph Gaudet opened a school closely related to St. Luke's, offering stimulating education to children of African American families. The school remained open for thirty-three years, when the valuable land where the school was located was sold by the diocese, the proceeds going—then and now—to fund education for black children. Because of her community service, including an inspiring prison ministry, Frances Gaudet was recently named an "Episcopal saint" by the national church, the only one from Louisiana. Now "Blessed Frances," the national church celebrates her life and her witness each December 30.

St. Luke's became strong under the leadership of the Rev. John Boyce (1928-1945), the congregation growing from 17 to 248. Unfortunately, Boyce was removed from his position by Bishop John Jackson, even though the members of St. Luke's petitioned the bishop to keep him on. An early example of why the Black Lives Matter movement is so important.

In 1978 St. Luke's moved to its current site, a lovely building that previously housed the Greek Orthodox Cathedral. The congregation has had its ups and down, especially during and after Hurricane Katrina. The church is however, once again growing and serving as a model church, not just for African Americans but for all of us. The congregation is largely middle class but all are welcomed. Located in a changing neighborhood, St. Luke's describes its mission this way: "To be a welcoming community and to bring people to God by living out the good news of Jesus Christ through worship, fellowship, and service within and beyond our community so that others may know of God's redeeming love." I served as part-time priest-in-charge at St. Luke's from 2012 to 2014 and still help out on Sundays when they need an assisting priest.

━━ ━━ ━━ ━━ ━━ ━━ ━━ ━━ ━━ ━━ ━━ ━━ ━━ ━━ ━━ ━━ ━━

Trevor Bryan and April William:
Young Professionals Showing the Way

In this chapter, Trevor and his longtime partner and now wife, April, tell their story. Both are young rising leaders in New Orleans. Trevor is also the "adult coach" from St. Luke's—like the older coaches or leaders who introduce the various chapters in *Angels in the Wilderness*. Now the junior warden, he recently served as senior warden (head layperson) of St. Luke's. I met with Trevor and April on March 14, 2016, in our home. Trevor is a registered nurse and April a respiratory therapist working now on a public health master's degree. I began by asking Trevor and April to talk about their experiences at their church.

Trevor: My grandfather worshipped at St. Luke's, also my father. Most members of my family (originally from Jamaica) were members at St. Luke's. My grandfather moved here and became a professor at Dillard University. A lot of family members came to New Orleans to attend Dillard. They would live with him and attend St. Luke's. I moved here as a child, in 1978; that same year St. Luke's bought the old Greek Church and moved to our space on North Dorgenois Street. I was baptized there at the age of eleven, and later confirmed. I started off helping at the services by holding the incense censer. Then I became a junior acolyte.

So your fifth-grade son, Trevie, is following in your footsteps!

Yes, and we're very proud of him. I became Junior Warden in 2008 after Hurricane Katrina. Ms. Elvia James was the Senior Warden; she needed someone with experience in construction, as we repaired the church. The Storm damage had been taken care of, but some volunteers set the church on fire by mistake while doing repairs, not long after the Storm, so we had fire damage as well.

April: I was originally Baptist. After I started the relationship with Trevor, I said to myself, "Well, this is the person I want to spend the rest of my life with so what better way to become conjoined than to become an Episcopalian and attend St. Luke's." At that point I fell in love with St. Luke's. The people there are energetic and loving; they embrace strangers with love. When I first started going there ten years ago, I developed friendships with Ms. Elvia James and Ms. Ellarose Gray. Ms. Gray took me under her wing and had me become a member of the Altar Guild. Later she took me to meetings of the diocesan Episcopal Church Women (ECW), where she has been a leader, as well as in our own ECW. I liked what they were doing, and I joined. I later became Secretary to the Vestry. Currently I am Vice President of the ECW. I do a lot of different things at the church.

What are your hopes now for St. Luke's?

April: I hope we reach out more to our neighborhood; currently we don't have a full-time priest; but my hope is that we can reach out and embrace local people and bring them closer to God. They may know God, but they haven't moved to fully accept him. We need to go out and preach the word of God and pull them into the fold, saying "Hey, look, the God we serve is a really great God!"

People in our neighborhood have a lot of economic problems, and there's a lot of violence. If they understood that God is *love,* we would be at least on the path to decrease violence in New Orleans. If St. Luke's became more financially stable, we could have the programs we used to have—for example, a strong feeding ministry and after-school tutoring programs and other programs for youth. We have a lot of educators and medical professionals in our congregation. We could provide care for our geriatric population. By doing those things we would become a sound church. We would become the voice of God in our neighborhood.

As a church one of our main issues is our lack of relationships with one another outside Sunday worship. We are at least beginning to see one another throughout the week. We can start fulfilling our baptism vows and can do more outreach.[1]

The new Presiding Bishop Michael Curry [our first African American Presiding Bishop] has said, *evangelism* is not a dirty word! It means spreading the good news. We want to go out and radically welcome new people into the church. I see us doing more things that are part of the community; inviting people in from the larger community. We don't just want to set up programs—we want to go out and *touch* the community and find out where people's interests lie. What's important to our neighborhood? To make us more relevant than just offering services and *our* programs.

Church members getting to know each other not just on Sunday—how is that happening, and how would you like it to happen even more?

April: Right now we're doing an exciting Wednesday night program during Lent. It is a national Episcopal program set up by Scott Stoner as part

---

1. In the Episcopal Baptismal Covenant, we say that we will "strive for justice and peace among all people, and respect the dignity of every human being."

of the Living Compass. The title is "Living Well Through Lent, 2016: Letting Go with All Your Heart, Soul, Strength and Mind." If we're not well spiritually, then we're not well physically. If we're not sharing, if we're not building relationships, that's a sign that we need to change.

For years we have offered ECW Family Fun night. Families who are members of St. Luke's congregation and their friends come to the church: we have games, we raffle off prizes, and we serve wonderful spaghetti dinners. It's a time for people to get together and relax and get to know each other in a fun environment. The kids, of course, love it. We also did the St. Luke's annual Family Fun and Health Fest—that was a big success. We go and talk to various organizations like American Heart Association, American Lung Association, acupuncturists, and they come to our health fair and offer services that people in the community don't normally have access to. Also there's a fun aspect for the kids—we have a water slide and face-painting. It's a way of reaching out to the community to pull them towards us.

Though not large in size, St. Luke's seems to have such a strong community—people really involved and caring about one another. How does that happen?

April: First and foremost, there's a general love for God. That's the driving force behind everything we do. Because Christ died for us and sacrificed for us, we want to proclaim his love; the best way to do this is to go out and do these activities serving others. We love God. God loves us. That's how we bring a lot of people to us.

What special role does a historically black church have in our city and in the larger Episcopal Church? Or, is there a special role?

Trevor: Absolutely. I was involved in bringing six diocesan resolutions last year—three on the diocesan Racial Reconciliation Commission work (I am the co-chair now) and three especially for St. Luke's. Historically, St. Luke's was the congregation before the Civil War that Bishop Leonidas Polk envisioned for the free people of color.

People of color within the Episcopal Church always seem to have some idea of how they arrived within the church. The first part of our congregation was free people of color living in New Orleans before the Civil War. Then we moved into different reasons why people joined—for instance the banana company that was operating here. The Standard Fruit Company president, Samuel Zemurray, had a link to Honduras and other countries in the Caribbean region. He would get work visas for people from that region to come to the U.S., and they would end up settling here, and many, as Anglicans, would join the St. Luke's congregation.

Another thing was that a massive hurricane (Frederik) happened in the

Caribbean in the 1970s— people needed assistance, and many migrated here and joined St. Luke's. Today I see young people inside St. Luke's who don't know our history, but they see people coming to visit or calling us. I frequently receive calls from around the national Church, from people who say, "We need somebody to speak to the topic of black churches in the South." Referrals would come through Reverend Angela Ifill of the Union of Black Episcopalians office. We are part of a group called New Visions Initiative, which is about investigating the historically black churches to see what condition they are in and how we can move forward.

Like most sacramental churches, people believe the myth that we Episcopalians are in a drastic decline. Would that mean that Black Episcopal churches were in a faster decline, because we weren't receiving much financial support? No. St. Luke's was one of the first eight churches to be part of the New Visions Initiative, a new model of how African American churches can stand together and help one another.

What are the special things that historically white Episcopal churches can learn from the black churches?

Trevor: One of the most important things we would offer is perseverance—perseverance in dealing with dynamics related to race as they were in the mid-1800s, and also with things as they exist these days. Racism was overt in the past. These days—like Michelle Alexander writes about in *The New Jim Crow*—they changed the names, but the rules still penalize people of color. Think of how many African Americans are out of work or the numbers that we incarcerate.

You look around most Episcopal churches, and you don't see people who look like us. It wasn't until the 1980s when more black men and women were ordained that we started getting priests of color regularly coming through.

April: You can see that St. Luke's is a vibrant, culturally sound church where African Americans can relate. Because it's a predominantly black church, newcomers who are black feel at ease. They say that they have the same points of view, the same mind-set, the same culture as I do. At a white church, they may feel out of place.

On another subject: It's really easy for white folks to set up programs and invite black folks to join us. But I have found in my social-justice work that we whites need to, sometimes at least, join African American worship and other activities. And we don't.

Trevor: Angela Ifill invited us, and I went for the first time from New Visions to sit in on a CEEP national meeting—the Conference of Endowed Episcopal Parishes. I'd never heard of CEEP. We went down to a place outside Jacksonville,

Florida. A representative of a large church from West Hartford was discussing with the group how much they had in their endowment—a staggering amount of money compared to what we have at St. Luke's! His problem was that he could not spend the money—that was because the church is located in suburban Hartford. He can't get inner-city African Americans to come out and participate in programs that he has the funds for. I asked him why he couldn't initiate the programs in the inner city, where the needs are, and he said his endowment would not pay for that.

It reminds me that—it's not the program so much as it is the participation. If I start a food ministry and the churches keep volunteering, but we keep seeing these guys coming for the meals week after week but not participating in the church, I ask myself, are they feeling good about receiving all the time—while I feel good being on my side of the table, serving them. They need to come on my side of the table as well.

Yes, people support what they help to create . . . how can low-income people feel they are contributing?

April: It's one thing to do a feeding ministry—but to go beyond that is a challenge. I don't have an answer—*how* can they feel they are ready to receive more deeply the faith message we are offering?

Trevor: I encourage more people to join in. I learned that with the Department of Health and Hospitals—you have to meet people where they are. I was surprised when we put one notice that we had a feeding ministry inside Common Ground's information booklet. We were amazed at how many people kept calling—social workers and other helpers—to make referrals.[2] And people on mission trips to our city, during the recovery from the Storm, would call and volunteer their time to help our feeding ministries. If we re-opened our Loaves and Fishes ministry back up, as our member, Larry Bishop, wants us to do, we would grow on the edges and in the middle of our congregation.

When we, people like you Trevor, are visiting in the prisons we get people, the inmates, to tell their own stories. You might think about forming people into small groups during the meals and getting them to tell their stories to each other. Even if they only come from time to time, it always seems to work.

Trevor: When I talk about perseverance, I want to describe something that was going on in St. Luke's over the years. At one time we had over 50

2. Common Ground is a large and effective organization that helps low-income people in New Orleans, founded days after Katrina by a former Black Panther and friend, Malik Rahim.

percent of the congregation that was first generation immigrants from the Caribbean countries from the Anglican tradition. So they had never really experienced the American Episcopal Church as it exists. When they come from their home countries it's unusual for them to have mixed congregations of blacks and whites. Their priests may be black or white, but their congregations are usually solidly black. Our home congregation in Jamaica is all black. So, arriving at St. Luke's, an all-black church, a newcomer may feel that they've arrived, that they're in good shape. But if you remain in our church on North Dorgenois Street, you find you are isolated from the other, white Episcopal churches if you don't develop leaders among the congregation to work with them.

So, after Hurricane Katrina we began to develop such leaders. I went to the University of the South (Sewanee) to a leadership development course. I went to a "Called to Transformation" course with Canon Mark Stevenson here in our Diocese. We learned how to develop leadership amongst the laity. We found that we had strong people running our church but very few members were participating in the life of the wider Diocese. So, we moved on that and Gillian Knowles became a member of the diocesan Executive Council, etc. A lot of people have energy to do more in the diocese than they are doing. I would tell people that when they pursue religious knowledge or study theology, they didn't necessarily have to work for the church. Don't think that if you get a degree you have to become clergy; if you have that yearning to increase your knowledge, you can take courses. We need to be the best stewards of what He gave us.

What about you, April?

April: I am so concerned about the community as a whole: as an example, the schools-to-prisons pipeline in Louisiana. I have a hard time dealing with racism. Case in point: the Race and Reconciliation Commission was going to go last week to the Whitney Plantation [where there is a slavery museum], but the flood kept us from going. I didn't grow up during that era of slavery, but I have older relatives who did. To me, walking around a plantation would be hard, painful, even when the plantations present slavery in a negative way. [3]

Trevor: What I was going to say about race: the belief that April has, it's not unique—that many of our people don't want to go to a plantation to explore things that have caused great pain, with the history of slavery. It's the same as going in to talk to a white group about slavery: a good number of them would not want to go to a plantation with a couple of black people. Just as April would feel the pain of people in her family, in the past, the white people may feel terrible about what their ancestors did so they don't want to think about slavery either.

3. The plantation trip was rescheduled and worked quite well as Lindsey Ardrey says in chapter 5.

So, when we are at a former slave plantation, what do we talk about to-gether? It's awkward. What the Race and Reconciliation Commission was hop-ing is that we would have a dialogue on race and be able to move on to more of a resolution. Racial reconciliation, in my opinion, will never really be done unless we study our history together. For me, it's history that needs to be ac-knowledged and respected. There are many places to this day in and around New Orleans where people of color have been harmed greatly in the past. On the Lakefront they used to lynch people—they had a lynching tree. I know that, but for me it opens up a painful dialogue.

It's the same as though you're meeting with a non-minority group—they would not want to go to the plantation with black people. Our collective culture here in New Orleans represents so much that has gone on in our past. As April says, so much pain has happened, it would be hard to talk together about the past.

Once when I was at a meeting with members of a black church here, a therapist who was in our group pointed out that for African Americans talking about slavery would be like an adult survivor of child abuse bringing up the abuse in a group. It's sometimes too hard. You acknowledge what happened to you, but there's so much pain and shame associated with it. But what I like to see, is when people of various backgrounds—white, black, Hispanic—come together and tell their stories, there can be a new and help-ful understanding.

Trevor: In the most recent editions of the Episcopal News Service (a na-tional email publication) they had front-page stories about racial reconcilia-tion. How do we accomplish racial reconciliation? The idea was to tell stories and look deeply into our past—to come up with real solutions instead of just applying band-aids, so to speak. Another suggestion: making sure we're shar-ing stories of the white person of today, rather than the white Episcopalian of the past. We have institutional racism that goes on. Or for people of color, we suffer from feelings of internalized racial inferiority, and sometimes we're not aware of it. We tend to think: that's just the way it's going to be.

You've experienced racism on your job?

Trevor: Yes, even in Germany (I was born in Germany). There were a cou-ple of patients there speaking in German and saying to each other that they didn't want the "N" nurse—me—taking care of them. I was amazed—I felt that I'd always been at home with German people. And another time I was taken off the roster for two months at Ochsner Hospital, where I was working, because another nurse objected to working with a black nurse.[4]

---

4. Ochsner's, in New Orleans, is known as one of the leading hospitals in the nation.

Have you, April, experienced that kind of racism in your work?

April: Yes, sometimes older patients won't let me work with them as a respiratory therapist because I need to touch them or lean over them to listen to their breath sounds. They don't want an African American person touching them.

Trevor: Yes, people in the older generation have more problems with race—well we're now dealing with Gen-Xs, Baby Boomers, Millennials—you have to be careful to evaluate who you are working with before you get started.

April: There is a small proportion of young people who've absorbed the values of their elders—occasionally you will find younger patients who won't accept treatment from a person of African American descent.

Trevor: I had a principal at Ben Franklin High School—she was really tough on people of color. She would say to us, "You black guys—you are now in a school that wasn't exactly designed for you. You're going to have to work a little harder." I didn't understand what she was driving at. I know I have two strikes against me—I'm black and I'm male. But she was letting me know that I might have special difficulties.

My brother was also a student at Ben Franklin, and he got into a pushing match or fight with a white boy who called him an "N" and spat at him. The white student had an "in-school" suspension, but my brother was suspended for four days out of school. My family realized that there was a disparity of treatment and complained. The principal apparently relented and asked my brother to return to the school.

April then discussed how difficult it was recently for their family to enroll Trevie in the gifted charter school, Gretna Number Two, though he is obviously gifted, very gifted.

April: We couldn't get him initially into the gifted program, so we arranged for him to have the Stanford-Binet and Wexler tests, and it turned out he is highly gifted. Now he's certified for an IEP under federal regulations.[5] Then they insisted that Trevie be tested in Jefferson Parish; we had to undergo delay after delay, probably because he's an African American child. It was an ordeal.

April, finally, what do you want people to know about you?

5. The Individual Educational Program includes especially gifted students, as well as students who need more support in school.

April: Well, that I'm a God-fearing woman. I am a wonderful mother and hope I'm a good spouse! I'm meticulous about doing things—everything has to be just so. I love life, and I feel blessed every single day.

And you, Trevor?

Trevor: God is Number One. Even if it's a negative situation, I pray about decisions and take my time. Sometimes I may take a little longer, so as to not cause harm to others. In regard to racial reconciliation, I'm very sympathetic to people who are suffering where they are not able to deal with wounds at this point. As for me, I could be exposed to atrocities, but I'll try to find a way to turn it into good.

I also like to do leadership development. I like a mission. I like being a servant leader, leading from behind. Like Mandela, I enjoy being in a group where I don't have to be the person setting the plan or the agenda. The Harvard model—you get involved and then step back and let people work out the ideas by themselves.

You are both angels in the New Orleans wilderness. Keep up your faith and your outreach to others—but I don't have to tell you that.

My Reaction:

It still amazes me that such gifted leaders in New Orleans have to put up with ongoing "personal" racism (bigotry) as well as the structural, institutional racism in the city. White patients who do not want to be touched by black professionals, or a school system that wants to exclude a highly gifted boy from an accelerated program because white parents don't want their children to be in classes with black young people. But, like St. Luke's itself, April and Trevor will persevere and bring changes to both the Episcopal Church and to our city.

Since my interview, some good news: With Trevor's leadership as co-chair of the Racial Reconciliation Commission, fifty Episcopalians (both whites and blacks) made the hour-long trip to the "slave plantation"—the Whitney Plantation. Its history goes back 264 years; it has now become the only slavery museum in the state. While many blacks as well as whites do not want to think about slavery but want to move on in an anti-racism future, leaders like Trevor and now April (and William Gillespie in chapter 5) realize that we *must* claim our history if we are not going to repeat it. As William Faulkner once said in relation to race, "The past is never dead. It's not even past."

Nancy Hampton: At Home at St. Luke's

Nancy has been a member of St. Luke's for five years and has held several leadership positions. She is a librarian at Xavier University in New Orleans. She is one of the members at St. Luke's that I have gotten to know especially well; I was the clergyman who prepared her for confirmation in the Episcopal Church. She has also been a supporter of prison ministry with others from St. Luke's. I began the conversation in our home, asking her to tell me what had been going on with her as I had not seen her for a while.

Nancy: On Valentine's Day I had an accident. It was really bad. I feel renewed and I'm lucky to be here. It was a head-on collision. The driver was in my lane. He had diabetes and had passed out. It was just a horrible situation. So, that's making me think about things very seriously. I have whiplash, and I hurt my knee and my ankle. I stayed home for a week and then eased back to work. I'm OK now; I'm back into a routine. I feel like I have a guardian angel!

That was the first thing—and then this week I started jury duty. I thought of you when I got there—I was called for criminal trials. I had done jury duty before for civil trials. That was light compared to this. They wanted to question everyone to see if they were appropriate for this jury—and it was a murder trial. The defendant sits in the courtroom listening to his counsel questioning people and then the prosecutor questions you as well.

Most of the questions are, where do you live and work, and so on. Then they start with questions like, "Could you put someone charged with capital murder away for life?" The defendant was being tried for manslaughter, robbery, and attempted murder. So the maximum sentence would be life in prison. Could you put someone in prison for life?

I have an issue with that! I told them I don't believe in that—I believe that people change, that everyone needs second chances. The crime had taken place when the defendant was eighteen, six years previously. Also, the guy being charged was shaking with nervousness. I did not think of him as a psychopath. They let me go. They didn't want someone who wasn't convinced about sending someone to prison for life.

But I was thinking of you—I thought, maybe I should have told them I can convict someone for life. In that way I could be put on the jury and could block someone from being put in prison forever. But then, I think I couldn't fake it for long days—stating that you held one opinion, and then in the end telling the jury you had changed your mind.

I probably would have said "Yes," crossing my fingers at the same time. In reality I could not vote for putting anybody in prison for life. As you say, people can and do change.

Nancy Hampton, librarian and member of St. Luke's Historic Episcopal Church

I was raised in a military family, so I grew up attending services in military chapels. They are very mild-mannered churches. They remind me of Episcopal services. But, I didn't know anything about the Episcopal Church then. We lived in Virginia, in Washington state, and Kansas and elsewhere. We also lived a lot in Germany: Mannheim, Frankfurt, and other cities. I moved every one to two years. It wasn't comfortable for me, but now I look back, and I am grateful for the experiences I had. Still, more than most people, I am always looking for community because I'm not sure what a true community feels like.

When I became an adult I was supposed to be a Baptist like my parents—and I was told that (but we didn't go to Baptist services because they weren't offered on the bases). So I was looking and looking. And in Denver I found an Episcopal church. I was a librarian in Denver and found an Episcopal church. I liked it very much—for a silly reason: I liked what it looked like. So I said to myself, "I'll go and see what it's like."

I tried different churches in New Orleans, including Trinity [*my home church*], and found St. Luke's was right for me because it wasn't too large. I was trying to make myself go to Trinity Church because it was near my apartment. But I didn't really like it, and I discussed this problem with Violet Bryan [a long-time and highly esteemed English professor] at Xavier University, where I work. I told her Trinity Episcopal was OK, but it wasn't pleasant for me.

It didn't feel like home?

No, I didn't feel like I could become part of that congregation. Violet invited me to St. Luke's—but she didn't tell me it was Episcopal. But when I finally went to church there, the people were very friendly. They said, "Come and have coffee with us." Now that I am a member and serving as an officer I see that everyone is nice to newcomers. William, you were there serving as a priest shortly after I arrived there. There were several other fathers coming and going.

Yes, I have worked there off and on. The church is not yet able to hire a full-time priest so I am glad to help when I can. What about St. Luke's works for you?

Well, I have been there quite a while and have enjoyed being asked to take on certain responsibilities, like I've represented St. Luke's at the Diocesan Episcopal Conventions in Baton Rouge. I went as a substitute—I could go and enjoyed it. It made me aware of the business of the church. It made me see that the church is larger than St. Luke's, so I saw the many different ways of being Episcopalian. There are many different beliefs!

At the convention, people from certain Episcopal churches think that St. Luke's should close. That these small churches that are not bringing real revenue in—how are they going to grow? That was one question. How will you make yourself relevant? "We (the large churches) are carrying you too much," they said. But then there was the complete opposite attitude—some people were from larger churches and they said they loved that the smaller churches were keeping on going.

Then, I saw the Bishop (Morris Thompson) in his role, and I respected him more. I saw him maintaining order like a judge, and reminding people about what the church is really about. I saw a really nice, socially aware part of him and you don't get to see that when he is just conducting a high worship service.

Bishop Thompson has always supported St. Luke's. So have the previous bishops that I have known. I brought retired Bishop Charles Jenkins to St. Luke's once when I was there; he was the bishop who confirmed you and a big supporter of St. Luke's. So, why is it so important to keep St. Luke's going, as a church, Nancy?

I like its history. It means a lot. I know it's a historically black church but even more, it is an historic church. It was one of the first Episcopal churches in the city.

The first Bishop in this diocese was Leonidas Polk. In 1855, before the Civil War he saw a need for a church for free people of color and certain slaves. But Nancy what draws you to the history of St. Luke's?

I like things that are established, so I like that St. Luke's Church is so old. That it's been here since 1855. That means it's not a flash-in-the-pan; that it's not an idea that one of my contemporaries who just decided: "I want to have something important and have people follow me." It's beyond that. I love that it's historic. I also appreciate that St. Luke's has evolved. It was established for freed people of color and for slaves. But now it's diverse. It has a lot of middle-class members.

Many members want St. Luke's to grow. That will bring about changes. You can't invite new people to be a part of it and not expect them to bring new ideas. I'm not sure I want to think about it—I just selfishly want it to remain the congregation it is! But, that's not realistic. I don't want it to become something I can't recognize. I know you always say, "People support what they help to create." And new people would want to help create St. Luke's in the future.

I like the stained-glass windows. The colors and the style . . . the people in the stained-glass pictures are brown and a sort of general color. You could read into them whatever you like. And they are colorful and well-designed. They don't have a lot of detail, but you can recognize the images. They remind me of European churches.

You will have to show me around St. Luke's. I love listening to people's stories but I don't know about art—I don't see what others see. I guess I am an ear person and not an eye person. I couldn't even tell you what is featured in the stained-glass windows.

I also like the garden space. I go there after church, and if the weather's nice, we end up talking in that little garden area. I've always liked the Episcopal services. I haven't yet memorized the worship, but it's always comforting—the words, prayers. I love the sameness of it, every Sunday, like the Episcopal church in Denver. And when the bishops confirm you and put their hands on your head, it's like the hands of the hands, of the hands, being passed on since Jesus laid hands on Peter.

I really like the music—we've always had great music at St. Luke's. There's an acknowledgment of our good singers in our choir, by the presentation of special programs from time to time. Like having a jazz musician come in for a particular Sunday—that's just lovely. There's a recognition of the arts. Maybe that is true in all Episcopal services. A recognition of just how the arts are a part of a higher power.

I wish that were true in every church. People demonstrate that at St. Luke's through the beautiful music—and it is a beautiful church. It is a place of art—art is a way we express our gratitude to God. What are your hopes for the future of the church?

Moving forward I hope St. Luke's stabilizes its financial situation. I know that's heavily on the minds of the vestry. I think they will figure it out. They are doing things to create revenue sources. I am sorry it is such a burden. I wish I could contribute more.

I want to support St. Luke's in whatever way I can—the last thing that's needed is for me to get in their way. Tell me more about your-self, Nancy. I'll help you out: Here's the theme of this new book of mine. Jesus is in the wilderness. And the angels minister to him. It's a rough place—forty days and forty nights. No food. Satan is after him. We are told in Mark's gospel that during this very rough time that the angels minister to Jesus. Can you talk about a wilderness experience you've gone through, and who were the angels that ministered to you?

My grandmothers are probably my angels. I had such an unstable child-hood—moving all around. I didn't recognize it at the time, but when I look and see the other people getting to stay in one place, I realized that I was not ad-justing well. But the consistent things in my life came from Louisiana. And both my mother's and father's families are from Baton Rouge. I had one grandmother who was from New Orleans and one who lived in Baton Rouge all her life.

Every summer we would have to be moving, but it would be arranged during the summer times. My father knew—I wasn't such a great student—that I would do better if I could finish the school year, and then move during the summer. So during the summer my sisters and I would be shipped to Lou-isiana most summers, so my parents could move the household goods. We would then meet them in the new house, wherever that was. So I spent a lot of summers with my grandmothers, and they were two *extremes*! One grand-mother (not faking it) was very religious. She went to church and read the Bible when she prayed.

The other grandmother had grown up in New Orleans. She liked Mardi Gras. She smoked cigarettes and would have a drink every day. She let me try her cigarettes (I know this sounds horrible). I learned that I really did not like cigarettes. She also let me have sips of her vodka and her wine. And I'm not an alcoholic nowadays, but her way of looking at the world was different from my other grandmother's. I loved them both. They were kind of my angels. They of-fered stability. They wrote to me when I was not with them. They would always tell me that I was from Louisiana—"You have a place, and it is Louisiana."

Tell me about your educational background. How did you go into library science?

I went to Howard University, in Washington, D.C. When I was in high school I didn't like school, so I didn't want to go on to college. I might have gone to Tacoma State, in Washington state, where I was living. But I didn't want to go to school—I wanted to join the Peace Corps or just go to California to hang out on the beach. I don't know why I thought that would be a good life! I was young. (laughs)

My cousin who is close in age to me—she went to Howard University. She was a freshman at Howard when I was a senior in high school and my parents sent me to visit her for a week. She was really enjoying her time in that college and my parents thought that it would help them convince me about college to spend time with her. And that worked. So, I went to Howard. I majored in speech-language pathology because that was my mother's profession. I really wanted to major in Art. But my dad didn't encourage that. He believed that if you major in Art you won't have a job. You have to pick a major that can get you a job. So I just chose something.

After I graduated I worked in an elementary school for two years as a speech therapist, in Washington state. I didn't care for it—it was OK, but I spent a lot of my time in the library with the school librarian. I would volunteer there, putting books away and also reading to the students. That fit more with my personality. That's when I decided to go to Clark-Atlanta University, in Georgia, for library school. I got my degree and have worked in libraries mostly after that.

I worked in public libraries after getting my library degree. That is hard work. First I was a children's librarian. In that situation you see a lot of things—in that situation you see that a lot of kids are neglected or they are just dropped off at the public library because the parents can't afford babysitters. So you end up in a way being a child-care provider—not officially, because legally you're not supposed to acknowledge that that is what you are doing. But it is happening. You can't help it.

When I went into working with teenagers and young adults they were interesting. It's like being a counselor sometimes because they need someone to talk to. Not officially; but they figure out that you are always going to be there so they start sharing with you. A lot of them have sad stories to tell. You just listen, and try to point them to places to get help. But you can't do much for them. Some of them follow your advice, and some of them don't. But I think I got burned out. It was sometimes overwhelming. I decided I wanted to be a librarian in an academic setting, because it wouldn't have that social-work aspect. To do that I had to get a second master's degree, a subject degree and a library-science degree.

But then I decided to do *what I wanted to do*—study art. To do that I went to Wentz, Austria. It's cheaper to go to school in Europe than it is to go to a university in the United States. The classes were largely in English. Wentz, Austria, is so bizarre, because that is where Adolf Hitler was from.

When I finished my degree I applied for jobs in the U.S. Early on, I was hired in New York City at the New York Public Library. I kind of burned out, and I left that job without having another job lined up. One day I decided that the city was just too much. I stayed then with my parents, in Zachary, Louisiana. I was actually thinking of living in Portland, Oregon, but I got the job at Xavier and at the same time I realized I liked certain aspects of living in Louisiana. It's quieter than New York City. I just needed to get away from the hustle and bustle.

So being here feels more like being home?

Yes, I have more friends here than I have had in a long time. People here are very friendly and open. They share information—they will share with you a good place to go and eat, or they will invite you to have coffee together. They are not closed and skeptical of everybody. New Yorkers are suspicious—they think that you're after something all the time. If you want to be around them, it's because you want something from them.

Meanwhile, how do you think we're doing with race relations in New Orleans, and overcoming our terrible history of racism?

It is changing. But I think we are uncovering things—I think we thought everything was OK, but with Hurricane Katrina, some difficult things happened. A lot of people who'd lived in New Orleans all their lives had to leave New Orleans for a time. Those were largely black people, I believe, or at least the ones I know of. Then, because of Katrina a spotlight hit our city and everybody got to look at it and they decided it was interesting. There's been an influx of newcomers from other parts of the country, from maybe more liberal parts of the country. They are bringing their money with them—that can be bad, because they're paying cash for homes in certain areas and seem to be pushing out poorer families.

But they are also bringing their liberal attitudes of: "We don't have an issue with race," they say. "We've worked with black and white people and all kinds of people and we're not going to get hung up on race. That's not our issue." So things changed for the worse and the better. Many of the students at Xavier are those who are coming back to New Orleans for school. We have students now who are from New Orleans and who evacuated to Texas and their parents never moved back. They've gone to these pretty good public schools in Texas. So they're smart, and their test scores are high, and they're capable of doing well at Xavier.

This is interesting because there are public school graduates from New Orleans who are not capable of doing the college work at Xavier. These students have to begin with remedial courses. But the kids from Texas schools— they are doing well. They are coming here because they know they were born here and maybe they miss something about it. They left when they were so young, it is amazing they still want to come back.

With all the craziness, New Orleans has a culture with so much to offer in different ways. Let me ask you this, how can we, whites and blacks, work together more to help racial justice further along to help New Orleans?

I think we're starting to do that work. I think you've been doing it. Well, beginning by requesting the justice system be changed. As it relates to incarceration, that's a big part of it. Also, I don't do drugs, but I know the city council just changed the law to say that people holding small amounts of marijuana will not be arrested but fined. I think things like that are helpful because only blacks were convicted when they got caught with something and white people were let go.

Right! Take Tulane, where young white students use marijuana all the time and are never arrested. Fortunately the city council and the state are changing on that issue.

Yeah. There's probably a bigger problem as to why people are smoking weed and such, but hopefully they are doing better. And you know, the taking down of the Confederate memorials is a good symbolic gesture on the part of the mayor, who is in favor of it. I'm not sure why there is such resistance to it. It is interesting though that most of the resistance is coming from people outside of New Orleans, outside of Orleans Parish. I don't know why they feel so strongly that they can come dictate to another parish what to do with statues and symbols. While New Orleans is a little behind other cities in regard to racism, we're catching up.

Thank you Nancy, for telling me some of your story.

Reaction:

I had to hold back my thoughts as Nancy talked. She said so much that I could relate to, especially in my role as an Episcopal clergy. I wanted to have more of a discussion of why she did not feel at home in my long-time home church, Trinity, New Orleans. Nancy said she stopped going to Trinity because she did not feel at home there. Over the last twenty-five years, several hundred Trinity members have taken part in Undoing Racism workshops sponsored by the People's Institute for Survival and Beyond [see chapter 5]. With headquarters in New Orleans, the People's Institute is thought by many to be the strongest group in the country that helps both whites and African Americans understand just how pervasive cultural/structural racism is.

So why would an especially attractive, fully committed, and engaging young Christian not feel at home in Trinity, *my* Trinity? I think maybe we at Trinity have concentrated so much on the underlying problem of institutional racism that we have neglected to find ways to make wonderful people like Nancy Hampton feel at home. On Sundays, there may be ten African Americans present (in a congregation of over 1,500) with most of those in the choir. Trinity is still learning, as I am still learning how to change what Dr. King called "the most segregated hour of the week." And most black churches I attend, like Christian Unity, no small church, are often, except for me, a hundred percent African American. In chapter 7, I do write about a small Episcopal church, St. John's in Kenner, outside of New Orleans, that is diverse in every way.

Then, of course, I wanted to stand up and applaud when Nancy said she could not, as a juror, sentence anyone to long prison sentences as "people do change."

And I was most interested in those things that make her feel at home at St. Luke's: its special and unusual history, its genuine friendliness, its "small church" atmosphere that makes its own witness, along with the larger Episcopal churches like Trinity. Finally, I value Nancy's understanding of racism—she is so thoughtful and loving and knows that God will help her stand when she is down.

Chapter Seven

Christian Unity Baptist Church

Christian Unity and I have been close friends since 1990 when Pastor Dwight Webster invited my church at the time, Trinity Episcopal, to join an emerging Industrial Areas Foundation (IAF) presence in New Orleans. Initiated by Saul Alinksy in the 1940s as a labor-driven, justice-seeking organization, the IAF's drivers now are faith communities. (As mentioned, Isaiah, described in chapter 3, and Micah, described in chapter 5, are also modeled on IAF.) Pastor Webster and I got to know each other through Ms. Linetta Gilbert, who was on the board of Agenda for Children, a strong statewide advocacy center that was housed at Trinity.

As I've said, we white liberals always want to get African Americans to join our justice efforts but usually don't think of joining theirs, so it was important that the black church invited the white church to join. Predictably, the partnership of Christian Unity (a citywide faith and justice leader) and Trinity Church (the largest Episcopal church in the state with a longtime community ministry) bore fruit. Twenty other faith communities joined the local IAF coalition, and we named ourselves the Jeremiah Group (aka Jeremiah), after the Hebrew prophet who sought to rebuild his nation.

Once Linetta Gilbert helped bring our two churches together through Jeremiah, we found many other ways to work with each other. In New Orleans, most candidates for public office say one thing in white churches and another in black churches. But when Christian Unity and Trinity came together, we would invite candidates to speak to members of both churches, and we would fill both sanctuaries. We then asked them to speak to questions that we, together, had prepared in advance but wouldn't give them until just before they appeared to speak. We'd ask them to think about the questions in the corners of the sanctuaries while Pastor Webster would offer a prayer loud enough for our guest candidates to hear, asking God to make sure that what our candidates promised to do, they would indeed do if elected.

Recently, I have been co-leading Bible studies with Pastor Webster on Wednesday evenings at Christian Unity. I often visit the church for their main Sunday service and am always invited to sit in the pulpit and sometimes asked to lead a prayer. In many black churches the pulpit is the entire front of the church where clergy and other church leaders, along with the choir, sit on a raised platform facing the congregation. They are always welcoming to me, even though I tell them that we Episcopalians are known as "God's frozen people."

In this chapter, after Pastor Webster introduces Christian Unity, and three of their longtime younger members tell some of their story: Linetta's daughter Ashleigh Gardere, a senior advisor to Mayor Mitch Landrieu, and Jarvis and Kelly Harris DeBerry. Besides being active at Christian Unity, Jarvis is the Deputy Editor of Opinion for the *New Orleans Times-Picayune;* Kelly is, among other roles, a poet. While Pastor Webster speaks of Justice and Beyond in this chapter—he is the co-moderator—Pat Bryant gives a much more detailed description in chapter 4.

On June 21, 2016, I met with Pastor Webster in his office and began by asking: "Pastor Webster, what do you want people to know about Christian Unity Baptist Church? Your church's special strengths, growing edges. I don't talk about weaknesses. Any special Biblical passages which you try to adhere to? And what do you want people to know about yourself?"

Rev. Dwight Webster, Ph.D., Senior Pastor: A Church that is Unabashedly Black and Christian

Pastor Webster: Christian Unity Baptist Church (CUBC) is located in downtown New Orleans, at 1700 Conti Street, about three blocks off of world-famous Canal Street. The location, right at the heart of the city, is a fortuitous one. We are on the Claiborne Corridor where new developments will bring in millions of dollars. We are located between two large, former housing developments, the Lafitte and the Iberville. Both so-called "projects" are being redeveloped and are now mixed-income.

We are Christian Unity *Baptist* Church—we are part of the Progressive National Baptist Convention. The Convention is going to celebrate its fifty-fifth annual session during August 6-12 (2016) here at the Hyatt Regency Hotel. So I am excited about that. The 2.5 million-member Progressive National Baptist Convention was founded in 1961 under the aegis of Rev. L. V. Booth of Cincinnati. It was started by black Baptist ministers who were looking for something more progressive than the black Baptist church was up to that point. It also became the Baptist Convention of Dr. Martin Luther King Jr. and the Rev. Gardner C. Taylor, who pastored Beulah Baptist Church in this city and then went on to pastor the Concord Baptist Church of Christ in Brooklyn for forty-two years. He was very well-known, highly respected, and played a prominent role in the religious leadership of the civil rights movement of the 1960s and beyond. (CUBC is also affiliated with the American Baptist Churches, USA, and the Lott Carey Foreign Mission Convention.)

Christian Unity Baptist Church celebrated its twenty-seventh anniversary recently. The members are here because they *want* to be here. Baptists are known to multiply (grow) by dividing! But we didn't grow out of a split, but rather got started because we were locked out of our former church by a small group who didn't want to be progressive. We met in various venues for quite a while—we are still grateful to the Franklin Avenue Baptist Church (pastored by Rev. Fred Luter, former president of the Southern Baptist Convention). We are even more grateful to Southern University at New Orleans—we met in the Brown Lecture Hall in the old science building. SUNO let us meet there often, for a minimal fee, until they had to renovate that building.

At one time the church had over two thousand members! We stopped counting individuals and started counting families—we had about 1,200 families. At one point we plateaued—several years before Hurricane Katrina. Then when the hurricane hit eleven years ago, our people were scattered all over the country.

But many of us were fortunate in being able to return to the city and to our church almost right away, because this building is elevated and the flood water damage to it was at a minimum. It is an adaptive re-use of a former bowling alley. It's had many other iterations over the years. It was a roller-skating rink at one time. We have members who in the past have bowled here and skated here. But there was also a nightclub here once, and a Bingo hall. Immediately before we acquired the building it was a concert venue for Blues concerts. Little did they know when they built their stage (proscenium) for the concert that it would become our pulpit, our choir loft, and the place where our baptismal pool would be.

We're both a gathered church and a community church. Community in the sense that we didn't just minister to the housing developments; we were part of them and they were part of us. We also had members from as far west as Laplace [thirty-five miles from New Orleans] and as far east as Slidell [twenty-five miles from the city]. Occasionally, we would have folk with us from across Lake Pontchartrain—the Mandeville and Covington area. But our data showed that the majority of members lived in New Orleans East. We had a fair number of members from Uptown. Also, New Orleans members came from the West Bank, from Seventh Ward and the Sixth Ward. Pre-Katrina we had a large contingent of professionals—teachers, preachers, doctors, and others. But we were also drawing in folk who were on food stamps. We were and still are a mass-class church. We have a broad base of people from the grass roots.

And we are part of several Councilmanic districts. Technically we are part of Tremé next to the French Quarter. We are part of Councilmanic District B; and there are two more districts that come together near where we are. The Lafitte Greenway—we are two blocks away from that new development. And we're close to Mid-City. We're a stone's throw away from the French Quarter, from Louis Armstrong Park, and Congo Square. I would say we are in the heart of the city!

You are indeed! How many families do you have now in the church?

The number of people who attend service (as opposed to those on the rolls) now is significantly smaller than before Katrina. Whether we had 2,000 plus people on the roles—the number who attended on a given Sundays was between 350 and 500. What we, post-Katrina, are seeing perhaps is 40 percent of attendance pre-Katrina. This is true of congregations around the city. There's an estimate that about 100,000 black residents of New Orleans who had to leave during the Storm never came back. We still have a trickle of people who come back to our city to live here again.

Talk about your stands on social justice.

We believe that social justice and evangelism are flip sides of the same coin. That's what the Bible teaches. They receive equal weight in the Bible in terms of what one should be *about*.

Many institutions have core values. We actually have two sets of core values. One is called Nguzo Saba-Kwanzaa values, of which there are seven: unity (*umoja*), self-determination (*kujichagulia),* collective work (*ujima*) and responsibility, cooperative economics (*ujamaa*), purpose (*nia*), creativity (*kuumba*), faith (*Imani).* Kwanzaa is celebrated between the day after Christmas and New Year's Day. One of our late and former church members, Dr. Morris F. X. Jeff Jr., gave us our seven R's: rhythm, religious life, respect, restraint, redemption, reciprocity, responsibility.

Yes, I knew Dr. Jeff, and I've supported what are the five Rs at Trinity, my home church, in TEEP—the Trinity Education Enrichment Program—and in similar church programs in Boston and at the Washington National Cathedral. The young people recite and talk about the five Rs every day they meet. The churches I have worked with omit rhythm and religious life, so that's why we are five and not seven.

When you come into our sanctuary you will see that we have banners derived from the Nguzo Saba that we embrace. And we have mottoes: there's an old, old saying I picked up when I was a child and I adopted it for this church—"There's no place like this place anywhere near this place, so this must be *the* place." The other motto is a little headier, and we adapted it for ourselves (we know other churches that have a variation of this)—"We are *unabashedly* Black and Christian." If you parse that, you can see what our self-defined identity is. We're not ashamed of the Gospel of Jesus Christ: the power of which is available to everyone who believes—to the Jew, the Greek, or the Gentile (Romans 1:16). But as born-again, blood-bought, baptized believers in Christ, we are black. We are sons and daughters of the African Diaspora, and as one of my professors told us as well as those who identify with us, we have room for those people who identify with us. We have room for what theologian James

H. Cohn called "ontological blackness."[1] Those are the people who may not have the melanin, *but* they've got everything else.

When we first established ourselves as a church, we were multi-racial, multi-ethnic, multi-generational, mixed classes. We didn't have a lot of the *other*. But people were coming to our church because we didn't apologize for being black.

And we are a gospel church. We know there is a movement that has become very popular called "The Full Gospel Church" and people would ask us if we were part of that movement—and I would reply to people, "No, we're whole gospel!" This comes from the Greek *hagios* and *holos*, meaning both *holy* and *whole*. We preach the Holy Bible to the whole community, to the whole person. And it is a holistic message we preach.

We are a gospel church in that the predominant music we sing is gospel music. We sing hymns, on occasion we sing anthems, but ordinarily we sing gospel. By that (I wrote my dissertation on this) I mean the twentieth-century music that emanates in large part from this area of the United States, with roots in jazz, spirituals, hymns, and several other forms of music. Gospel is a genre, a style, and a movement. That's the music that sustains us. But we will sing anything and embrace anything wholesome!

We've had the Louisiana Philharmonic Orchestra hold a public dress rehearsal here in our church so that we could make that kind of music available to our people. We've had Wynton Marsalis do a concert here. One of the most successful events was when we had Hannibal Lokumbe—our friend and our brother—who has written music honoring the pastor and the first lady, this church, other people associated with us, and civil rights figures.[2]

We've had groups come from Europe. We had a band from southern France. We've had a musical group from Denmark. We've had folk come from all over the world; this is why we say we're unabashedly who we are: To be pro-Black is not to be anti-anything except for what God says we shouldn't be. That's what we're about.

I try to provide for the church through Bible study and Christian education the best of whatever it is I've learned. Several of us clergy said to ourselves during seminary days: "We're not going to spoon-feed people. We're going to give them what we learned in seminary, so that they can rightly 'divine the Word of Truth' and not merely be indoctrinated." When we use that scriptural study, we rightly divine the Word of God.

We also embrace Matthew 25: "As you have done to the least of these . . . you have done unto me." And, "As you have not done to the least of these, you have not done unto me." We also hang our hat on the Great Commission in Matthew 28 ("Go therefore and make disciples of all nations, baptizing them in the name of the Father and of the Son, and of the Holy Spirit"). We hang our hat

1. From his book *A Black Theology of Liberation*

2. Lokumbe is a great American jazz trumpeter and composer.

on Luke 4:18, 19: "The Spirit of the Lord is upon me because he has anointed me to bring good news to the poor. . . ." All those we embrace. Even when we fast, we fast based on Isaiah: the acceptable fast that the Lord proclaims in Isaiah 58. Because again, it's not about just personal piety. The extension of that notion is—and here again we see evangelism and social action being flip sides of the same coin—what God has commanded us to do is to be concerned for the community. This is what Martin Luther King Jr. embraced as "the beloved community."

A funny thing happened in the teachings of our church. I was preaching out somewhere else one afternoon. As ministers are wont to do, on the drive back I wanted to get some feedback from my family, who had accompanied me. I asked, "What did you think about the worship service today?" There was silence for a time. Then one of my sons said, "There weren't any women in the pulpit today." Which means that my children see men and women together in the pulpit as normative. So I got a pat on the back, but it wasn't the one I was looking for.

Tell me about your clergy—the women and the men.

Pre-Katrina, at one time we had twenty-five or twenty-six associate ministers. We had five clergy couples (men and women who were married to each other), and the others were single. We have been blessed with folk from across the country, some of whom were seminary trained. We were blessed to have a New Testament scholar at one time, Dr. Demetrius Williams, who was from Milwaukee and has now returned. He was teaching at Tulane University. A great blessing! I could turn my Bible study over to him with complete confidence. [Dr. Williams is known for African American Biblical interpretations.] He is top-notch. We embrace other clergy like you—William; you can come and go with ease.

We also, before Katrina, had a very productive relationship with St. Francis de Sales (a nearby Roman Catholic Church) and a pastoral team that was there at that time. Sr. Addie Lorraine Walker, SSND, and Father Fernand J. Cheri III were there—he is now Auxiliary Bishop here in this archdiocese and she completed her Ph.D. and heads up the Sankofa Institute, at the Oblate School of Theology in San Antonio. Locally, we were part of Dr. Jeff's Sankofa Communiversity program, focusing on youth education, nutrition, community gardens, and integrational learning.

With St. Francis de Sales we had pulpit exchanges. Some of their members who were relatives of our members would fellowship with us, we would fellowship with them. They would come here for Maundy Thursday service. We just had a wonderful time. We reached out to AME churches and Episcopalians—just a wide range of folk, like The Living Witness Church of God in Christ on Oretha Castle Haley Boulevard. So we believe in ecumenicity—not the kind where they just mix everything together. That doesn't work out very well. But with our ministers, our ecumenicity does work well.

One of my longtime assistants was especially outstanding: Rev. Audrey

Jackson Johnson, a pediatric AIDS nurse and a nurse educator. Her husband Felix Johnson Jr. was the chairman of our Deacons Ministry. They did a wonderful thing in that they had a Bible study in their home for twelve years. When we formed our church, they folded their Bible study into our church. Audrey Johnson led the charge in so many things. I think we were the first church around here to have a human sexuality institute. We would teach young people and others about their bodies; we would ask, "What does God think about human sexuality?"

The other thing we pioneered was a Health Fair. Since then, many churches have had health fairs learning from our experience. We had doctors and nurses come in, and we saw hundreds of people. They said they wanted to give aid to the poorest of the poor. But the people who came to us were not the poorest of the poor, because *they* had access to green cards, etc. We found that the people who needed our services at the Health Fair were the working poor. They didn't make enough to be able to afford health insurance; but they made too much to have indigent care. So when it came to kids going to school who needed shots and all those things, and their parents dealing with hypertension and diabetes—they didn't have the wherewithal to get care. Our Christian Unity Health Fair kicked off that community consciousness. We have extension programs to this day—nutrition, healthy lifestyle teaching, and a little bit of exercise. We partner with the McFarland Institute here in town (a Baptist Community Ministry program that teaches spiritual and physical healing).

Has the congregation been supportive of your support of Planned Parenthood?

I am supportive; and my assistant Dr. Kevin V. Stephens, MD, JD (former Health Director of the City of New Orleans) is openly supportive of Planned Parenthood. I am not the poster boy, and you will not see me carrying a poster supporting abortion, but we have referred many, many persons to Planned Parenthood over the decades. I am a direct beneficiary of Planned Parenthood! When Trudell and I got married in Berkeley, California, years ago, we went to a clinic that had a Planned Parenthood connection. When I started counselling, Planned Parenthood was the only place I could send an expectant mother *and* father to get family planning. It was *Planned Parenthood*—exactly what the name stands for.

I believe that over the years, Planned Parenthood has made a big contribution reducing the need for abortion. It keeps these women and some men from having to make sometimes terribly difficult decisions.

Because of what they do! I've had a girl come in to talk with me who was in her third trimester of pregnancy and had not had pre-natal care of any kind.

I got her to go to Planned Parenthood, and she got the care that she need-ed. She was not counseled to do this or that. She was counseled to take care of herself. That's what we should be doing. It's not so much that the congrega-tion says to me, "We champion your support of Planned Parenthood." They trust my judgment. They trust the information of my clergy assistant Dr. Stephens, who is an Ob-Gyn and delivered my fourth son! Between Rev. Audrey John-son (a pioneering Baptist woman preacher and an AIDS nurse, now deceased) and Dr. Stephens, an obstetrician/gynecologist, the congregation knows that I understand the scientific reasons why certain procedures are warranted. Now we're not talking about the capricious actions of the immature, or people who just don't want this or that. We're talking about life-threatening issues. So, I will stand with Planned Parenthood. But I wish that they would create a space where *other* clergy who have trouble with the organization can stand. We will support Planned Parenthood; we just can't say that we are banner-carriers for abortion.

Now on Justice and Beyond: You and Pat Bryant have given so much energy and time and talent to Justice and Beyond; I focus on it in an earlier chapter. I have come to realize that Justice and Beyond is probably the strongest voice for African Americans in the city, and from my experience in several other states, a good model for all black leaders and the people they represent. Well over a hundred attend most Mondays.

Pat Bryant came to me and said that a coalition of this nature would be able to accomplish things that heretofore were lacking. We could provide a platform in the context of the church that would address critical issues in the city. He had to convince me; I had something else planned for the Monday evenings when Justice and Beyond meets. Also, I insisted that we follow up the Monday evening meetings with a planning meeting on Tuesdays. He brought to the table his fifty-year experience in civil rights work, particularly in tenant organizing across the South. He has a very wide experience. He is the son of a minister and one who is very knowledgeable and familiar with the law and what can be done with it.

Initially we tried to move it around from venue to venue: From UTNO—United Teachers of New Orleans—we tried to move it to the West Bank, to Rev. Cassimere's Love Outreach Christian Center. We tried to move it around, but we kept meeting at Christian Unity Church because this place is so easily accessi-ble and accommodating.

And welcoming.

And welcoming. I am not exactly sure how we came to the starting time of 4:45 p.m.—we knew that people would be getting off work, or picking up children from child care, or whatever. We knew we had to provide a hot meal, whether it was in the winter or summer season. We never knew who was going to come, and whether they would need something to eat. We weren't going to set a prerequisite—that you have to listen first to a song or a sermon. But, queue up and we'll feed you. We went to the staple of red beans and rice and of course rotisserie chicken.

Has the church been proud of Justice and Beyond?

I think they've become proud of what we are able to do. Justice and Beyond started because Justice Bernette Johnson was trying to obtain her rightful due—to ascend to the office of Chief Justice of Louisiana's Supreme Court. [She is African American.] In the process of meeting, other issues and concerns appeared. Slowly but surely our church members began to ask, "What is this about?" They would sit in and see that something was developing. At first I was doing the running around, getting food and so on. But gradually my staff and members saw that this was something benefitting the church, so they relieved me of much of the chore. People from Justice and Beyond began to join the church. They picked up the foodstuff. They started to serve. They saw a clear benefit for our church.

The two principles that we established were justice and righteousness, which means "right-relatedness." We saw that from the major religions (Christianity, Judaism, and Islam), we would be able to offer and embrace those two pillars. And even people who say they are agnostic or don't believe in God are welcome. We are always going to open with a prayer and bless the food at a quarter of five. And on or before 7:00 p.m. we are going to close with a prayer [in a growing large circle] from a Baptist, a Unitarian Universalist, a Muslim, a Roman Catholic, or sometimes even from a good Episcopalian!

In the past when certain groups would try to hold a forum on a particular issue, there would be some folks who could come and would dominate the meeting and keep others from contributing. I took the authority that I have here as the Pastor to set some ground rules. We would get as many voices in as possible during the Q and A part of our meeting to allow questions and comments. The coalition agreed.

And you do succeed in moving the discussion around.

I do have to, from time to time, be forceful or resolute—you can't ask four questions at one time. You can't talk for ten minutes. We need to hear as many voices as possible. Black and white, young and old. Fight for $15 minimum wage. Take 'Em Down NOLA[3] University Women—we have a wide array of viewpoints. You can't engage in character assassination. You can't use profanity. I will shut the meeting down if necessary. The idea behind that is that using violent language gives way to physical violence. So by following the first rule

3. Meaning the Confederate flags and monuments

you are less likely to have to deal with physical violence. It is out of respect of the Lord's House. I tell them, "I wouldn't go into your house and cuss; so why would you cuss in my house of worship?"

When the newcomer, or someone who doesn't know the rules, or someone who gets over-excited—those kinds of ejaculatory things slip out. But if you try to repeat that kind of thing or intensify it—rabble-rousing—we're not going to have that.

What growing edges does Christian Unity Church have?

I'm going to take a risk, William, and say, I would like to have this whole block as Christian Unity. We've had some good neighbors and some not-so-good. We have had discussions with businesses in this area, with store-owners who've moved out—if there is some way that we could acquire the facilities of those who have left. What we would do is make it a full-service space. In short, we would make it a Family Life Center, a recreation center. Multiple spaces where we can have events of various kinds—concerts, lectures. That's what we would do for this area. If we could sneak a pool in there, we would.

Recreation and after-school activities?

Definitely. We would make it a literacy center with reading, but also computer literacy. We would be offering it to the wider community. With the multiple-income groups coming in as the housing developments are re-done, we would connect with the schools and churches in our neighborhood. Somebody once said, ask God to do something that's just too big for you as an individual to do. That would be my *ask*: We're going to ask God to work with us on it. We couldn't do it ourselves financially, but we have to find a way to bargain!

You want to be surprised by grace.

Yes, and the way the Claiborne Corridor is developing we would be in a prime position. We would be making a witness for ourselves and our families: where we would have not just one gender-headed family but families in every configuration.

You have very strong lay leadership here, who can make something like that happen.

We have some of the best leaders in the city! Job developers, consultants. There are physicians, lawyers, city planners, government workers. And we have just regular people who are really, really smart and know how to get things done. Business minds. They are just regular, everyday people who know how to get things done. And that comes from the mass-class nature of this church.

Thank you, Pastor Webster, and what else do readers of my book need to know about Christian Unity or you?

That this church is pastored by a minister who loves his wife, Trudell, and who loves our four children—all of whom are adults now.

That I try to use everything I have ever learned to be a leader in this city and this church. My undergraduate major in college was Math; I minored in French. I went to Howard University, which changed my whole perspective on the world. Some of the best teaching takes place there because it's from a global, and not just a Western, perspective. It's black, but it is the way black is in the *world*, not just in this country. I did my seminary training at Colgate Rochester Crozier Divinity School. Dr. Martin Luther King went when it was in Pennsylvania. I learned theology from a social gospel perspective. Howard Thurman graduated from Rochester.[4] When I graduated and went to California, I attended the Pacific School of Religion in Berkeley and benefitted from all that training. I wrote my PhD dissertation on gospel music and themes of survival, liberation, and elevation [the word means what it says]. I drew them from Gayrand Wilmore, from his book: *Black Religion, Black Radicalism*. Also, I am grateful to the Rev. Dr. Archie Smith Jr. who saw me through my doctoral work.

Reaction:

I know not all readers will appreciate all of the detail Pastor Webster gives, like the names of the various teachers he mentions and the organizations Christian Unity is part of, but when I asked him to talk about his church, that's how he told the story. And it is a very important story for the people in New Orleans and I think everywhere. *And*, it is the particulars of Christian Unity that have made the church a home for Jarvis, Kelly, Ashleigh, and many other young people.

I appreciate all of the ways Christian Unity strives to pastor their people, and at the same time serves the larger community, challenging us all when justice issues are at stake, especially through Justice and Beyond. I also appreciate how both clergy and laypersons are grounded in their Scriptural faith. As much as I enjoy visiting Christian Unity—as an Episcopalian, I would miss our liturgy and the Communion that we celebrate every Sunday. And as a white person, I am not sure how comfortable I would be long-term in a church that is "unabashedly Black." I appreciate the necessity of what Pastor Webster calls their "self-identity." Were an historically white church to call itself unabashedly white, it would rightfully be called "racist." But by claiming the beauty of blackness in a society that still discriminates, for many African

4. Thurman (1899-1981) was a major leader in many social justice movements.

Americans the black self-identity is a necessity. For now, I do feel accepted despite my lack of melanin.

Still, I hope the day is not too far off when all of us will unabashedly call ourselves just people! I have served many months at St. John's Kenner (a small Episcopal church in a New Orleans suburb) that may be showing the way. The congregation is the most integrated Episcopal church I know—not just black and white, but Spanish and English speaking, with young and older members, and with people of means and those barely surviving. But the best thing about St. John's is how they view themselves: They don't even think of themselves as diverse.

Once at a vestry (board) meeting, I said to the eight or nine people there, "I sure appreciate the diversity here." The senior warden looked baffled. "William," he said, "what do you mean by diversity?" I hope the day is coming when our churches, like St. John's, will take our diversity for granted. No longer would it occur to someone like Martin Luther King to speak on how Sunday morning is the most segregated time of the week.

One of my readers said he wished I had brought up the "unabashedly black" versus "the taken-for-granted-diversity" issue with Pastor Webster. I'll have my chance, as he and I will be co-leading another Bible study this fall at Christian Unity, this time on the Book of Genesis. I love to quote Scripture to the participants—me, the non-doctrinal, Biblically vague Episcopalian and "them," the learned Bible-quoting Baptists. "So, Pastor Webster," I'll say, "When God created the man and the woman in the divine image, was either of them unabashedly black? Tell me. Genesis 1, verse 26."

I didn't think to ask Pastor Webster about his "angels in the wilderness" experiences, but last fall in the same Bible course, I asked each member of the group who their angels in the wilderness were. Pastor Webster told two stories of how white farmers in the rural South helped him out when his car would go no further—white angels!

━━ ━━ ━━ ━━ ━━ ━━ ━━ ━━ ━━ ━━ ━━ ━━ ━━ ━━ ━━ ━━ ━━

Jarvis DeBerry:
A Justice Voice for All of New Orleans

As the lead-columnist and deputy opinion editor for the leading newspaper in New Orleans, the *Times-Picayune*, and a deacon at Christian Unity, Jarvis is highly respected locally and nationally. He and I have known each other since before Hurricane Katrina. In fact we were two of the six volunteers who "gutted" Pastor Webster's house after it was badly flooded by the Storm. (I remember tearfully throwing out soggy sermons that went back many years.)

Jarvis graduated from Washington University in St. Louis with a degree in English literature. Throughout his career, he has been recognized regionally and nationally for his work. For his coverage of Hurricane Katrina in 2005, he was awarded the Pulitzer Prize for Public Service. His wife Kelly, who tells her story next, is a beloved poet. You can almost see their four-year-old-daughter, Naomi, in some of her writing and some of his.

Jarvis has helped me get several op-eds published, and on occasion he mentions me. Here is one of Jarvis's recent columns (June 18, 2016), in which he refers to a Bible study Pastor Webster and I led at Christian Unity that he and Kelly participated in. While this particular discussion was about race, mostly we talked about Mark's Gospel and told our personal stories. And in good humor, we argued about whether the Baptistic interpretation of various passages was right or whether we the chosen frozen were right.

"How can you Episcopalians not talk about being saved before we die?"

"Well, how can you Baptists talk about a God who would desert us just because we stop breathing? By the way, we don't like the word saved anyway. We are all eternally loved!"

Of course I felt proud and humbled that Jarvis would write the following, and I can't think of a better way to use my limited space for some of his storytelling.

Several months ago at a Wednesday night Bible study at Christian Unity Baptist Church, the Rev. William Barnwell—an Episcopal priest—led a study of "The Welcome Table," a short story by Alice Walker. There was great significance in Barnwell, who is white and from the South, discussing that story at a mostly black church. Walker's story, published in 1967, concerns an elderly black woman in the rural South who walks through the doors of a white church only to be promptly put outside. It is after she is expelled that she sees—or thinks she sees—Jesus and she walks toward him when he beckons.

Martin Luther King Jr. often called out the ungodly separation of black and white Christians. In 1963 he told a group of students, "At 11:00 on Sunday morning when we stand and sing that Christ has no east or west, we stand at the most segregated hour in this nation." Walker's story lays the blame for that division at the threshold of white churches.

Even though I appreciated her story for getting to the heart of the matter, I figured that in having a decrepit black woman be physically removed from a church Walker was employing the kind of exaggeration common to fables.

But then a deacon at my church [during that session] spoke of arriving in New Orleans in the late 1960s to attend Dillard University. He walked with friends to a nearby Baptist church to worship. They weren't allowed inside.

I never had an experience like the woman in Walker's story or like the deacon at my church. I grew up not even attempting to enter white churches, especially not ones affiliated with the Southern Baptist Convention. I figured they were filled with the same folks who had started their own schools rather than send their children to school with me. I couldn't imagine their churches being any more welcoming than their academies.

Things have changed and are yet changing with the Southern Baptists. In 2012, as they were poised to elect Franklin Avenue Pastor Fred Luter as their first black president, I told my aunt—a woman with as many years as the woman in Walker's story—that I admire Luter and like his church but that I remained wary of Southern Baptists.

"But you know?" she said. "They're trying."

In 1995, at the sesquicentennial of the convention, the denomination issued a statement acknowledging that "our relationship to African Americans has been hindered from the beginning by the role that slavery played in the formation of the Southern Baptist Convention. . . . Many of our Southern Baptist forbears defended the right to own slaves, and either participated in, supported, or acquiesced in the particularly inhumane nature of American slavery. . . . In later years Southern Baptists failed, in many cases, to support, and in some cases opposed, legitimate initiatives to secure the civil rights of African Americans."

Racism, that document confessed, "has divided the body of Christ and Southern Baptists in particular, and separated us from our African American brothers and sisters. . . . Many of our congregations have intentionally and/ or unintentionally excluded African Americans from worship, membership, and leadership."

June 17 marked one year since Dylan Roof slaughtered nine people at a Bible study at Emanuel AME Church in Charleston, S.C. The state of South Carolina responded to the attack on the black church by removing the Confederate battle flag from the grounds of its State House. On Tuesday, the Southern Baptists responded to that tragedy by also taking a stance against the flag.

The Rev. Dwight McKissic, a black man who pastors Cornerstone Baptist Church in Arlington, Texas, proposed the resolution opposing the Confederate battle flag. "You can't take something that is contaminated and make it innocent," McKissic told *The Washington Post* before Tuesday's vote. "I think to honor those nine people in Charleston that were killed, surely you can repudiate what drove Dylan Roof to kill those folks. You say to the black community, we identify with your pain. We share your pain."

The denomination approved a resolution noting that the flag "is used by some and perceived by many as a symbol of hatred, bigotry, and racism" and that it "offend[s] millions of people. . . . We call our brothers and sisters in Christ to discontinue the display of the Confederate battle flag as a sign of solidarity of the whole Body of Christ, including our African American brothers and sisters."

Russell Moore, who leads the denomination's Ethics & Religious Liberty Commission, later wrote on his blog, "the Cross and the Confederate flag cannot co-exist without one setting the other on fire." His allusion to a cross on fire cannot be accidental.

The deacon who was turned away from a New Orleans church remembers shrugging and saying, "God ain't in there." That's the importance of these changes. When the Southern Baptists apologize for their racism and repudiate racist symbols, it's not just black folks they're welcoming.

Reaction:

Other than being proud of Jarvis's mention of our Bible study, I always appreciate the way he makes the case against racism and for people, for all of us! Since he is Baptist—though with Christian Unity, a Progressive Baptist—he focuses on how much the wider Baptist church needed to learn in order to make all people, even Jesus, welcome. If I were telling the story, I would be talking about just how far we Episcopalians have had to go and the journey ahead of *us*. But like the Baptists—in the words of Jarvis's aunt—"we are trying." A New Orleans African American, the Rev. Fred Luter, was the President of the Southern Baptist Convention, as Jarvis mentions. And just this last November (2015) another African American minister, Bishop Michael Curry, became the Presiding Bishop of our national church.

I also appreciate how Jarvis often relates his own story to the great issues of the day.

■ ■ ■ ■ ■ ■ ■ ■ ■ ■ ■ ■ ■ ■ ■ ■ ■ ■ ■

Kelly Harris DeBerry, a Poet: Her Struggle and Her Sustaining Faith of Love and Justice

Kelly avoids using DeBerry as her last name because those who get angry with her husband because of his columns—both African American and white—want to "take it out" on her. Jarvis does not hold back when he believes black leaders as well as white leaders are in the wrong.

I have gotten to know Kelly through the Christian Unity Bible Study and through her lovely poetry in her CD "Revival Poems," many set with music in the background. All of her poems grow out of her strong faith, but many are not obviously Christian. One of my favorites, printed with her permission, follows her story. In the Bible study, Kelly mostly listened (and listened well!) so I was glad to hear more about her "liberating faith." We met in our living room on July 20, 2016, and after telling her about the Angels project, I asked her what she wanted people to know about her most of all.

Kelly: I'm a believer. I'm a believer of Christ. I think that's important to say first and foremost. Beyond being a wife, daughter, mother, all those

Kelly Harris DeBerry, singing poet and
active member of Christian Unity Baptist Church

things. I was just at the Alton Sterling funeral in Baton Rouge.[5] It was this moment of discovering what it means to be a believer, sitting at this funeral, hearing various preachers talking. The full gamut: from the Nation of Islam to the most Baptist preacher you could think of. And I was just sitting with the things we, as African Americans, toil with and are encountering these same injustices. How do we sit with our belief in Christ? And it was especially interesting because the minister from the Nation of Islam really got the crowd excited. And really pushed the crowd to what they wanted us to think and feel. So on one hand there was this "We Want Justice" theory, and nothing else will do. And then there was on the other hand "Jesus is going to fix it," which we've been telling ourselves forever. And they're both true and . . . well, and we are still waiting, you know.

So I sat there with that, thinking about how people become radicalized. How do people turn from faith? Not just from Christian faith but from general faith in that things are going to get better. I sat there, still, throughout everything believing and trusting that God is a God of love and justice. I have to believe that, because if I'm going to be a believer, I have to stay steadfast in that. Otherwise, we open ourselves up to abiding by whatever we feel at

---

5. He was a much beloved African American man shot and killed by a police officer on July 5, 2016, many believe unnecessarily. Thousands have protested his killing in New Orleans as well as Baton Rouge, including me.

that moment. Or cynicism! So, that's the first thought that comes to my mind. When I say I'm a believer, it's not a cliché statement. It's a difficult task to be a believer. It's not some cool thing, like something I use to rep myself. Like, "I'm a believer, and you're so bad," or something like that. But at the core of me, no matter what has happened in my wilderness moments, that I'm sure we'll get to, I still believe. I still believe.

Talk about how this belief gives you love and a way to look for justice, but how is it a struggle for you.

It's a struggle because life is so uncertain. It's a struggle because I'm human. It's a struggle because us black folks have been waiting so long for justice. It's a struggle because I'm flawed. All of those things, and you put that all together and it really creates tension, for me at least, to believe sometimes. And I still struggle. But even if I take race out of it, it's still challenging. We've had health challenges in our family. My mom, my sister . . . financial challenges growing up in Cleveland, Ohio. And you know, it's interesting for me to watch this RNC going on now (in Cleveland), as a native Clevelander. To see convention places on TV where I know that just around the block is a poor, struggling area. And to have all that power and wealth concentrated in that one area of Cleveland is really interesting for me to witness. And the dichotomy of that with the Cavs (the Cleveland Cavaliers basketball team) winning the championship shows how the energy in the city can shift so fast from sports to politics. Just seeing what that does to Cleveland and us. *So* it's just interesting to see that. I've had struggles in my own beliefs. And you know college, I think, for many Christians and young people is where you can hit a wall.

I remember I was at Kent State University in Ohio for undergrad. I dated this guy who started to get really interested in the Hebrew Israelites. And they would come to campus and were in the Pan-African studies building. And so initially they just seemed like they were trying to raise awareness for African history, and there was some good in it. I did feel like I really had to make some choices about whether I would go full-fledged into their belief system since I had such a firm Christian foundation. You know, I'm not sure entirely what they were about, but the Hebrew Israelites believed things like black people were the first Jews, and there was some real tension with the modern State of Israel. But I'm really not comfortable trying to say everything they believe because I don't want to misrepresent them.

What was the conflict for you then?

Part of it was that I was like, okay, here I am. Is it that I've been trained so long to be a Christian that I can't think of anything else, or is it that my Christian faith is so strong and steady that it blocks me from leaning away from the faith? So that was interesting in college, and that was the first time I was really challenged in my faith. Because they were telling us that Christianity was the slave religion and the white man's religion and all those things. And at that time I was really interested in learning about black culture and began to see how people can be radicalized. Eventually, the guy I was dating got disinterested with them, and I really needed to remove myself from those events. I didn't feel safe enough in my own beliefs to stay there. But it also made me realize how much more I needed to study the Bible because I really couldn't articulate what I was trying to defend, other than my momma and my grandmamma and my grandpa went to church all their lives. And for the Hebrew Israelites that was proof that I was still enslaved.

Wow. That's interesting. Let me ask you this, how did your strong belief in Christ develop as a younger person?

Uh, well gosh. I've never not known church. I was born in the church. My father was an associate minister in the church I grew up in, the Church of God in Christ or, as they say, COGIC (a Pentecostal denomination). We were in church all day, all night. It didn't matter if I had to go to school, if I was sleepy, if I was hungry. We were there. And I remember being afraid one time that God was going to get me. I think I was seven or eight. And my mother told me I couldn't have another cookie. And I snuck and got a cookie. I was so afraid that night that I would go to Hell. I was so convicted about this chocolate cookie. And it was really, really frightening. I knew I was going to hell for eating this cookie. And I look back on that now, and I think it was unhealthy fear. And I was taught to fear the Lord. And it really shaped me to the core. It kept me out of trouble.

I grew up in East Cleveland, Ohio, which is maybe ten minutes from downtown. It was once an all-white neighborhood. My grandparents had moved there. You see, my grandfather worked for Chevrolet. And he worked hard, and my mother was a housekeeper for a hospital. And they eventually saved enough to buy a property in this well-to-do neighborhood that was once all white. And then white flight happened and the neighborhood really turned. And it turned bad. And it was scary.

There was crime. And at that time there were a lot of young people getting killed. That was at the time of the Michael Jordan tennis shoes and the Starter jackets and that's when people were getting killed for their stuff. That kind of thing. It was just a rough neighborhood. And there are people I grew up with who are dead now. Some were murdered, and a few murdered in areas we'd grown up and played in. And so I was always just afraid. At that time, there was this big deal, in our neighborhood at least, about girls getting pregnant. And like that was a big thing for me. I was like I could not get pregnant. I would not get pregnant. It was such a shame to a family and to a church.

And I knew from an early age I wanted to do something big or different. I just didn't know what that thing was. But that fear of God always kept me in check. So the cookie was kind of hysterical and blown out of proportion in my mind, but it was also very good because that kind of thing kept me out of trouble. And I remember growing up, that before school or going out or anything, my parents would not allow us to leave the house without praying over us for safety. And we had to say our prayers. And my grandmother was big in the church. Even as a little girl, if it was my birthday and she gave me ten dollars it was "Happy birthday, but don't forget the Lord! You owe him ten percent of that ten dollars." So the concept of tithing and all these things were ingrained in me at a very young age. And many of the older church people would take me aside, and I found myself hanging out with older people. And my grandmother especially. I can see her kitchen with the Bible being open, and reading and praying from it. And I would go to the grocery store to help her. And she would just start praising God out loud, sometimes in the grocery store. And I remember it was so embarrassing at that time for me to have my grandmother thanking God in your heart for these groceries. And I mean like she would really start praising God about it. It was embarrassing.

But I get it better now. I understand it now a lot better than I did at that time. The church really shaped me. Both in good ways and bad ways. My parents wound up divorcing, and that was really frightening because it wasn't as acceptable in the church as it is now. I remember us being talked about. And I remember my mother not being able to teach Sunday School anymore. And I remember my father still able to do things and my mother not. I didn't have the language for what was happening but that was devastating because I was a daddy's girl. And that really broke up the whole foundation of our church. Because after they split, I wound up going, for the first time, to a Baptist Church, which was a shift in culture for us. But my mother couldn't go back to COGIC. She was dog tired and ridiculed.

So, the initial church that I grew up in was Community Temple of Church of God in Christ. Which I remember on a day like today: If it was hot in the summer, you could pull into the parking lot and hear the church happening. And you know, we would go in teams and pass out tracts. And this was as a little girl. And it was frightening to me to go up to people's doors and knock on their doors and tell them about Jesus. And it was frightening, especially with the neighborhood we were living in. There were actually a lot of things that were frightening to me. But, we were Christians so we had to do these things.

There seems to be a lot of love for you coming through in all of this.

Yes, I'd say so. And that transition to a Baptist Church in high school was very different. Church was very structured. And it was more academic in many ways. And my pastor was very good. And my father probably would not like me to say this, but I think that I learned how to be a Christian and learned more about Christianity at the Baptist church under this pastor than I did all those years before. I credit Pastor Eddy L. Hawkins for a lot of who I am.

It sounds like he was an angel in the wilderness for you. Yes?

Yes, and to your question I would say that sometimes angels are our ancestors. Well, I know there is African traditional belief in that. And I say that because there are times I can almost hear my grandmother's voice. She used to always say, "Whatever you ask in faith, he'll grant in grace." And all these little sayings that she used to have about church or being a Christian, I still feel those today. I still feel connected to the people who are gone on before me, if that makes sense.

You're talking about angels in your ancestry, as in people who you didn't even know. Can you talk more about that? I think that's so important.

My grandmother, Willie Eva Harris, was from Alabama. And when she died, I was asked to do a poem at her funeral. I think I was a sophomore in college. And a relative who I'd never met before was a cousin of hers. You know when you have these funerals, people pop up who you've never met or never heard of. And once my grandparents migrated north, they didn't go back south much. That was their life, and they had to make it in the North. And that was the catch for many people. So people sometimes only reconnected once there was a death; they would come up from the South to check up on folks and things like that. So, I did the poem, I still have it somewhere, but this cousin who I had never met said to me, "Granny has come back through you."

And he was talking about my grandmother's mother, who wanted to be a poet. And they described her as a small, tiny powerhouse who would recite poems in the living room to the kids. Who would recite poems in church except she wasn't allowed to do that much because she was a woman. But she could recite like nobody's business. She loved poetry. And so it sent chills all over me. And to finally be able to make the connection. Like, nobody in my family knew where my poetry came from. It was just assumed I was an outlier. But at that moment I found it. It was like, there it is!

An angel you didn't ever know!

Right. And as a poet, I felt like I was the manifestation of this great-grandmother that I never met. That sometimes the dream is planted, but it is fulfilled later. So I think about her a lot. Even when I'm at Christian Unity and I'm allowed to read my poetry and just how my great-grandmother may not have been able to stand in the pulpit and do that. I'm still not comfortable with it standing in the pulpit. Sometimes the pastor will ask me to come up in the pulpit and talk and I'm like ehh . . . I'm not comfortable with that. I'd rather be off to the side. And I don't know if it's angelic or if it's just a seed, planted, and you never know when it will bloom. Just like Dr. King said, "I may not get there with you."

But I have a vision of that Promised Land, he said. And he showed us which way to walk, towards it.

Right. And I don't want to say I'm in the Promised Land. But I think there are things like that in our families that are spiritual redemptions and spiritual manifestations that are connected to those who have come before us. That gives me strength and makes me feel very purposeful. I have to be very intentional about what I do. Pastor Webster has been asking me to build a poetry program at the church, but I've been slow about it. I find it difficult to poet in church the same way I poet outside of church, because I feel that the call is so much greater in the church, and I'm very careful about what I say and how I present it. And I always have to ask myself: Have I heard from Heaven with this poem to give it to the church? Have I been inspired in a way of conviction to make this go right?

This is versus when I'm asked to speak at Dillard [a university in New Orleans]. I can rely on my creativity and my master's degree to present there. But when I'm in the church, I'm required by God to have a higher level. So that has been part of why I've been so slow about starting the poetry program at Christian Unity. If he asked me to do a poem every week, I could do that because I've been trained and I, well, have the talent. But I don't always believe that talent is the be-and-end-all. Especially in church, I think we confuse talent with—for lack of better phrasing—anointing. As a person who's grown up in the church all my life and seen many things, I've seen many talented people who have the spirit of Christ in them. They can play the organ really well, or they can direct the choir really well, or they can even preach really well. But it's not enough if the spirit at the core of it is tainted. So I'm very conscious of that and even if I get up there in the front of the church, I'm not perfect. And I try really hard when I'm doing poetry in church to be conscious of it as ministry not as art.

But one of these days ministry and art are going to come together!

Yeah, and I shouldn't separate them. But I do in my mind. But some of that is back to my roots and disciplining. Even the pastor that I went to after COGIC was a former Marine, and there was an obedience and structure to the church that was very factory like. That's how I think of it. Very . . . This is your place, this is what you do, this is how you behave.

Talk some more about Christian Unity.

It's the first church experience I've had where the pastor is physically accessible. And what I mean by that is: Growing up, children could not go in the pulpit.[6] You didn't bother the pastor unless you really needed him. He was

6. The raised front stage of the church facing the people

busy. He had things to do. He needed to hear from God. So you didn't shoot the breeze with the pastor unless you really knew him or needed him. Church of God in Christ is really strict. And even later at the Baptist church, the pastor came in shortly before it was time to preach. He was ushered in—you know how ushers bring the minister in—and he preached and then, most times, was back in his office. There was no hanging out amongst the people.

And Pastor Webster hangs out?

Yeah, and so I think Pastor Webster may think I'm strange.

Pastor Webster? No, no...

I don't know, but I still struggle with proximity to a pastor in that way. I don't know how to explain it. I don't know what to do. I see people hugging Pastor Webster in Christian Unity. And I don't remember getting hugs from a pastor. I don't know what that's like. I don't know if I'm out of place or if I should embrace it. There is a whole history of correctness in the church for me. So I don't know how to act when there's downtime in the church or in social situations. I'll see people hanging out with Pastor, laughing or talking. It's hard for me to know what's safe and not, what's appropriate or not. Because in my mind, he's Pastor or *the* pastor. So that has been a real transition for me. I haven't been in a church with that many women ministers in the pulpit either. That has been really different for me.

I should say that I got my wings as a poet in the church. We always, always, always had Easter speeches. And my dad, to his credit, always saw something extra special about me. So he would make me do an Easter speech and quote a Scripture. An Easter speech and name the twelve disciples. An Easter speech and whatever. And so it was like "Oh God, why do I have to do all this extra?" And you know, it created tension between me and other kids in the church. But I had to do what my father said even though I didn't want to be doing that or be shown off. So at times I found myself retreating from my own gift. And I still find myself doing this sometimes. Because I'm still fighting the past.

Well, my hope for you, Kelly, is that you stop this fighting the past and continue to move forward. And be aware that you're already appreciated! But you understand that.

I'm just saying that about the past to say how all of that connects and that I'm very sensitive to people's church experience. Like when I see somebody doing something, I don't always jump to a conclusion because I don't know what that person's experience might have been. Because a lot of us are wounded Christians. And we're still walking the faith walk, but we've been wounded by that church family that we are a part of. So I try to be conscious of that. But all that to say that Christian Unity is a lot different. Even the Bible studies have been an adjustment for me because in my mind they are more academic Bible studies versus the way I've known it to be in the past when you get your shot in the arm and it's more inspirational. It's like mini-church. You know, you walk away with something to get you through the rest of the week. That's not to say our Bible studies don't do that, but it's more of a drill down study which was not necessarily the case in the past.

I was made a deacon lately. Jarvis has been a deacon, and Pastor wanted us to serve as a husband and wife team. But, to be honest, by the time I moved to New Orleans and got married, I felt "churched out." And I had been very busy in the Baptist church I came from. I had gotten really good training. And I was part of the education focus committee. We were giving out scholarships, working with the young people, and my pastor said he really saw something in me and told me he thought I could be a really good church leader. So he was bringing me in and throwing me into everything possible.

When I got to New Orleans, I just wanted to be married and not all this other stuff. That was my initial feeling. I didn't know anybody at Christian Unity really, and even though they were embracing me, I wasn't ready for that. The North is very "We've got to wait and see what we see about you, then we will know." Whereas Christian Unity's slogan is "There is no place like this place, so this must be the place." And I really thought that I was only being embraced because I was Jarvis's wife, not because of who I was. That's how I felt when I first got there, and you can probably understand the sudden identity of a wife of a public figure and everybody was like "Who is this person he's bringing from Ohio?" And this was eight years ago.

I really was incredibly scared and nervous when I got to New Orleans. I didn't know how I was going to poet. I didn't know how I was going to wife. I didn't have any family here. I didn't know anybody. I'd never lived in the same city as Jarvis. I couldn't find my way around the city. I had to have a GPS for everything. But I took a leap of faith. People thought I was crazy to leave. I had a great job in Ohio. I had a great apartment; I was doing all this work in the community around social justice and art. I had built up such a name as a poet there. And people really thought I was leaving a lot on the table. And at the time, New Orleans hadn't fully come back from Katrina the way that it has now. So people were like, "Well, what are you going to do? It's still not a stable situation!"

What was the job you had in Cleveland?

I was managing K-12 public library programs. So I was creating programs for a whole public library system. I absolutely loved it. It was a writer's dream job. I was doing work for the Rock and Roll Hall of Fame as a curator on the side for their black history month programs. So I was putting panels together about resistance through music. All sorts of fun things. I had an apartment overlooking a really cool part the city. I was making the most money I'd ever seen in my life. I was like "I'm going to pay off my school loans! I'm gonna help my mom out!" I had all these things in my mind. I actually didn't know Jarvis was going to propose so soon. It actually took me by surprise.

How did you all meet?

We actually met at a writing conference in Pittsburgh. And I didn't really notice him that much. And everybody had to go around and introduce themselves. You know, at that time, my mother had breast cancer. And I was really torn about being there at the conference. But this was like a fellowship. And it was hard to get in. And if you could get in, you had to go. And my mother gave her blessing. And I wasn't really fully there. But I knew I needed to be there. And I actually saw Jarvis at the table with the Bible open working on a poem. We had to turn in writing every night for the next day at the conference. So people would be hanging around writing.

So you saw this handsome southern man with his Bible. . . .

I was amazed, because it's just so rare to see people writing with a Bible. So I went over to him and you know, I think I quizzed him on the Bible. And he had good answers. And he said I'm very sorry to hear about your mom, but I hope she gets well. And he went on. I mean, he was from New Orleans, I was from Cleveland, I didn't see any possibility in there.

Two months after this week-long writing conference, Katrina happened. And he said I want to keep in touch. I was like "Oh my God, I just met this guy from New Orleans. I hope he's okay! And I didn't hear. . . . I didn't really know him. But I hoped he was okay. And then that October, he contacted me and said "I'm okay. And I sure enjoyed meeting you. I hope we can still remain friends." And I was like, "But you just lost your house and everything." So it became that kind of friendship. What can Cleveland do to help? So we organized money here and all of that. And so that's what it was for a while. He didn't have time to date anybody or anything.

But he kept calling and wrote me letters. It was kind've an old fashion thing because he was all over the place because of Katrina. And we eventually began to date. And we dated long distance for two years. And then he suddenly popped the question. And I wasn't ready to get married yet. I wasn't ready to leave at that time. I really enjoyed my life. I thought things were going really good. And I didn't want to get married that fast. He proposed in Easter and wanted to be married by October. And I just wasn't ready. But his mom was very ill. Also with breast cancer. Ironically, by the time my mother was getting better, his mother was diagnosed with breast cancer.

My mother didn't die from the cancer, but his mother did. My mother is still with us. She survived that. But I will say I think God brought Jarvis and me together. All of what I went through with my mom as a caretaker prepared me to help him with his mom. And it actually prepared me at the end to help the family. Because at one point, when I was there, the doctor said, "There's nothing else we can do." And the family was not ready to hear that. It was very emotional and people left the hospital room and suddenly I was alone with only her. I just sat with her . . . and held her hand and prayed. And I just sat there. I didn't know what to say.

And it was just . . . I don't know how to describe it. I've tried to write about it, but it's hard to explain. Just being in this room, and her learning that she's going to die, and it's such complete chaos for her, but I knew I had to focus on *stillness* because I had seen my own mother in such a horrific state with breast cancer. I understood the language of the doctors. So I just let them all go their ways and sat there with her.

That's such a gift. I think a lot about the importance of presence like that. You know, like when Jesus is in the Garden of Gethsemane and those chosen disciples kept going to sleep. And I came to understand how hard it would have been for them to be with Jesus during this very, very hard time. Having a pretty good idea that he was going to be cruelly executed. And they just couldn't handle it and kept going to sleep. But he wasn't asking for answers. He was saying, "Be with me. Watch with me," but they couldn't do it. (Mark 14:32-42) But with your past experience in this situation you were able to be fully present, watching with Jarvis's mother, and there is a lot of healing in that.

Yeah, and I helped her in very intimate ways. As if I was her daughter. With catheters and all those things.

Let me ask you this, what are your hopes for Christian Unity now? Thinking of the whole church? And what are your hopes for yourself vis-a-vis Christian Unity?

Oh gosh . . . um. I have spiritual hopes and practical hopes, you know? My spiritual hopes are that we grow. My spiritual hope is that we start to have a narrative that isn't "Before Katrina, we were . . ." or "Before Katrina X." I want us to get to a place where we are not just comparing ourselves to what was. Because I think that keeps us always looking back and not moving forward.[7]

I'm really hoping our children's ministry can grow. I'm a little biased because I have Naomi, but a lot of younger couples who have children have expressed concern about not having enough for our kids to do. I do appreciate

---

7. Like so many churches in New Orleans, over 50 percent of the Christian Unity members were unable to return.

how Naomi likes church. Her church experience is so unlike mine. She jumps and claps and dances and wiggles in the choir stand.

Sounds like she's getting into it.

Yeah, but I go to her and say "Naomi, can't you just be still up there?" Because she's always the one spinning and doing all those things. She says to me "Because Pastor Websty—that's what she calls Pastor Webster—says praise Jesus."

And I recognize that Naomi is at a church where people get up and dance. Even the first lady (Ms. Trudell Webster) can get out there and dance. There is a lot more freedom for Naomi in this church than when I was growing up. So I recognize I have to step back and let her church experience be *her* church experience. It's truly hers. She loves one of the songs they sing. "Oh how wonderful it is" [also known as "Jesus promised to return"]. It's for the adults. But Naomi, when she hears it, she gets up and goes to the choir stand and sings it with them as if she's part of the choir.

She's a very gifted child. I was astounded when I got to meet her.

But the freedom that she has to do that. She would not have had that freedom in the church I grew up in. And so I feel like she's very blessed to be able to be at a church where she can see people dancing and hear African drumming. When I grew up, all I knew was Sister So-and-So. I didn't know what they did. They were just church people to me. But I think Naomi really gets a wide view of what a church person may be. Because Sister So-And-So may dance. She may be at Community Book Center. You know, whatever. So her experience is much broader than mine, even at her age. And I'm very pleased with that because I think she will not be the child scared to go to Hell over eating an extra cookie like me.

Ah . . . she's not going to be that scared. But you know, Christian Unity has all this freedom, but it's within a structure. And so, for example, at Justice and Beyond, Pastor Webster and Pat Bryant carry that through. Because this is a church, you can't use any four letter word, not even H-*-L-L. You'll be called out. And also because it's a church that hosts Justice and Beyond, you can express forcefully what you think, but you can't put anybody down. So I'm impressed with the structure that keeps Christian Unity a Christian church, but then there's freedom mixed with that. It's a good combination.

Right. You have freedom to be you. And I think Naomi is allowed to explore that, whereas I was not. I was really programmed to be a certain way. So I feel like Naomi and all the kids there are really lucky even if they don't have a children's church. But they are very lucky to be able to experience a wide range of what it means to be a Christian. And I'm using the word lucky, but I really mean that they are blessed, too.

Well, let me just ask you, before I ask about your poetry, how can Christian Unity pass on what you have accomplished there to the larger community?

I don't know. I don't think there is one blanket answer. I think all of us represent Christian Unity when we go out. So whether I do poetry in or out of church, they say, "Hey, Christian Unity!" They may not know my name, but they know Christian Unity and, therefore, whatever I'm doing is reflected on the church. And I'm very conscious of not doing anything that may be a bad reflection of the church. And so they know us by our love, our light, and the work we do.

And you all make such an important contribution to the community . . .

And I think you see that in the fact that even people who aren't members of Christian Unity respect Christian Unity because they know that they will be respected and taken care of if need be. They embrace you as a church family better than any church I've been to.

That's a great answer. And one reason I go to Christian Unity when I'm free is that I sometimes need a spiritual uplift we don't always get in the Episcopal Church. But I so much appreciate your congregation for the reasons you're saying. And I see one of your major outreach efforts through Justice and Beyond. And I try to attend every Monday.

My prayer is that Pastor doesn't get so burnt out. I hope we can be able to get the infrastructure of the leadership on various levels so that we are able to sustain ourselves. And that's the practical part of the things that I want for the church. Because it's a lot. And for me, I've grown up in the church all my life. My dad started a church. I know the stress and the strain that it takes on a family, a person. Gosh, I would have to know I was called by God to preach or minister or be a pastor because it's incredibly stressful.

I agree Pastor Webster needs a lot of support. And he reaches out so far. For example, Justice and Beyond started out as a small group, but now I think it's the most important voice of the African American community in the city. . . . But, thank you so much . . .

Thank you. I hope I answered your questions.

Absolutely, what you did was tell some of your inspiring story. All the way back to the cookie. Of course I love the way you and Jarvis ministered to each other when your mothers were so ill. Here is one of my favorite poems. I wish I could pass on more. Your poems work even better on the CD when you sing as well as recite with music playing.

Names Don't Name Me[8]
My 6th graders know
good words from bad ones,
except when the word
starts with N.

Sometimes, it's hard for them
to explain why
it drifts easy without an anchor
or thought or history
or excuse me or oops
or don't or stop saying
that N word.

It's just there, they say—
on purpose sometimes,
a habit mostly between
friends, ya know?

The N word don't mean
what it meant.
Used to be a bad sign
in a yard, on fire in the South.

It's just familiar talk before
what's up or please.
It's the beat we speak
when the radio's on
and the jokes fly.

It's the punch line emphasized.
You've heard
a woman cussing mad
or a fight starting in a street

8. Copyright, 2015

Could be an N word
acting like an N.
Depends,
on the mouth's

meaning and if
you're in or outside
of strangers (white folks).

Don't want them
thinking our talk
is theirs, it's different.

Can't explain why
our English
don't mean—mean
the way it used to
in slavery, in Mississippi,
in Georgia, in Memphis,
in Kentucky, in stores,
in bathrooms, in schools,
in courtrooms, in elections
in hospitals, in restaurants,
in banks, in day or night.

The N word don't hang
in doors or from trees
or chase my feet or grandpa
no more.

That's history, they say.
6th graders know these things.
They learned it all before
knowing the right way
to rub words together
to start a fire.

Reaction:

I appreciate the way Kelly is trying to put together her early all-absorbing church-going experiences with her more recent understanding of the Christian faith, especially at Christian Unity. I can identify with her having to make a distinction between her art and her faith. She can read some of her poems to the congregation at Christian Unity, but not all of them. For me, I wish I could say everything I wanted to say from the pulpit—my "art," such as it is.

Kelly describes so well her childhood fear of going to Hell. When she was telling me about her seven-year-old crisis over "stealing" the cookie, I started to laugh but quickly realized this was a life-changing and terrifying moment for her.

And then, of course, I appreciate her determination that African Americans claim who they are and how she has made her way into the quite different world of New Orleans, including her reluctance to use the DeBerry last name, as she wishes she could. William Gillispie, the transcriber, calls attention to these words from Kelly: "[My] struggle is because life is so uncertain. It's a struggle because I'm human. It's a struggle because us black folks have been waiting so long for justice. It's a struggle because I'm flawed." "This is an excellent description of the black experience and of faith," says William, whose own story is in chapter 5.

And finally, her very sensitive poems help an old white guy like me and probably everyone else see life the way Kelly and her "people" see life and *how* they understand spoken and unspoken language.

Ashleigh Gardere (Senior Advisor to the Mayor): Making New Orleans Proud

Ashleigh and her family are strong members of Christian Unity. She holds top positions with the City of New Orleans as a Senior Advisor to Mayor Mitchell Landrieu and as Director of the Network for Economic Opportunity for the City. She is married to Lamar Gardere, and they have two young children, Jayden and Justin. Ashleigh is the daughter of Linetta and Paul Gilbert, with whom I have worked in community ministries since the 1980s. She graduated from New York University and then from Harvard's Kennedy School of Government with a master's in Housing and Urban Development. We met in her office on the eighteenth floor of an office building overlooking the city and City Hall. I told her about my angels in the wilderness project and then asked her to begin by saying what she wants people to know about her.

Ashleigh: I want people to know that I am the daughter of Paul and Linetta Gilbert. They were amazing parents and fully responsible for me becoming the person that I am. I think first of them, and now that I am a mother, I appreciate the level of intentionality they committed themselves to in making sure that Marita [her sister] and I were really exposed to a full range of people and places and experiences in New Orleans. I now can appreciate what it took to make sure we had access to an excellent public education, which often wasn't as diverse as it could have been, making sure we had a church family like Christian Unity that was really steeped in not only Baptist culture, but also African American and

Ashleigh Gardere, senior staff member for the mayor of New Orleans
and member of Christian Unity Baptist Church

New Orleans culture as well. I value the experiences of getting my hair done in the projects and also going to Bar Mitzvahs and doing African dance and ballet.

My parents did what it took to make sure they could raise black children in a city like New Orleans but also in the American South and that we were fully exposed to a range of people, places, and experiences. And I think that was amazing. And, given who they are, their faith and their calling as they interpreted it meant that they felt that any professional work would be linked to that faith and calling. That example absolutely wore off on me. And I think from a very young age I felt like I had a responsibility to support the New Orleans community and its success.

What special emphasis should there be on black education in New Orleans, a big question these days?

Well, I would say that pre-Katrina, probably at every stage of education there were one or two great schools, public schools, but what I didn't understand until my adulthood was the level of prayer and supplication required during the application process. And while there are a few more options now in the public education system, I think we all would acknowledge that all schools aren't equal. And so having to go through that myself as a mother, you see another side of it. Marita, my sister, and I attended Alice Harte Elementary School [just about all for white children] on the West Bank. At the time, it was one of the highest performing elementary schools in the state. And I was the sixth grade valedictorian, then we both went to Eleanor McMain for middle school and my sister stayed there for high school, and I went to Ben Franklin.

Those are paths two of my children took. McMain and then Ben Franklin.

I thoroughly enjoyed my educational experience, particularly middle school and high school. And, you know, while at the time I enjoyed elementary school, I think it wasn't until I got to a more diverse school in middle school that I appreciated the weight that you can bear as the one or two representatives of a much larger group, especially as a very young person. So for the five-year-old who has to be the black representative in their class or one of two—that's a lot to carry. McMain and Ben Franklin were more balanced and more diverse.

And where do you hope your children will go?

We made it through a nail-biting process with that same prayer and supplication required of our parents and at the end of it, Jayden is going to Lusher Elementary. You know, after all of the lotteries and rolling of the bins, at the end of the day, it's about your faith that God's will is perfect. So we ended up grateful that he was accepted into Lusher.

So what else do you want people to know about you?

Well, I love New Orleans. There is no place else on the planet that is as spiritual as this city. Not just in a religious way. Its history, its culture is grounded in faith, the early tradition and practice around Catholicism and folks' faith traditions linked to their social traditions. I think that's one element that shapes the city. But also the social fabric is a spiritual experience. I'll use Christian Unity as an example. My parents were not from New Orleans. And that means my biological grandparents I saw probably once or twice a year. They were in New York State, in Buffalo and Rochester. But because of Christian Unity and our religious practice at Christian Unity, we developed a rich and deep family that is the Christian Unity family and our church family.

So, as a result, I say I had a "third grandmother," though that's not really a good way to describe Grandma Lee Ester. She was the grandmother I spent the weekend with and her grandchildren were really my cousins. We met through Christian Unity. Our families connected through the church. And with the "aunts" and "uncles" who fully played those roles and attended all of my graduations and went to family milestones and no one would believe they were not my biological family. And yet, they weren't. And that grew out of the church.

Who was that family? I might know them.

Well, Lee Ester Edwards was my adoptive grandmother, and she passed away shortly after Katrina. And Reverend Audrey Johnson and Felix Johnson were my Tee Dee and Uncle Jr.[9] And all of their kids were like cousins. In fact, Troy Johnson and I joke that he is my cousin-uncle. These "family members" made great holidays, Thanksgiving and Christmas and Easter, all of the traditions that are linked to our faith, but also shaped my own family experience here in New Orleans. So, in that way, the city is faith-based and spiritual.

But, you know, other aspects of the city carry a spiritual undertone. Whether it's the jazz or the food traditions, they carry a certain spirituality to them. Mayor Landrieu said, "They get up in you." There's something beyond the physical experience for people who live here for any significant amount of time.

I go on and on about what brings people together in New Orleans: jazz, always the food, Mardi Gras, Saints football—win or lose—and then everybody knows somebody's cousin, like I know some of your New Orleans "cousins."

Yes, yes, absolutely. And so, all of that wrapped together creates a kind of spiritual connection to this place and the people of the city.

So, anything else special that you want people to know about you?

In addition to my love for New Orleans, I love the people of New Orleans. First, New Orleans is not really a physical place. It's really a set of relationships and even if you don't know yet that you knew so and so's cousin, the sense of connection to each other is so intrinsic and deep within who we are. And I feel absolutely connected to the people of New Orleans but also responsible for ensuring that people can do more than survive or exist, but instead thrive and be successful. People who share the experience and history with New Orleans absolutely feel responsible for making sure the people of New Orleans are successful. In my family, we used to joke about the number of people who had a key to our house. So that sense of love and family that I experienced in New Orleans was very deep and important. And not just through the church.

What other ways did you experience New Orleans?

You know, my aunt Judy was Judy Watts, who started Agenda for Children. So the full extension of people who are about community and community success were like family members for me. My aunt Jessie was Jessie Smallwood,

9. Reverend Audrey was a beloved assistant pastor at Christian Unity, whom I did know.

who ran the housing authority and worked in state government and left her footprint around the U.S., but those are the folks who were in our network.

How well did you know Judy? She was a good friend! In fact, Judy introduced me to your mother, Linetta, a long time ago. Agenda for Children had space at Trinity, and I helped that happen. (It was nice that Ashleigh didn't speak of Judy as white. She didn't know that I knew Judy. She was just Aunt Judy.)

I met Judy Watts because my mother worked with her at Agenda and in Early Childhood spaces. And I was just a five-year-old who was always walking through these buildings. I just knew her as an aunt. The first word that comes up when I think of her is joy. There was just something about her laughter and smile and genuine love. And you could see that—inside of her work in the same way my parents showed that. So, I think that one of the things I would want people to know about me, and especially my parents to know about me, is that their love was actually passed on, that love for community and sense of responsibility.

You graduated from Ben Franklin, and I know something about your college, but tell me more about it and your graduate school. What led you to this very important work?

The first thing that led me to this work was that before college and graduate school was Tambourine and Fan. I worked at the Tremé Community Center when I was fourteen and one of my first jobs was camp counselor for Tambourine and Fan. And that was my first explicit exposure to social justice.[10]

Before Tambourine and Fan, social justice to me was only connected to the meetings I would attend with my mom. And you don't even know at that point what you're hearing or how those conversations stick with you. It's the same thing going to my church that is really rooted in social justice. There are messages that you hear from the youngest age that you haven't yet processed. But the work experience at Tambourine and Fan was explicitly about nurturing the next generation of leaders in the social justice movement, so it was specifically for me! The leader was Jerome "Big Duck" Smith [a well-known freedom fighter], who continues as the leader of what is still to me a movement. In addition to the lessons and indoctrination that happens for teenagers who are working at the camp, I was blessed to also be able to participate in 21st Century Leadership Camp.

Tambourine and Fan has a relationship to 21st Century Leadership Camp,

10. Tambourine and Fan is known widely for its service to young people and for its parade on Super Sunday, a time when the Mardi Gras Indians also put on their colorful suits and "strut their stuff." Tremé—the heart of New Orleans—next to the French Quarter, is known most everywhere for the television series. Super Sunday is the third Sunday in March around St. Joseph's Day.

which is in Selma, Alabama, and that's a civil rights camp. Young people from all around the country, but certainly from the American South, every summer gather in Selma and are exposed to the civil rights movement and are exposed to a sense of nation building and sense of responsibility and how they connect to each other. That leadership camp was part and parcel of Tambourine and Fan and the Tremé Community Center experience.

I was not able to go to the fiftieth anniversary celebration at Selma this past year. But the camps and programs I did were foundational experiences for me. At age fourteen it helped me to be clear that I wanted to contribute to the community and the world and to be rooted in New Orleans; and it was about helping people and really supporting black people, especially to have families that would thrive—that we could do better as a community than what was immediately in front of us. That had a lot to do with that fourteen-year-old experience.

I was a counselor for five-year-olds, and there was a little boy named Maurice who would get sick. I remember one time he had a serious nosebleed, and as a fourteen-year-old I was nervous and afraid and wanted to make sure we were taking care of him. When I called for his mom to come get him, she just said, "I'm not coming." The idea that she was not in a position to come and care for him was a revelation. You know, with my fourteen-year-old self that was the first time that I really got that: There are some folks and some kids who are living a different kind of experience where their parents weren't available in the way mine were to take care of them and that there were parents who had significant burdens and barriers that blocked them from being able to provide the fully nurturing environment that you might expect for a five-year-old.

You know, these particular examples that you tell are important because this is how we learn, by telling each other stories. So, that sounds like that was a turning point for you.

Oh, absolutely. From that summer on, I was very determined to get to the work, and so, as you can imagine, this couldn't have been more frustrating for a teenager because, ironically, when you are a young person interested in community development, what is available to you is only youth programs. And more stuff about young people. Except that wasn't what I wanted to do. I wanted to focus on community development. I was in a real race to gather all the necessary little sheets of paper (i.e., degrees) that would allow me to do all of the work I wanted to do. So I graduated from high school and went on to New York University and every summer came back home to do an internship here.

The first one was at the New Orleans Neighborhood Development Collaborative, NONDC, which no longer is around. It became Harmony Oaks Neighborhood Development, but at the time NONDC was an intermediary for community development corporations and housing development organizations. My internship project was to create a directory of philanthropic organizations that could help to support and expand the capacity of New Orleans community based organizations.

Then, the next summer, I came back and worked at the Greater Tremé Consortium with Cheryl Austin, a leader in the Tremé neighborhood. And we really grew together. She invested time and energy in a twenty year old. I learned what it takes to stay grounded in community. To have and lead a small community organization without real access to financial resources, with banks not willing to provide a line of credit for an organization that produces housing. To endure the stress and strain of producing affordable housing units in a neighborhood that at that time was not gentrifying. The residents knew Tremé was rich in culture—this would have been in the late 1990s. And so it was at a time that people knew there was something special about Tremé. And I suppose Tremé had started to have transplants to the neighborhood, but it was not yet a tipping point, as it became later.

Back up for me to your college days.

When I was at NYU, I surely had one of those wilderness experiences, as the September 11 attack happened while I was there. I was a Resident Assistant (RA), a floor captain in the dorm. I was a senior at NYU, and I was responsible for all of these freshmen. I remember sitting on what was essentially the roof of our building, which was in lower Manhattan, and watching the buildings come down. I remember trying to figure out: "What the hell am I going to tell these young people?" Because I was telling them, "Everything is going to be okay," when I was actually thinking, "We might really die today." That was a wilderness experience for sure. But that was a time when all that my parents poured into me and all the lessons about faith and God, you know the covering we exist under, that's when me and that cover were really tested.

I have a strong feeling that you were an angel for younger people. You were responsible for them. Let me ask you this: Were there any special people for you during that experience or was it carrying forth what you had absorbed so much?

I think it was carrying forth what I had learned previously, and you know what's hilarious? I am only realizing that one of the most present angels in that experience was my now husband, Lamar. The reason I wouldn't have recognized it at that time was that we weren't dating. We had dated in high school, but at that time we weren't staying in touch. It had probably been a couple of years since I had spoken to him, but he called when 9/11 happened.

At that time, he was still in New Orleans at Xavier University. But I wouldn't even have remembered this in this way, but his call was a reminder that there are people who are angels. They just really care about you, care for you, and there are just these moments when they step in.

That is such an important point.

Yeah, and it was really just an instant. So, New York is falling apart, the tower just fell down, and we were literally in that moment homeless. We were in the gym of NYU. They set up a call center. And I guess people just called with names of people to make sure they were okay. And he was one of those people who called. That was special. You know, when I'm going through something, I close in and focus on the thing. I don't ask for help readily. But it's of note that he, with me being someone who wouldn't have reached out, was among those tens of thousands of people looking for folks and was reaching out to me.

Because of 9/11, I realized that I had already earned all the credits required to graduate and I moved to D.C. for a little under a year, to work and be able to practice being a "grown up." And then I went to the Kennedy School after that year. And I would say that was a wilderness experience in and of itself. Harvard University has so much weight assigned to it. Such a buttoned-up perception of it. I remember my family graduation party from NYU was also my sendoff to Harvard. I remember that same church family was all around to celebrate. And they would say, "Now girl, you're getting ready to go somewhere that some of us have never been. Many of us have never even dreamed about Harvard!"

It was not just me who was experiencing something of a wilderness, but I would say most of the black folks and students of color. That first semester is very difficult. First off, you don't want to embarrass yourself. But you certainly don't want to embarrass all the people you are representing. It's not just *your* seat at Harvard, it's a community seat.

You were Christian Unity's person there.

Right. And also the New Orleans person there, too. And the family lines, all three of them: my mother's, my father's, my New Orleans family. I was representing for everybody. And most of the white folks there didn't seem to be carrying that weight. They were just there, representing themselves, right? I struggled to find my voice and not show up as the angry black woman or whatever the caricature is.

Tell me about your voice that you were finding.

I think I would describe the first semester by the quick pace of a classroom. I discovered that "Oh, I'm not the only smart one. . . ." Everybody is smart. I absolutely had something to contribute, but I didn't want to sound angry, and I didn't want to fit the caricature. By the time I put together my response in the conversation that I thought would be received well, the class moved on to a whole other conversation. So, the first semester, most of us were just on mute. Realizing that you are *supposed* to be there is big. You are equipped to be there. You are supposed to be there. You have earned that seat. The reason you are here is that what you have to contribute is important. And even if that's not so, you've got to believe it's so.

And, you've got to know that you are smart. And that some of your class-mates aren't. They're occupying seats for other reasons. I guess somewhere between the second semester of the first year and the first semester of the fol-lowing year, somewhere in there I found my stride and learned how to be fully self-expressed. I share this with the people on my team here at work and the young people at City Hall. If I had to do the Kennedy School experience all over again, I probably would have waited another couple of years before going. At the time, I was twenty-three or twenty-four, and I thought, "Well, everyone tells me how mature I am. I'm clearly mature enough for this, right?" But it wasn't about behaving well. Having more work experience before going gives you an opportunity to unpack things you've seen already, an opportunity to test choices you've already made professionally against this new set of tools at the school. But I went when I was supposed to go. And I did well there.

The angels in that experience were my roommates at the time. They were Oni Blair, who was from Texas, and Akunna Enwereuzor, who was from New Jersey. They were two other black women there at the time. We'd all gone to different undergrad colleges, but we all were part of the same graduate fel-lowship. Our apartment was our safe space to yell or cry or laugh or whatever needed to be. And both of them had grown up in a Christian community. So having that was really important.

After I graduated, I was unemployed for three months. I was living in my parents' house, which, as you can imagine, was its own traumatic experience *with a Harvard degree*. That was when my parents were living in Brooklyn, New York. I finally got a job with the City of New Orleans. That was during Mayor Nagin's administration, in 2004, the year before Katrina. When I got back to New Orleans, my parents were in New York, and my sister was in Minnesota. And David Harrison, who is our adopted brother, was also in New York at that time. I was home in New Orleans, while most of the biological family was gone. Christian Unity was that good, safe space and the church family was still there, and they provided that family structure and the angels. Actually when Katrina came, the first angel I had was Mary Washington, who was an adopted daugh-ter to Rev. Audrey Johnson, the now-deceased associate pastor.

Sounds like another of your cousins.

Yeah. She actually lived with them at that time. And Mary was one of the most loving and caring people, but she loved . . . hard. She would not call to inquire "Ashleigh, are you planning for the storm, are you going to evacuate?" Not Mary! She called on Saturday (August 27, 2005) at 7:45 in the morning and said, "Ashleigh, go put gas in the car!" Unwillingly, I listened to what she said, and by Sunday morning, I parked my car at the church and I left with them. I evacuated with Audrey and Felix Johnson, Mary Washington, and Troy

Johnson. There were fourteen of us. And we were in one of these blended New Orleans families that filled four cars. They absolutely were angels. I stayed with them. I think people still wouldn't understand why I didn't go to New York where my parents were. But my blended family were angels to me. I was an angel to them too.

All fourteen of us first went to Galveston. There was a baby with us, Devin, who I think was six months old, all the way to Felix Johnson's father, Paw Paw, who was ninety. We started in a motel in Galveston, then a hotel in Houston, then finally a couple of apartments in Houston. After Hurricane Rita had passed, I was called back to New Orleans to work for the City and lived on a cruise ship (anchored in the harbor of the Mississippi River) with the first responders and the city government and public school employees. I don't know how to describe that. It was a surreal time. I think one of the big reasons I didn't go to New York to be with my family goes back to the answer to your first question, which is that I love New Orleans and absolutely feel responsible for this place. We were on the ship for a few months. Then I ended up house sitting for my "aunt," Jessie Smallwood.

We ate a lot of food on the ship. If we didn't do anything else, we worked and ate. And you know, that experience was a moment in my personal growth. Sometimes you have to grow on your own, and being by myself was an important part of the experience. I don't know that people will ever really appreciate the city employees who worked from the ship and the sacrifices they made in order to get the city up and running. I am at the bottom of that list, after hundreds of other people. But folks who lost their homes themselves and were living on a cruise ship, like Natasha Muse, who still works in City Hall. She and I were sharing a room with her two teenage sons.

Some people were living with strangers. I ended up sharing a cabin with Lora Carmichael, who was a church member. She was called back to help "stand up" (rebuild) Children's Hospital. We saw each other coming back, and we decided we would room together. Later she moved off the ship. She was replaced with a stranger. Living under those conditions and with people you may or may not know, and the long days people invested to make sure the city came back—that absolutely got lost in the Katrina media stories and tales about people who got in trouble.

I want to hear about your position now and what some of your hopes are for yourself and the City.

I serve as Senior Advisor to Mayor Landrieu for Economic Opportunity. I lead a cross-sector initiative known as the Network for Economic Opportunity. Our portfolio includes all things related to workforce development, with federal funding and in partnership across the other lead workforce agencies in the city, like the Urban League, Good Work Network, and Total Community Action. We bring people together: major employers, training providers, job seekers, and social service agencies. First, we focused on fully leveraging city positions that are careers with benefits and retirement for people to come into city departments, but now we partner, and I would say most importantly, with the private sector and make sure that our major employers are offering opportunities for the underserved.

Making sure they offer the opportunities they are really required to offer. Do you do any work with Barbara Major? We go way back with the People's Institute for Survival and Beyond. She has long been a core trainer with them. (See Derek Rankins's story in chapter 5.)

Yes, we work together in another portfolio focused on small businesses and small business contracting. She is a leader and organizer for small business and contractors—black-owned contractors who together are called The Collaborative. Our work together is about making sure that not only is the city fully leveraging participation from Disadvantaged Business Enterprises (DBE) and minority-owned businesses in city contracting, but again, that we are opening up opportunities in the private sector as well and really leveraging the purchasing might of major companies.

Last year we created a new local hiring policy for the city of New Orleans. Now, for anybody who is working on a construction project for the city or anybody who is asking for an incentive for a development project, there are goals for participation in those projects and goals for disadvantaged local workers as well. The goal is that by 2020, 50 percent of those working on city projects are local residents. And 30 percent of those workers are disadvantaged workers. And that's everything from folks who have been emancipated from foster care, to custodial single parents, to the formerly incarcerated, to very low-income people.

That includes people who might be working but just are not earning enough. And then likewise on the small business contracting side, we updated all of the rules governing the Disadvantaged Business Enterprise programs in partnership with the collaborative. And we now have a 35 percent goal with DBE participation in city contracts. We spend a lot of time, as I said, working with the private sector employers, showing them how to open employment opportunities to low income or low-skilled individuals and to extend contracting opportunities to local and small businesses here.

You're really on the cutting edge.

We are. Not just in New Orleans, but this is the work we're going to have to struggle with nationally over the next few decades. We are working to change three hundred years of behavior! And practice! So, my work is really about relationships. For three hundred years, the business leaders in the city have not been connected to the workers and the folks who wanted to work. And while

I used to want so badly to restore relationships, I now realize we actually never had those relationships to begin with, over those three hundred years. And this work is so hard because it's really about introducing people to each other and helping them to see how they can benefit from being kind to one another and supportive.

How do you bring people together across those barriers?

We have what we call the Anchor Collaborative. It's a table of employers who've opted in. They've said, "I'm willing to try to figure out how to do this work—make good jobs available. I don't know how, so let's design it together." And we've literally spent the past eighteen months with them to understand what their needs are, what the skill sets are for the jobs or contracts they can offer.

Are you're talking to the workers or the businesses here?

The Anchor Collaborative really operates in both spaces. There are the vice presidents of human resources at major companies. There are also vice presidents for contracting and procurement. And then on the workforce side you've got a whole ground game, which is a community-based recruitment and outreach strategy. Community residents are directed to those workforce agencies that I mentioned earlier: the Urban League, Total Community Action, JobOne, Inc. (a job search service). They are coordinating efforts to strengthen the quality of local workforce services overall for jobseekers with employment barriers.

We integrate Delgado Community College and the building trades to provide the technical skills that those people need. Then we introduce the candidate to the employer. Ochsner Hospital is one example.[11] They'll send us a request saying: "We're getting ready to hire six medical assistants or administrative staff." And then we'll reach out across the five workforce agencies and build a pool of the most qualified candidates. In the case of Ochsner, when we started, we literally would host interview days here, in our offices, so that they could meet folks they never would have found otherwise. We're getting people from the community, "pouring into them," as the mayor says, making sure they are trained and ready, and then putting them in front of employers.

And then the same thing essentially on the contracting side. So the Louisiana Children's Medical Center—the people who run Children's Hospital and University Medical Center—have a business exchange. Ahead of particular events, we ask, "What specific opportunities are you having in the next six months that can be locally sourced?" And then based on that list, we work

---

11. One of the largest and most prominent hospitals in the nation

through partners like the Good Work Network and NewCorp New Orleans to connect procurement officers to ready DBEs and majority owned companies that can perform the work.

You bring a lot of different people to the table and with your help, you figure out what's going to help the community, both the employers and those who badly need work.

Right. So my goal, two years from now, when the next mayor comes in, is that there would be new practices that we have practiced over and over again. And it's the ownership in the community that will continue to make it so. Because employers will say, "Well, every time they give me someone qualified, I've saved money on my turnover." Then it becomes the new way. It doesn't really matter what the next mayor says or doesn't say or what she or he likes or doesn't like; it's just the new normal. It's how we do our work now.

That's great. What haven't we covered?

Uh, well, my hope for New Orleans is that we are the first example, the model city of the U.S. and whole globe, that demonstrates that we can have a thriving economy and still have smart systems like the health care system, education system that are still rooted in people—created by and led by the people who interact with those systems every day. I want to prove that this city can be a global city and not lose herself in the process.

You and I were talking about the things we love about New Orleans and can contribute to this hope that you have. And I think people have gotten tired of me saying this from the pulpit over the last fifty years, but the educator John Dewey once said, "People support what they help to create." When you bring people together as part of the creation process, as you are doing, not just imposing change from the top down, then people support change.

Yep. And so we can be this amazing city that fully leverages something that was always there, something for the future, but we're not building an amazing city for somebody else. That's my hope: that we continue to love stronger than anybody else. That we remain an amazing culturally rich, fun, and joyful city. And that we become a proud city. We're proud of our neighborhoods and we rep our neighborhoods, but I don't know that we've ever been proud of New Orleans, right? So, that's my hope.

Thank you. It's a wonderful story.

Reaction:

Besides her obvious thoughtfulness, training, commitment to her faith centered on love and justice, and her leadership, Ashleigh is so open, so willing to talk about herself, always learning from various experiences, especially her wilderness experiences, always appreciating her parents and those in her church family and now her own family. She is determined, as she says, to make New Orleans proud!

My hope is that she will help bring New Orleans together the way Joe Riley, the mayor of Charleston, South Carolina, brought my hometown together during his forty years as mayor. He would fly from national conferences to be present at a funeral when someone from Old White Charleston died (like my brother-in-law). And Riley also took part in the black-led effort to remove the Confederate flag from the top of the state Capitol building in Columbia. In 2000, he walked the 114-mile route from Charleston to Columbia in a protest group. (It wasn't until 2015, after the Charleston massacre in Mother Emanuel Church, that the governor moved the flag off the capitol grounds altogether.)

And of course, I greatly appreciate the way Ashleigh brings together her so-called secular work and her strong faith. It is a faith that does not exclude but empowers us all to support those whom Jesus called "the least of these our sisters and brothers." I can think of no one who does that better.

An Update:

On September 22, 2016, Ashleigh Gardere was recognized by Living Cities as one of the nation's top 25 Disruptive Leaders. Living Cities, a collaborative of eighteen leading foundations and financial institutions, has recognized leaders who dare to act urgently and with unrestrained imagination to improve economic outcomes for low-income people in America's cities. "Ashleigh works diligently and deliberately to serve the people of New Orleans, and we are proud to have her on our team," said Mayor Mitch Landrieu. "She has earned this distinction by dedicating her energy toward creating economic opportunity for all of our residents."

Chapter Eight

What's Next?

I began this project trying to prove Flannery O'Connor 's wisdom right—We can know the people in our communities best not by statements or statistics but by the stories they tell. And, of course, for me, knowing them also means knowing their angels. In these days of still brewing racism, what could be more important than listening to young African Americans—with their diversity of voices—in places like New Orleans. I hope the stories show that not only do black lives matter, but that the young and black in these pages are leading the way.

Now I am beginning two new and quite different listening projects. William Gillispie, back in New Orleans for a master's degree at Tulane, has agreed to help me again and has begun by transcribing stories for each project.

Project #1 involves formerly incarcerated women I am getting to know—"graduates" of the Louisiana Correctional Institute for Women, widely known as St. Gabriel's (the town where it is located). I am getting to know these women through the Kairos Prison Ministry, very active at St. Gabriel's; through a drama group that women take part in while they are in prison and remain active in when released; and finally through an endearing group of formerly incarcerated women (FIPs), the Sister Hearts, who not only support one another but have started a successful business—a thriving thrift store.

I began Project #1 by first getting to know some of the Sister Hearts. It happened this way: In recent months, I have been quite upset with the Louisiana Department of Public Safety and Corrections and with the staff at the Louisiana State Penitentiary at Angola. For some infraction of prison rules, a man I had visited on Death Row for four years, Terrance Carter, more of a friend than a spiritual advisee, was transferred to a place of punishment on the Angola compound, Camp J—a place where over three hundred inmates live for months, even years, at a time. On April 2, Terrance hanged himself on the same day that another inmate living in Camp J hanged himself. I don't know how many men have taken their lives in Camp J, but I do know from inmates who "walk the tiers" that they prevent many suicides. Terrance told me when I saw him last February that he longed to be back on Death Row, where at least he was treated as a fellow human being and not as an animal.

On April 8, the New Orleans *Times-Picayune* published an op-ed I had written protesting the cruelty on Camp J. On April 18, I was banned from all volunteer work at Angola. I had been visiting the compound two or three times a month for various church-related programs, including Kairos Prison

Ministry that I helped start at Angola in 1993. I was not surprised. But in order to keep the issue of Camp J alive, I helped set up a Justice and Beyond forum on a Monday evening, with two former inmates who had themselves spent months on Camp J. (One was Jerome Morgan, whom Kristen Rome talks about in chapter 4.) They spoke to a group of 150 or so people about how cruel and dehumanizing Camp J was for them. We decided to send a letter of protest to the governor (who, as a candidate, had spoken at Justice and Beyond last fall, looking for votes) with a copy to the Secretary of the Department of Public Safety and Corrections.

Sitting in Justice and Beyond that night was the lady who began Sister Hearts in New Orleans, Sr. Maryam Uloho. She had served twelve years at St. Gabriel's and during that time had experienced living in a kind of Camp J there. At the evaluation meeting of the forum the next day, Sister Maryam thanked us for the forum but wanted to know why we had not talked at all about incarcerated women and how they themselves have experienced similar cruelty in lockdown at St. Gabriel's and other places. I gave a long answer to her question, but the short answer was—I hadn't thought of it. Probably like most working on prison reform, I focus on men in and out of prison but not usually women.

To begin to correct this wrong, I asked Sr. Maryam if I could visit her in the Sister Hearts Thrift Store that she had started and where formerly incarcerated women and men work. I was amazed at the size of the thrift store, some four thousand square feet, and further amazed by the items for sale, just about anything you could want for a home, including appliances. All of the items for sale came as gifts from individuals and stores from all over New Orleans.

So, I began what I hope will be many conversations with Sr. Maryam. Her story and the stories of other Sister Hearts need to be told as much as any of the stories in this book. "In prison," Sr. Maryam says, "you lose the capacity to think for yourself. Year after year, you are told exactly what to do and exactly how to do it." In her store, the employees gradually learn that *they* are in charge of what they do. They can for example, arrange the items for sale in their part of the store and help set the prices. "In prison," Sr. Maryam says, "you are treated like trash, but in our store and in Sister Hearts, people begin to see us not as trash but *as treasure*. From trash to treasure."

Late in our first and long conversation, I asked Sr. Maryam if she had been part of Kairos Prison Ministry International at St. Gabriel's—I knew Kairos was strong there. I was blown away by her response: "Not only was I a part of Kairos," she said, "but it really was the thing that changed my life and brought out the best in me." Then she said, and of course I loved this: "The administration of the prison would not let me do Kairos because I am a Muslim and Kairos is Christian. *But* Mary Kennedy, one of the assistant

Sister Maryam Henderson-Uloho, formerly incarcerated,
founder of Sister Hearts in New Orleans

wardens—and an active Episcopalian here in New Orleans—intervened on my behalf and eventually they let me be part of the program. I am as much a Muslim as ever, but Kairos gave us ladies a way to be friends with each other, across religious and race lines."

Besides being appreciative of Kairos's openness to other faiths, I suddenly realized that through Kairos I have connections with women who are still incarcerated and others who are out of prison but still in touch with Kairos. So I am counting on a second group of women to tell their stories, the Kairos ladies, as they like to be called.

Then, serendipity. An old friend, Kathy Randels, an actress, dancer, and teacher invited me to a show that formerly incarcerated women whom she works with put on—with singing, dancing, and what I, of course, enjoy the most, storytelling. They told stories of their lives so far: their lives before prison, in prison, and now, trying to make it out of prison in a society that wants to shut them out. If all of their stories are as engaging as the ones I heard at the show that evening, they will inspire us all.

As I move on with Project #1, I am sure I will get to know other formerly incarcerated women—like those employed by AmeriCorps—and I will listen and listen, and if they will let me, record some of their stories and then ask

William Gillespie to transcribe them all. And I will *try* not to talk too much myself.

Project #2 comes by way of an Episcopal clergyman, Hill Riddle, with whom I worked as his associate rector at Trinity, New Orleans, from 1984 to 1996. Long retired, Hill is now blind and physically disabled, but, like the women I am now listening to, he is a wonderful storyteller and tells of how he has tried to make the largest Episcopal Church in Louisiana become "a transformer of culture"—to use H. Richard Niebuhr's words (from his 1951 highly influential book *Christ and Culture*). White, largely middle- and upper-class Trinity was certainly not going to be what Niebuhr called "Christ Against Culture"—like authentic churches in Nazi Germany and churches in this country that stood bravely against slavery. Trinity could have easily become what Niebuhr called "Christ in Culture"—a church that merely reflects the culture—always a temptation for Trinity, which is led by many of the elite of New Orleans.

So my working title is *The Rev. Hill Riddle: His Ministry as a Transformer of Culture,* or some such. I meet with Hill most weeks and get him talking about such things as how Trinity has managed to keep together both liberals and staunch conservatives, especially when our national church embraced gay clergy and bishops; how Trinity, while not particularly integrated, has received so much respect from black New Orleans; how Trinity School, too expensive for 95 percent of New Orleans parents strives to become diverse; how Hill has dealt with struggles in his own life, still succeeding in being a pastor to so many people—*including me*, when in the midst of controversy I needed the rector's support.

Besides these two listening projects, I will continue to listen to and support the young people in all the various groups I have written about in this book, learning from them, helping them to get to know and support others outside their particular groups. Already, I have signed on as a mentor/tutor for the fall semester at College Track; I have agreed to lead services when I am needed at St. Luke's and will be teaching a course with Pastor Dwight Webster on the Book of Genesis at Christian Unity. You don't exactly sign up for the Red Flame Hunters, or the Icons for Peace, or Justice and Beyond— but all of my friends in those groups will see a lot of me, maybe too much.

Since I have already begun volunteering at College Track for the fall semester, I want to pass on this "personal statement" that Orlando Smiley, a rising high school senior, wrote for his college applications.

> The morning of August 31, 2012, was very unusual from the moment I turned on the television and looked at the news. It was reported that a man was shot on the 4300 block of America Street. As my mom walked in, she sat next to me in the bed and she started to cry softly. When I asked what

Hill Riddle (left) and William Barnwell, working on the next book.

was wrong, she just left the room.

Later when my sister and I got in the car to go to school, she started talking to us about the importance of education and how we should make a positive change in our community. At the time I didn't underhand why she was lecturing us. She turned around once we got to the corner where the school is and explained that last night she was called to the hospital for my cousin Melvin because he was shot by his friend because he refused to sell drugs for him. The words that came out of her mouth felt like they hit me. I asked was he okay and the expression on her face said it all. As the tears ran down her face, my heart sank. At that point I knew that my cousin was gone. I was devastated and sad for a long time.

My cousin's death was one of the hardest things I have had to go through. Eventually, I came to the realization that even though I felt helpless, I would dedicate myself to getting a quality education working hard despite my weaknesses. I want to help change my community in a positive way and the most effective way to do that is to get my education, get a good job and come back with knowledge to spread to my people so we can grow in a positive way. I learned from that experience that I would like to make changes in my community so that crime and poverty numbers will go down and overall make it safer for my family, and I know this is all possible through education, plus I have an angel watching over me.

Since that sad event, I have been in multiple positive movements, such as the 2015 fiftieth anniversary of the March on Selma. I have volunteered to clean up around my neighborhood and also helped at three different food banks. Through College Track I have helped younger kids learn the values of community education and teamwork. I have also spoken at many events, such as the Tie Tying Ceremony, where young black men and police officers come together to talk about the disconnect between young men and police.

Even though I am dedicated, I do struggle in school sometimes because I have such a busy schedule. I study hard and try my best at everything I do. Melvin's death gave me a reason to look at the world in a positive way, even though there is so much negativity. I have found my purpose in life. Now I just need to keep working. The changes I make could save somebody from going through what I did.

The only help I gave Orlando was inserting commas and periods where needed. The angel watching over him is, of course, Melvin. I can't believe I—the big angel devotee—had to ask him who that angel was/is.

Orlando also introduced me to the Tie Tying that College Track has sponsored before. Somehow I had missed knowing about it. Twenty College Track students and twenty police officers sit around several tables and—no surprise!—tell each other some of their stories. What could be more important than young African American men and police officers—the so-called "enemy" in many neighborhoods—getting to know and trust each other.

Already, I have made plans with Sherdren Burnside, now retired as director of College Track, to bring those same police officers or others like them to meet in small groups with such "street people" as the Icons for Peace *and* members of my home church—Trinity—they need to be part of this too. Already, the Icons and several members of Trinity have agreed to join our own Tie Tying at Sherdren's church in the essentially all-black Ninth Ward. At the end of the College Track Tie Tying sessions, after the relational *ties* are made, the police officers ceremoniously place bowties on the dress shirts of the students. Sherdren and I think *we* should give the bowties to the officers, as well as to the Icons and other young black men.

So the work continues. No old age-anxiety yet. And then there is my work through Kairos at a state prison I have not been banned from, not yet anyway—Dixon Correctional Institute (DCI), an hour northeast of Baton Rouge. I have been seeing a member of Trinity there for the last four years and have taken part in two long Kairos prison weekends there during the last year. More stories arise than my getting-old brain can handle.

Like stories from the mother, father, and sister volunteers who are part of every DCI Kairos, supporting their son and brother, who has been in prison for thirty-one years (since he was seventeen). As an inmate, he always helps out the Kairos volunteer team by serving tables. What we call the Kairos "family" takes on special meaning with that family present.

Like the stories of two of the men on the Kairos team who were once inmates themselves at DCI.

Like a volunteer who told me recently—outside of a Kairos meeting—that if Hillary Clinton were elected, Christianity as we know it would be destroyed! I could have had a shout-out argument, but this man has served on many Kairos teams spreading as best as he can what he and I both call the love of Christ to inmates who have received very little of it in their life. What should I have done? What should I do?

Like a story I was part of, sort of. One Kairos Saturday afternoon when the groups of inmates and volunteers were enthusiastically talking to one another around six tables, suddenly, an inmate from the table next to mine stood up and shouted, "I AM GODDAM SICK AND TIRED OF ALL THIS BULLSHIT AND I AM NOT HAVING ANY MORE OF THIS FUCKING STUFF." He left the room waving his fist in the air.

I expected alarms to go off or security officers to run in and take the man away. At very least, I expected our Kairos leader to reassemble all of the volunteers and residents to stop what we were doing and "reflect prayerfully" on what had just happened. *Instead*, the conversations in the six groups went on, just as before. That afternoon, the man rejoined his group, and no one said anything about it.